SOME OF MY FRIENDS ARE...

SOME
OF MY
FRIENDS
ARE...

The Daunting Challenges and Untapped
Benefits of Cross-Racial Friendships

DEBORAH L. PLUMMER, PHD

Beacon Press ▪ Boston

Beacon Press
Boston, Massachusetts
www.beacon.org

Beacon Press books
are published under the auspices of
the Unitarian Universalist Association of Congregations.

22 21 20 19   8 7 6 5 4 3 2 1

This book is printed on acid-free paper that meets the uncoated paper
ANSI/NISO specifications for permanence as revised in 1992.

Text design and composition by Kim Arney

Some of the names, when indicated, and some identifying characteristics
mentioned in the work have been changed to protect identities.

Library of Congress Cataloging-in-Publication Data

Names: Plummer, Deborah L., author.
Title: Some of my friends are . . . : the daunting challenges and untapped
benefits of cross-racial friendships / Deborah L. Plummer, PhD.
Description: Boston : Beacon Press, [2018] | Includes bibliographical
references and index.
Identifiers: LCCN 2018023628 (print) | LCCN 2018026223 (ebook) |
ISBN 9780807024010 (ebook) | ISBN 9780807023891 (hardcover : alk. paper)
Subjects: LCSH: Race relations. | Interpersonal relations. | Race awareness.
Classification: LCC HT1523 (ebook) | LCC HT1523 .P583 2018 (print) |
DDC 305.8—dc23
LC record available at https://lccn.loc.gov/2018023628

To My Friends of Many Races

CONTENTS

CAN WE BE FRIENDS?

My husband, Mike, is an engineer—a full-blooded engineer. Not only is it his career choice, but he also lives and thinks like an engineer. Often when we go out with my friends, the occasion is loosely planned and somewhat spontaneous. A phone call made that day inquiring about the evening's plans usually gets things started. Mike's friends (fellow engineers), on the other hand, plan events literally months in advance—even if we are just meeting for dinner. Time, place, and confirmed reservations are emailed in a precise manner.

One Saturday, we met his friends Julie and Steve (both engineers) for dinner.[1] Mike and I arrived at approximately 7:25 p.m. The 7:30 reservation was in Julie and Steve's name, and the hostess informed us that they had not yet arrived. Knowing their habitual promptness, we decided to go to the table. I began to get nervous after fifteen minutes, since this is equivalent to waiting over an hour for someone in nonengineer land. My husband pulled out his printed email with the confirmed date and place. "Yep," he said. "We are in the right place. Besides, the reservation is in their name, remember?" We asked the waitress again if anyone else was waiting for a couple. "No," she assured us. "Your friends are not here." After a half hour, I was convinced that something was dreadfully wrong. I checked our voicemail. No message. No missed phone call or text. We inquired again with the waitress, who checked with the hostess; she impatiently came back to tell us, "We checked. *Your* friends are not here." As she was walking away, I turned to watch her—only to notice the back of Julie's blond head and the shoulders of Steve, her husband, seated next to her. Not surprisingly, they were being told the same story. Apparently, the restaurant hostess assumed we could not be friends.

If we cannot even imagine individuals being friends across races in social settings, how can we envision and create a racially diverse and united

America? Our natural preference for sorting people into categories of people who look like us, sound like us, and share our same values and beliefs leads us to remain socially segregated.

Now when I am the first to arrive at a restaurant to meet friends who are white, I openly let the restaurant know that I am waiting for some friends . . . and that they are white. Hostesses and maître d's always appear a bit taken aback. It might be that they feel my mention of race is unnecessary, or perhaps they are surprised that I have named the elephant and they are grateful. As my husband frequently says, "Assumptions make asses out of you and me."

Nobody likes feeling like an ass, so it is time to examine our assumptions about others who are racially different from us. The time for talking about the elephant in our societal living room is long overdue. I am not talking about ugly, evil, racist remarks that most people abhor. I am talking about those thoughts in our heads that would cause us to be a bit embarrassed if people were reading our minds. Like believing that blacks are lazy and Hispanics are dumb. Or wondering what country Asians are *really* from when they tell you they are American. Or wondering how authentically Native is that professed Native American and how did they come to know they were Native American? Did they use Ancestry.com? Although annoying to those who represent the identity, this kind of thinking is common and interrupts building the capacity to be able to have a meaningful conversation with an acquaintance of a different race without having what we will later explore as an amygdala hijack.

From kindergarten through third grade, I attended a racially mixed school. From first through third grades I was friends with Kitty, who was white. Our friendship started because I loved her blue rhinestone-trimmed eyeglasses. I was also friends with Maria, who was Filipino. Our friendship was based on the fact that I coveted the windbreaker jackets she possessed in several different colors. I was friends with Carlos, who was Puerto Rican. Our friendship was based on my pure attraction to a cute boy who was also quite popular with everyone in the class.

By seventh grade my formerly racially mixed school had become predominantly black, as the inner-city neighborhood surrounding St. Thomas Aquinas Elementary School in Cleveland, Ohio, became subject to white flight, the large-scale migration of middle-class whites from racially mixed urban cities to the suburbs. My best friends, Gayle, Zoe, and

Debbie, were black. Judy, one of the few remaining white kids, sometimes hung around with us. We would often take the bus from the East Side to downtown Cleveland, where we could walk around and window-shop, peering at the trendy, pricey outfits on the mannequins and talking about our dreams of one day being able to buy clothes like that. We each had about fifty cents for lunch, which in the 1960s meant you could get a full meal at McDonald's, consisting of a hamburger, a shake, and fries. Going to McDonald's for lunch was a special part of these Saturday outings, but on one particular day, Judy said there was a better place we could go for lunch. She suggested the cozy corner diner where she and her mom ate when they shopped downtown. On our trips without Judy, we had passed that diner often, always peering in the window and assuming we could never afford to eat there. Judy assured us that the food wouldn't cost us much more than McDonald's and would be even better, a claim I found hard to believe. Thinking that the worst thing that could happen would be that we would have to share an order of fries, we agreed to go.

Debbie, Gayle, and Zoe quickly claimed five empty stools along the counter, and motioned for Judy and me to hurry up and sit down before other patrons claimed the seats. The waitress was a tall white woman with a hairstyle like the actress Lucille Ball, who held special fascination for me because she was married to Desi Arnaz, a Cuban who often butchered the English language like my immigrant Spanish-speaking parents. I assumed that because she looked like Lucy she would be friendly, but her expression was one of annoyance. Still standing at the entry with Judy, I started to giggle, thinking about how quickly my friends had gotten themselves into trouble, as there was barely a minute between when Gayle, Zoe, and Debbie sat down and Judy and I entered the diner. While I assumed that my friends must have done something unimaginable to cause Lucy-look-alike to be so upset, Judy had quickly assessed the situation and knew what the argument was about between the waitress and three black teens. They were being asked to leave.

Judy loudly announced, making sure the others in the diner could hear her, "If my friends are not allowed to eat here, then I won't either. We are taking our business elsewhere."

She dramatically motioned for us to leave. We were all stunned that what we'd witnessed on television happening to black people in the South was actually happening to us—good Catholic school girls, dressed appropriately and with enough money to pay for lunch, albeit maybe without French fries.

What I learned from the diner experience was that there were individuals who happened to be white who were racist and there were individuals who were white that you could call friends. White friends like Judy would challenge those racist structures and support you in the struggle for equality. I haven't seen Judy since those school days and have no idea whether as an adult her views remain the same, yet throughout my adult years I frequently recall her advocacy against racist practices on behalf of her friends of a different race.

As a seventh grader hanging around Gayle, Zoe, and Debbie, attending what became a predominantly black school and living in a black neighborhood, I didn't fully experience racism. I heard many stories of my parents' experiences with racism and knew the impact of racism witnessed by their lowered expectations for financial prosperity despite their hard work and their limited career mobility despite their talent. As a young person, hanging around with Judy forced me to think about how the world treated us differently because of our race and how we developed differently as a result. This developmental process involves cognitive, emotional, and behavioral components and continues throughout all our life stages. As an adult, after an exchange with my close friend Yvonne, I became intensely curious as to why so many of my black friends, who were raised in similar circumstances and had the same values as I, did not have friends across racial lines, and why for so many of my white friends I was their only friend of color.

My curiosity persisted and I began examining friendships across racial lines as a major component of my research agenda. Over the course of my three-plus decades as a clinical psychologist, as an academic whose research has explored cross-racial relationships of all kinds, and in my more recent work as a chief diversity and inclusion officer, I have seen that one of the most effective ways to bring about the change in understanding our need to improve race relations is by forming friendships across racial groups. Yet a racial divide exists in cross-racial friendships, most notably between blacks and whites.

This book is about how friendship patterns, yours and mine, reflect America's racial divide, the tension created by that divide, and the hope for future racial harmony. Stories of my cross-racial friendships, along with many others in the book, are used as examples of the circuitous and challenging path cross-racial friendships can take. As a well-recognized qualitative research method, storytelling can help explain the multilevel and dynamic perspectives of race relations. Stories also give witness to the benefits of cross-racial friendships, as a way toward navigating what is an increasingly racially complex world. It is my hope that by reading this book you will join me in examining race relations through the lens of your own friendships.

In addition to stories, interviews with cross-racial friendship pairs and discussions with focus group participants across the United States complement my research studies and the research of other social scientists on intragroup relations outlined throughout the chapters. Grounded in social science research, the book examines this dynamic through several levels of human systems—personal, interpersonal, group, and societal. On a personal level, cross-racial friendships help us recognize and reduce implicit bias, develop empathy, and enhance our understanding of ourselves as global citizens. On an interpersonal level, cross-racial friendships provide a vehicle for maximum self-expression and being fully authentic. In our racial-group identities, cross-racial friendships help us achieve healthy resolution. On a societal level, cross-racial friendships are the interpersonal building blocks and the foundation for any larger social or government efforts working toward positive race relations.

Of note to readers is the use in this book of the term "cross-racial." Many social psychologists use the terms "interracial friendships" and "cross-racial friendships" interchangeably, with a preference in the literature for the term "interracial." I intentionally use the term "cross-racial," as it speaks to the conscious action that has to be taken in these kinds of relationships. Similarly, other terms used throughout the book, such as "racism," "microaggressions," "privilege," "intersectionality," and "racial identity," are rooted in social science (psychology, sociology, anthropology) rather than conceptualized from a political, historical, or journalism framework. I believe this adds both a different and complementary understanding of the race narratives prevalent today in television news, blogs, podcasts, YouTube videos, and social media platforms. Popular race narratives are important and enlightening discussions that often point to generational differences in how race is experienced and conceptualized in contemporary society. However, what guides the analysis in this book are social science theories rooted in empirical research. In addition, the book focuses on patterns of adult cross-racial friendships rather than school-age children or romantic interracial relationships, as little attention has been given to understanding the nature of adult cross-racial friendships.

Over the years, following presentations on the topic, I have often been asked, "How can I make better or more friends across racial lines?" At first blush the question seems simple and almost naive, but it is not. Each chapter of the book speaks to the historical baggage, institutional structures, mind-sets, and psychological underpinnings that make crossing racial lines in friendship so challenging. Examining these factors also leads to insights and how-tos gleaned from the collective wisdom of strong cross-racial friendships used as models and inspiration in exploring a way forward.

Positing cross-racial friendship as an answer to our deep racial divide may seem naive and even ignorant to those more directly affected by the divide, and miseducated to those who have studied history. It is a rosy answer that comes with hard, coarse thorns. For as the book will lay out, not every cross-racial friendship has the capacity to move the mountains of racism, but all give witness to the goal of racial equity. Advancing race relations in the broader society cannot be achieved just by changes to our national conversation, for sometimes that conversation feels like a shouting match, with neither side listening, rather than a true dialogue. Black Lives Matter conversations are met with All Lives Matter and Blue Lives Matter rebuttals. Racially charged deaths of black men and police officers ignite animated yet stagnant conversations about race. Political rhetoric about what constitutes a racist remark and what makes someone a racist or a bigot doesn't change the narrative on race. Americans don't need more conversations about race. Americans need more friends of different races with whom to engage in conversation about social change and bridging the racial divide.

Cross-racial friendships widen our lenses. They are foundational for building trust and bridging our widening racial divide. It is both an optimistic answer and a necessary, healthy start in the right direction for improving race relations. This book, through a robust combination of research findings and shared stories, aims to be a reliable guide toward that progress.

Chapter 1

LIVING "SEPARATE AS FINGERS"

When I graduated from eighth grade, in 1965, my parents, being Panamanian and Jamaican, didn't know they were not supposed to flee the inner city with the white folks. They moved us to a predominantly white rural area about thirty miles outside Cleveland. At thirteen, thirty miles away from Gayle, Zoe, and Debbie, I found myself a ninth-grader in an all-white, all-girls' Catholic high school. Starting school on the first day, I was friendless. As the only black student in the class I definitely stood out. I didn't have a uniform because my scholarship only paid for tuition and books. We hadn't realized that, and the uniform would be two weeks late by the time my parents could afford to place the order. Instead, I wore my eighth-grade graduation dress, a blue-and-white-striped empire-waist dress that was not store-bought like the ones in *Teen* magazine but made through the excellent seamstress skills of my mother. The dress, with its matching triangle scarf tied under the back of the neck, was the fashion trend at that time. But on that first day of high school, an outfit I once was so proud of became a symbol, along with my skin color, of not belonging.

Less visible were the other factors that made me different from the majority of my classmates. My mother's first language was Spanish and my spoken language growing up in inner-city Cleveland was some form of Spanglish peppered with Ebonics (now known by sociolinguistics as African American Vernacular English, or AAVE, the preferred term of the academic community). Still, I excelled in school, largely because I loved to read. St. Thomas Aquinas did not have a gifted program, so instead the nuns deemed me a candidate for skipping the fourth grade. As a result, I was a full year behind my high school classmates in critical socialization developmental processes.

Like many racial-minority students in private schools, I received a financial scholarship, mine from a Catholic Interracial Scholarship Fund, awarded to gifted black and brown Catholic children to attend Catholic high schools. Although it was an academic scholarship, my family's lower-middle-class status also qualified me for financial support.

Without any friends at lunchtime in my new school, I was destined to eat alone. Not knowing what else to do and feeling isolated, I anxiously stood by my locker arranging and rearranging my books, while wondering if the change my mother had given me that morning for lunch would be enough to buy even a sandwich in the school cafeteria.

"Do you want to eat lunch with us?" Rita, a blond girl with a warm smile approached and asked as she turned to her group of friends, who obviously had not been consulted. They all stared at me.

"Do you like the Beatles?" Joan, the apparent leader of the pack, asked.

In 1964 the Beatles led the "British Invasion" of American pop culture. My best friend at St. Thomas Aquinas, Gayle, atypical of adolescent black girls more in love with Motown artists like Marvin Gaye and Smokey Robinson, was obsessed with the Beatles. Because of Gayle, and because my dad bought all of the Beatles' albums in the bootleg network of neighborhood music sales, I was a fan as well. Luckily, I could give her an honest yes. As it turns out, Joan was just as obsessed, if not more, with the Beatles as Gayle. The Beatles became my pathway to deep friendships across racial lines.

Joan, Rita, and I had radically different upbringings. Joan's was an Italian, upper-middle-class family with a mother who held staunchly conservative Republican values. Her father, John, was born in Italy and migrated with his family to the suburbs of Cleveland at age eight. There, Joan's grandfather, along with his brothers, built the construction business that remains family-owned today. Joan's mom, Betty, had German and Irish roots, although culturally she assimilated Italian in almost every way, she was the only wife in the extended family who worked outside the home and not in the family business. Betty, a feminist in her own right, believed in women controlling their own checkbooks and as a teen instructed me to make sure I had my own money when I married.

Rita's family resembled what was characterized as the "all-American family," not, of course, because of their strong Russian and Bohemian cultural roots, but despite them, in their assimilation practices. Eleanor was a stay-at-home mom who worked over the hot stove preparing dinner and, in dress and apron, greeted Rita's dad, George, upon his return from work. George was a senior development engineer at General Electric and credited with a number of innovations. The family gathered every evening for Eleanor's meals around the dining room table and discussed the day's events. They must have looked like the Cleavers from the 1957–1963 American sitcom *Leave It to Beaver*, the idealized American suburban family living in Ohio. Mom was very loving and Dad was very wise. The kids were obedient.

My parents were immigrants: my dad, from Jamaica and undocumented; my mom, from Panama and holding a green card. My dad was a parking-lot attendant, and my mom inspected parts in a factory. Our family income was marginally middle-class, elevated only through buying goods from the neighborhood's underground network that benefited from illegal activities, a practice normalized in our community and in which even law-abiding citizens and churchgoing people like my parents participated. When my siblings and I were kids, the seven of us would go to bed in a house with a refrigerator and cupboards completely empty and wake up in the morning with a refrigerator and cupboards crammed with a variety of food products. This would happen once a month when "Santa Claus" arrived and delivered food throughout the neighborhood for a fraction of the cost at the grocery store. You could only place large, medium, and small orders, each with a fixed price. We ate whatever Santa Claus provided, which was what "fell off the truck" on its way to the grocery stores.

Joan and Rita reached out to me in friendship in high school without much thought to their intention other than kindness and with little understanding of any racial or social implications. They remain today as my longest-term friends of a different race. After graduating from high school, Joan, Rita, and I each entered the convent and remained friends throughout that shared experience and after we left religious life. We have other shared life experiences, such as being the primary caregivers for our parents. Yet our race shaped different worldviews, which set up taboo topics for discussion, and race continues to dilute intimacy in our friendship, drawing us closer to friends of the same race.

Joan's hair remains one of her best features, although her eyes are still solidly bright despite the wrinkles that have surfaced over the years, more visibly on her olive skin (rooted in her Italian heritage) than on my dark brown skin. As we sit on my deck five months into the Trump administration, discussing the moral decline of our country, Joan traces the origin of that decline to *Roe v. Wade*, the landmark 1973 decision by the United States Supreme Court making abortion legal. As I listen, I focus on her hair. I'm afraid that if I look into her warm eyes, it will serve as an invitation to be honest about my feelings and disrupt our fifty-year friendship. The running commentary going on in my head ranges from a patronizing "Bless her sweet heart" to wondering if she is fricking kidding me. How privileged to be able to forget that America's social contract morally permitted three centuries of slavery. How convenient to forget that Jim Crow deprived blacks of voting rights and institutionalized racial discrimination across the nation as a norm resulting in lynching.

Joan was an elementary school principal. How could she not think about state-sponsored school segregation? She probably forgot about the ban on interracial marriages enforced in many states until 1967. I took a deep breath and, for what felt like the billionth time in our friendship, chose to not confront her. Joan, after all, was one of my dearest and oldest friends, and it was an unusually beautiful spring day in Cleveland. We had just enjoyed a great lunch with Rita, who had left a few minutes before. Fifty-plus years of friendship and still I am careful not to bring up race.

This type of tiptoeing around race in cross-racial conversations is very common and something that I found within my own research and interviewing of focus group participants. Mia, one such participant, is a savvy young black woman who startles me in her wisdom. She tells me that her white conservative friends don't want to talk about race.

"They like to stay in a bubble and be safe," she says.

Though she has many friends of many races, her overall assessment of whether or not these friendships will change race relations is negative.

"I am my white friends' one black friend, and it is not going to make a difference to advance race relations," she tells me. "They think Mia is safe, which is why I am their friend."

It was at that moment that I realized I have a long history of being Joan and Rita's "safe" black friend. I collude in that safety by not being emotionally honest in our conversations. It is a complicated dance, our friendship, and we have memorized the moves in order not to step on each other's toes. Our cross-racial friendship is not unique: there are many cross-racial friendships on the dance floor doing the same awkward dance.

We limit possibilities when we only go with what is safe and what is known. We are all racially myopic. Racial myopia deepens the racial divide.

Having cross-racial friends is far more complicated than most people imagine. As with my friendship with Joan and Rita, friendships across racial lines take work to secure, are challenging to nurture, and are difficult to maintain in a "separate but equal" society. Don't believe me? Ask your friend of a different race. That is, if you have one. The majority of us do not. It has been that way for a very long time.

"In all things purely social, we can be as separate as fingers," Booker T. Washington proposed to a mixed-race audience during his 1895 "Atlanta Compromise" address, "yet one as the hand in all things essential to mutual progress."[1] Being "separate as fingers" socially and only coming together when we need to, particularly for economic advantage, has persisted as a relationship model across the racial divide since 1895. Many people still hold the belief that economic benefit is the only reason to socialize across races. Socializing with whites can provide racial minorities with the right connections that help advance their careers. They can learn "inside baseball" tips on securing promotions and getting buy-in from senior leaders for sponsorship of their ideas and projects. Most importantly, socializing gains them greater understanding of the attitudes and behaviors of whites, which can in turn give them an advantage in the professional world. According to some black focus group participants, however, although socializing with whites might be a business necessity, being friends with them is not.

"Outside of work, it [socializing with whites] is just not worth it," one participant said. "They walk past you like they don't know you on the streets when they are with their white friends. . . . That same white guy will be quick to use the N-word once he gets a few drinks in him."

For whites, the benefit of socializing with people of color is conceptualized as a learning experience, one that may be nice to have but is not considered a necessity. It is a form of cognitive cross-training that provides greater ease and expertise in multicultural settings, similar to being a seasoned traveler:

> "I like to get to know different races of people because I learn different things from them, such as food, ideas, thinking processes, and family dynamics."

> "As I have made cross-racial friends, I love learning new things about different races. I find it fun and life enriching."

> "My cross-racial friends see things differently from how I see my race, and rather than being stressed or upset by their views, I find them helpful providing alternative solutions to my problems."

These contrasting positions by people of color and whites highlight that whites often view cross-racial friends as a life bonus and people of color experience white friends as a life necessity.

In advocating for crossing racial lines as a business necessity, Booker T. Washington was not without critics. Many of his "brothers" accused him of colluding with powerful whites in order to gain support. His words and his conservative approach, they believed, served to undermine the quest for racial equality. While maintaining a separatist attitude toward whites, Washington secretly funded antisegregationist activities. He is best remembered today for helping black Americans rise up from economic slavery.[2] There are many people of color who would agree with Washington's critics in their strategic approach to dealing with powerful whites. In focus groups, both black and brown men tell me that their primary reason for socializing with whites (and really the only reason they can think of) is that it helps them advance in their professional lives. Like Booker T. Washington, their agenda is clear regarding economic freedom, and they are unwavering in their commitment to helping their communities achieve it, even if it means having a few white friends. In their opinion, socializing with whites is a business necessity.

Social science research bears this out. Self-expansion is a basic human motive, and having close friends is a way to achieve it. Having friends across racial lines provides us access to resources, identities, and perspectives we would otherwise lack.[3]

There are others, echoing Washington's critics, who profess economic self-sufficiency and advocate for race pride and racial separatism.

In the 1960s, racial self-sufficiency had its spokesperson in Malcolm X, whose ideology resonates with many of today's young activists, who have experienced little change in the economic and social condition since the civil rights movement. Here are Malcolm X's words:

> I tell sincere white people, "Work in conjunction with us—each of us working among our own kind." Let sincere white individuals find all other white people they can who feel as they do—and let them form their own all-white groups, to work trying to convert other white people who are thinking and acting so racist. . . . Working separately, the sincere white people and sincere black people actually will be working together. In our mutual sincerity we might be able to show a road to the salvation of America's very soul.[4]

Yet historically, many individuals have not followed Malcolm X's separatist views and have crossed racial lines with a shared passion for racial justice. Many of these relationships resulted in friendship, which is typically the catalyst for social change. Dr. William "Smitty" Smith of the National Center for Race Amity describes interracial friendships as "the lifeblood, the mortar that give cohesion and transcending moral strength to the work of establishing equity, access, and social justice."[5] Historically, individuals with widely different backgrounds, through a like-minded vision for social justice, have ended up establishing friendships. This is typically how we have come to know and understand the origins and nature of cross-racial friendships. They have been rooted in a shared vision and goal for achieving racial equality.

If we were to classify friendship on a continuum according to levels of depth or intensity, with points on the continuum being "acquaintance," "casual," "professional," "close," and "intimate," these kinds of friendships might be considered professional relationships, with more benefits directed toward the common good or society than for mutual personal gain. In this professional relationship, each friend holds deep respect for the other born out of an admiration for their advocacy and work together. Many might not consider these kinds of relationships in a social context. Nevertheless, professional cross-racial friendships are worth holding up as a historical framework for the possibilities cross-racial friendships hold. I'll introduce two as examples: First Lady Eleanor Roosevelt and educator Mary McLeod Bethune, whose public display of admiration and respect for one another primed race-relations policies for years to come, and the Reverend Dr. Martin Luther King Jr. and Rabbi Abraham Joshua Heschel, who were model civil rights advocates and spiritual brothers.

Mary McLeod Bethune (1875–1955) was an American educator and founder of Bethune-Cookman College, a private co-ed, historically black college in Florida. She was a prominent civil rights activist in the 1940s and 1950s and founder of the National Council of Negro Women. Mrs. McLeod Bethune enjoyed a public friendship with President Franklin Roosevelt and was a close, loyal friend of First Lady Eleanor Roosevelt. Although they were nine years apart in age, which some might consider significant, Mrs. Roosevelt frequently referred to Mrs. Bethune as "her closest friend in her age group."[6]

In "My Day," a six-day-a-week syndicated newspaper column with a reading audience of over four million, written by Mrs. Roosevelt from 1935 until 1962, she references Mary McLeod Bethune sixteen times during Bethune's lifetime, and once in a 1955 column after Bethune's death. She writes of visits from Bethune, who came to see her "with the desire to get some information as to where the Negro people could function in helping the unfortunates in other countries and in taking a real part in national defense."[7]

In the columns, the First Lady writes about attending benefits at Bethune-Cookman College, attending dinners in Bethune's honor, and presenting Mrs. McLeod Bethune with awards for her "great service in the educational field for her own people."[8]

On March 1, 1955, she writes, "I lunched with the National Council of Colored Women at the Hotel Willard to celebrate the beginning of its 20th year. The meeting was also held the last day of Brotherhood Week, so it was fitting that Mrs. Mary McLeod Bethune, who organized the council and was present as the honored guest should receive tributes for her work not only for the Negro race but for Americans everywhere. Her spirit of charity and kindness has smoothed many a difficult situation and has eased many tensions, and she has certainly helped race relations in the United States."[9]

Eleanor Roosevelt was known for bold moves lobbying for the civil rights of African Americans through her radio broadcasts and newspaper columns. She defied segregation laws at the Southern Conference for Human Welfare in Birmingham, Alabama, intentionally seating herself on the Negro side of the hall next to her friend Mary McLeod Bethune, then director of Negro affairs for the National Youth Administration. When instructed that she could not sit on that side of the hall, Mrs. Roosevelt took a folding chair and sat herself in the middle of the aisle between the two sections.[10]

On February 11, 1949, in a radio interview with Mrs. Roosevelt, Mrs. Bethune announced the launching of the National Council of Negro Women's first nationwide interracial membership list. "For the first time, we are inviting women who believe in the fundamental spirit of democracy to join us in our fight for human and civil rights." She further named the council's goal for reaching a million-membership mark. Mrs. Roosevelt inquired, "Why are you so anxious to get all these new members at this time?" Mrs. Bethune's response: "In these times, Mrs. Roosevelt, we feel that in order to achieve the goal of civil and human rights for all, it is necessary for women of all races and creeds to know and understand each other."[11]

Mrs. Roosevelt's entire newspaper column on May 20, 1955, was a eulogy to Bethune, who had died just days before; the First Lady called her "a really great American woman."[12]

The 2014 historical drama *Selma*, directed by Ava DuVernay and written by Paul Webb, refreshed our collective memory of the historic civil rights march from Selma to Montgomery, Alabama.[13] As a film it took certain liberties with historical facts and came under criticism for the omission of various individuals or groups historically associated with the Selma marches. One such omission was Rabbi Abraham Joshua Heschel.[14] With his wiry white hair and beard, Heschel marched in the front row, arms locked with Ralph Bunche, the first African American to receive the Nobel Peace Prize, whose arms in turn were locked with Dr. Martin Luther King, marking not only Heschel's prominent place in the civil rights movement but his friendship with Dr. King.

King and Heschel had met at the National Conference on Religion and Race and initially bonded over the biblical prophets. King was drawn to Heschel's intimate knowledge of the topic and Heschel in turn admired King's devotion to the Exodus story of Moses and the Israelites, and how he had adapted it to the narrative of the civil rights struggle of the 1950s and '60s.[15] Their friendship was a deeply spiritual one but also rooted in social justice advocacy.

Dr. King recalled: "He has been with us in many struggles. I remember marching from Selma to Montgomery, how he stood at my side. . . . I remember very well when we were in Chicago for the Conference on Religion and Race . . . to a great extent his speech inspired clergymen of all faiths to do something they had not done before."[16]

Rabbi Heschel's daughter, Susannah Heschel, is the Eli Black Professor of Jewish Studies at Dartmouth College and has traveled to Selma several times with her husband and daughter. On one visit, they went to the home of Dr. Sullivan Jackson, where Dr. King spent several months. The home has preserved the furniture as it was. "That was very moving," Susannah tells me, "and Mrs. Jackson told me the morning of the march, she got up, went into the living room, and saw at one side Dr. King praying, at another corner my father was praying, and a couple of others praying. So I thought that image was wonderful, and it shows you that the civil rights movement was about civil rights and humanism and its ability for one room to hold and host all these different people and all of them praying."[17]

In her 2018 article for *Telos*, "A Friendship in the Prophetic Tradition: Abraham Joshua Heschel and Martin Luther King, Jr.," Susannah Heschel states:

> The friendship between Heschel and King was unusual in its day, and was surprising to many, but also inspiring because the two came from such different backgrounds and yet found an intimacy that grew out of their religious commitments and transcended the growing public rifts between the two communities. Heschel brought King and his message to a wide Jewish audience, and King made Heschel a central figure in the struggle for Civil Rights. Often lecturing together, they both spoke about racism as the root of poverty and its role in the war in Vietnam, and both also spoke about Zionism and Israel and about the struggles of Jews in the Soviet Union. The transcendent issue was "saving the soul of America," the motto of the SCLC [Southern Christian Leadership Conference].[18]

Although most cross-racial friendships do not come shrouded in the obvious historical cloak of Roosevelt and Bethune's and King and Heschel's, all cross-racial friendships are embedded in America's racist history and can be both a unifying and polarizing force in society—unifying in that the friendship heightens awareness of the universal nature of humanity, and polarizing in that race also underlines the disparities in how each is treated in America. The polarizing aspect is most often unacknowledged among cross-racial friends. Treating each other as equals and pretending as though society does the same tends to be the norm. With this baggage strapped to every cross-racial friendship, it is understandable why there are so few.

Delving into this topic was spurred by an examination of the nature of my own cross-racial friendships. Did they extend beyond a shared vision for racial justice? Was it possible to have a cross-racial friendship without working for racial justice? How did the nature of my cross-racial friendships compare to others?

From my research, I know that individual cross-racial friendships do extend beyond advancing race relations in the broader society. You can be friends with someone of a different race and share a relationship that is not necessarily born out of a shared vision of and collective work for racial justice. Racial justice can be a happy by-product of cross-racial friendships, and a substantial body of evidence has suggested that reduced prejudice is a significant benefit of socializing across racial lines. The benefits further include reduced racial isolation in communities, the creation of a better-informed citizenry, an expansion of the concept of citizenship to a global level, the improvement of team performance in organizations, and an increase in innovation in organizations and the arts.[19]

Still, the case for extending ourselves across racial lines in friendship has yet to be made to the extent that cross-racial friendships personally matter to the average American. Examining one's friendship list and noting that there are no friends of different races is not a cause for lamenting for most Americans.

It is said that, on average, most individuals only have about one or two really close friends in a lifetime. More gregarious people travel through life with a social group of about six to ten friends. Widening the circle to include friendly acquaintances can take one up to about twenty-five.

Considering these numbers, there does not seem to be a compelling case for moving out of one's racial boundaries in the search for friends. There seem to be plenty of choices from the look-alike category, and it takes precious time and considerable psychological effort to extend ourselves into the "don't look like me" category.

REDUCED RACIAL ISOLATION IN OUR COMMUNITIES

Humans are by nature tribal; we are attracted to and want to live near people who share our racial identity, so the need for having cross-racial friends can be a tough sell. Reducing racial isolation in communities is not a high priority for most Americans. Research suggests that whites want to live in all-white neighborhoods and will tolerate only a few from different races. This phenomenon was dubbed in 1971 the "thirty-three and a third tip," with evidence that once racial diversity approaches roughly a third in a neighborhood, it results in white flight.[20] A similar tipping point does not appear to occur for blacks. Blacks desire to live in racially mixed neighborhoods but are okay living in predominantly black neighborhoods.[21] Regardless of socioeconomic class, race influences Americans' decisions on where they live. What is not clear is whether or not neighborhood racial segregation is a result of our natural instincts to live with our "own kind" or because we want to avoid those who are different from us. This lack of attributional clarity makes it difficult to suggest that having multiracial friendships supports reducing racial isolation, when many individuals prefer to be racially isolated, or at least do not mind it.

BETTER-INFORMED CITIZENRY

Populist-fueled rhetoric during the American 2016 presidential campaign not only uncovered angry voters who felt that they were being ignored by the established political parties but revealed how little informed average citizens (and even political candidates) were about how government actually works. The resurgence of the populist movement underscored the necessity and value of a better-informed citizenry. But while baby boomers and traditionalists might look back fondly on their junior high school civics classes, civics education is not a given in the digital age. Though forty-three states mandate that students study civics and learn about political parties, scholars note that civics classes present an oversimplification of the student's role in our democracy.[22] Clearly, it is advantageous for Americans to understand how government works, since they are charged with voting for candidates who have the power to make decisions that affect their day-to-day lives. Given that America remains racially segregated in neighborhoods and social lives, without authentic communication across racial lines, we risk the endless gridlock of a divided government as well.

EXPANDED GLOBAL CITIZENSHIP

The same rationale would hold for presenting a case for expanding the concept of citizenship to a global level. Global issues of a social, political, economic, or environmental nature tend to baffle the average American struggling to raise children on flat salaries, maintain their jobs with some level of enthusiasm for their work, pay for healthcare, and secure retirement to finally achieve some kind of life balance before they die. It is to our advantage to understand the deep interconnectedness of economic, political, and social life on our planet Earth by acting locally and thinking globally, as the saying dictates. Global citizenship is a way of thinking that people come to understand through formative life experiences such as those fostered in cross-racial friendships. Cultural empathy, principled decision-making, and cultural competence are enhanced in cross-racial relationships.[23] These competencies are not only necessary for a growing economy but for strengthening our democracy. Cross-racial friendships are a way to act locally and to expand our global consciousness.

IMPROVED TEAM PERFORMANCE
AND INNOVATION IN ORGANIZATIONS

But what about businesses and the case for increased productivity and innovation? This argument for having cross-racial friends presents our strongest case. Working as a diversity professional for three decades, I have facilitated hundreds of sessions to support inclusive work practices. Evaluations from diversity training sessions lend support to the idea that these sessions produce greater understanding of the complexities of diversity and its business case. Participants also develop skills for effectively communicating across ethnic and racial differences, along with a heightened awareness of any unconscious bias they may hold. Yet those benefits are not enough to build a case for cross-racial friendships.

An even stronger case is made by efforts to create synergy among network groups charged with creating and implementing organizational diversity and inclusion goals. Fostering contact among diverse employees with the aim of achieving the mission and business objectives of an organization can be more successful than diversity training itself. Working together on goals rather than just learning together on how to get along is far more productive.

Social scientists and change-management researchers agree that diversity has a competitive advantage in the business context if the conditions are right.[24] It is logical to assume that cross-racial friendships support people's ability to feel comfortable with diverse teams and generate positive feelings regarding differences and increased engagement and enthusiasm for working with others who do not share one's racial identity. All of these characteristics are what social science researcher Todd Pittinsky calls "allophilia," a liking for those whom we perceive to be "other." Friendships, Pittinsky claims, can serve as a path toward something positive and can do more than just eliminate prejudice.[25] Allophilia and prejudice have independent causes and are not opposites, as allophilia describes how one *feels* about certain groups and ascertains one's desire to move toward the "other" rather than simply tolerate their existence or holding a cognitive belief in the universal nature of humanity.[26] From this perspective, diverse work groups not only enhance performance and spur innovation but encourage different races to develop friendships if they so choose.

Social connections in general, and specifically across racial lines, have been linked to improved academic performance, income, and overall quality of life.[27] In a national survey conducted for this book, 70 percent of respondents *strongly* agreed that friendships across racial lines are essential to making progress toward improving race relations. An additional 25 percent agreed with the statement, totaling 95 percent who endorsed cross-racial friendships as critical to improved race relations. There were no significant differences in this affirmative response between whites and people of color. Almost everyone, particularly those with higher education, agrees that it is to our advantage to have cross-racial friends.[28]

In this same study, however, there was a difference by educational level in responses to how *important* it is to have a close friend across racial lines. Those with higher education (college degree, master's, doctorate, and professional degree) endorsed its strong importance; those with less education (some college, high school or GED, no high school degree) did not believe that it was as important to have cross-racial friends. These survey study results should be interpreted with extreme caution, however. Those with less education may simply believe that friends are friends and race should not matter. That belief was expressed anecdotally from focus group participants. Nevertheless, the findings strengthen the case for having diverse classrooms, as individuals with higher education may realize not only the complexities of cross-racial friendship but also its importance to improving race relations and the overall quality of life for all Americans.

So, if the majority of us agree that it is to our advantage and that it is important, what keeps us from forming cross-racial friends? Based on our survey, the top three barriers to having close cross-racial friends were time (respondent has no time in their daily life for more friends), neighborhood (respondent's neighborhood is not racially diverse), and work (respondent's workplace is not racially diverse).[29] To summarize, we believe that cross-racial friendships are essential for improved race relations, but we don't have time to establish them and we don't live or work in racially diverse environments. As a result, despite a strong professed belief in the power of cross-racial friendships to improve race relations for the benefit of all, most Americans do not have friends of a different race.[30]

In our daily lives, the advantage of having friends of different racial backgrounds is rarely raised as important, brought to our awareness, or even discussed. One reason is that we consider the work of bridging the ever-widening racial divide as a mammoth task that requires herculean effort rather than a light-one-candle approach. As a nation, when we break our silence to talk about race, it is in the form of a large systemic initiative such as One America in the 21st Century: The President's Initiative on Race, established by President Bill Clinton with Executive Order 13050 in 1997.[31] Or when Americans of all races listened in hushed silence as then senator Barack Obama delivered his speech on race on March 8, 2008, addressing the role race had played in the presidential election season.[32] Or closing the racial divide is considered work to be undertaken by academics with prestigious educational grants directed toward racial healing and racial equity, such as those sponsored by the Kellogg or Ford Foundations. Bridging the racial divide is simply perceived as too enormous to be the work of the average American.

Race is a big deal in the United States, and we are extremely uncomfortable talking about it, let alone making friends with someone of a different race. We intuitively know that in order to achieve the benefits of establishing cross-racial friendships we have to surmount some overwhelming challenges, and, as in the case of Mary McLeod Bethune and Eleanor Roosevelt, and Rabbi Joshua Heschel and Martin Luther King Jr., we have to be so driven and connected by the quest for racial justice that we are willing to make sacrifices for it.

Yet cross-racial friendships between average Americans can serve in just as profound a manner as any major national race initiative and might offer a more sustainable and permanent way to bridge the racial divide. We need cross-racial friends in order to master developmental tasks that, left unattended, render us incomplete as individuals and as a society. Still, the racial divide continues to widen, most notably between blacks and whites. Three responses from focus groups illustrate this reluctance to cross racial lines in friendship:

"Why do I even have to have black friends?" (47-year-old white male)

"You want to tell me with what I know about the history of how blacks have been treated by whites in this country, that now I should forgive them and turn around and be friends with them?" (45-year-old black male)

"I have a very small circle of people that I consider friends. Do I have any close white friends? I don't think so—not right now. I have a lot of white acquaintances at work or organizations and a lot of them come from friends of my kids. I don't have a need for them." (52-year-old black woman)

More than a century after Booker T. Washington first used the metaphor, we are still as separate as fingers, and it is worth examining why that is so and doing something about it. Perhaps we need to be "one as the hand" not just for financial gain but in things "purely social." We need to confirm whether or not racial desegregation is just a business necessity or essential to our mutual progress as a nation. My belief is that racial desegregation is not just about our economic survival but our ability to preserve and strengthen our democracy through a shared vision that comes only from an understanding of another's reality. Understanding another's reality is dependent on interpersonal relationships. Perhaps, in socializing across racial lines and becoming friends, we can create a collective vision and achieve mutual progress. Why is this so hard to do?

It is because cross-racial friendships represent more than the relationship between the two individuals. How cross-racial friendships are viewed and interpreted is symbolic of and influenced by broader social nuances and themes related to race relations.

———

Unlike the historical cross-racial friendships of Bethune and Roosevelt or Heschel and King, my friendship with Joan and Rita is not rooted in working for racial justice. As friends, we share a history of going to the same high school and knowing each other and each other's families for a very long time. This history provides an emotional foundation for going deeper on the tough topics if we so choose. Still, even after decades of knowing each other we tread lightly and carefully when we bring up race.

Weeks after our lunch, I decide to circle back to my conversation with Joan about our nation's loss of moral compass and talk about my reaction from a racial lens. She listens intently as I explain my reaction to her comment dating the start of the decline to *Roe v. Wade*. I listen just as intently as she explains to me that her strong religious beliefs and the tenets of her faith tradition are what guide her thinking. I understand what she is telling me, although my views on the religion we both share are very different. We continue a forward-moving conversation about how race and religion influence our thinking. We agree that our politics are probably more similar than they appear but the trappings of race in my case and religion in hers take us to very different places. We end this conversation in reflection buoyed by really hearing and understanding what the other has said. Because we are friends, we know we will circle back to the topic again. Still, our racial differences make preserving the friendship a challenge.

Chapter 2

LIVING "ONE AS THE HAND"

A doctor, Janet had traveled the same dark roads after her evening shift at the hospital for the past eleven years, yet tonight she doubted her ability to safely navigate the thirty-minute ride home.[1] She couldn't control her tears or her mounting anger. The banter that evening at the nurses' station resembled other hospital chatter in its tone and levity, except the subject was the recent presidential election. The conversation shouldn't have upset her as badly as it did, but the election had shaken her faith in the political system and her relationship with white people as well.

Lisa was her friend, one of the few white nurses on the floor that she trusted and had even socialized with outside of work hours. They had managed to transcend the perceived power differential of physician and nurse. They had established a friendship stemming from a shared value of compassionate patient care. Yet Lisa was participating in the celebratory banter about the election of Donald J. Trump, which was something Janet could not fathom.

"The best man won and it will make the country so much better now. Build that wall as high as the sky."

Didn't they see her standing there, just a few steps away?

"He'll get them all off of welfare."

Did she really see Lisa smiling and agreeing?

She held her breath for what seemed like an eternity, waiting for Lisa to interrupt, to come to the defense of people of color, of immigrants, of women, of Muslims, of LGBT individuals who had been insulted by the candidate, now president-elect. Surely Lisa would come to the defense of the many patients who represented the groups disparaged by these remarks. Together they had cared for these patients. How could she not challenge the stereotypes and acknowledge the racial slurs?

Lisa had chimed into the conversation with her hopes for less-expensive insurance premiums with the promised repeal of Obamacare. It was then that Janet realized the unimaginable. Not only had Trump been elected, but her good friend had voted for someone she considered to be in direct opposition to her cherished principles and values. She had thought of Lisa as a friend, but today confirmed what she'd always suspected in her heart to be true: black people could never truly be friends with white people.

How is it possible that Janet and Lisa's eleven-year friendship, which included numerous shared experiences—meals, laughter, tears, vacations, birthday and graduation celebrations, conversations about their marriages and a divorce, celebrating births and grieving deaths—neglected to include meaningful conversations about how their racial identities influenced how they perceived the world and their decision-making processes? Unfortunately, this is not unusual. In fact, it is the norm.

Here's some confirming data. A Reuters poll found that white Americans were far less likely to have friends of another race than nonwhite Americans: about 40 percent of white Americans had only white friends, whereas about 25 percent of nonwhite Americans were surrounded only by people of their own race.[2] Another study designed to assess the scope of diversity of Americans' social networks found that these networks primarily consisted of people from the same racial or ethnic background, especially for white Americans. Among white Americans, 91 percent of the people in their social networks were white.[3] Simply put, white people are racial isolationists.

The situation isn't much better in black and brown America. Among black Americans, 83 percent of the people in their social networks were black. Among Hispanic Americans, approximately two-thirds (64 percent) of the people in their social networks were Hispanic.

A Pew Research Center survey found that Asians and American Indians follow a similar pattern and claim little in common with those who don't share their racial backgrounds. Among Asians, 54 percent reported that all or most of their close friends are Asians.[4]

It is easy to connect to literally hundreds of "friends" on social media and to cross racial lines in internet connections, but the pick-up-the-phone-at-3:00-a.m.-because-I-am-lonely-and-depressed kind of friend generally shares our same race. Although cross-racial friendships are not by any means rare, many people do hold the expectation that their friends will be the same race as their own. We expect others to have friends of the same race as well. Clearly President Obama's life experiences have been enriched by his diverse racial background. Diversity is literally in his DNA and in the spaces he has called home over the years. Yet despite his multiracial, multicultural background and family tree, President Obama's reportedly three closest friends—Valerie Jarrett, Martin Nesbitt, and Dr. Eric Whitaker—are all black. Where friendships are concerned, race transcends personality, as well as similarities in occupations and values. We all, to a great extent, tend to be racial isolationists.

Not only are we racial isolationists, but those who venture out into having cross-racial friendships avoid racially sensitive topics and enter the relationship limiting their personal investment, protecting emotional boundaries that are more open with their same-race friends. In research conducted with colleagues at the University of Massachusetts Medical School, we found that those who reported at least one friend of a different race described a general reluctance to discuss any racially charged societal events, such as police shootings of unarmed black men.[5]

In our research, focus group participants reported that they experienced lower levels of trust and intimacy with cross-racial friends than with same-race friends. They attributed this difference to historical influences of American race relations. Illustrative quotations are as follows:

> "White folks don't 'get it' and some things would be different if my friend was black. Whites have a fear factor from segregating themselves based on old stereotypes." (55-year-old black female)

> "I am listening to this conversation [about friends of different races] and I have nothing to draw from. I don't really have any close friends of a different race." (46-year-old white female)

> "There's not enough exposure today to other races to carry us through these challenges. A lot of discrimination got carried

on from past generations and we are reverting back to that mentality." (42-year-old white woman)

"When our kids were younger, then we got together with the parents of their white friends. Not so much now. The different realities first came out with Hurricane Katrina. A white friend said things that were so flipping backwards and I didn't call her on it." (52-year-old black woman)

Those who have crossed racial lines find it challenging to do so as an equal partnership. The influence of social, historical, and political factors in shaping cross-racial friendships is strong. In both its intentional overt and unintentional covert forms, racism continues to exist. It takes work to achieve the intimacy and depth required to surmount the external barriers to cross-racial friendship.

As a result, despite increased opportunity to live and work in mixed-race settings, cross-racial friendships like Janet and Lisa's lack the capacity to navigate such racially fraught issues as the 2016 American presidential campaign, immigration reform, the travel ban of Muslim countries, or the police shootings of unarmed black men and the killings of police officers. This reluctance extends to even casual conversations about movies, television shows, tweets, and advertisements with racial themes.

After Janet overheard the election conversation at work and witnessed what she experienced as Lisa's racial insensitivity, she was so distressed that she began to look for other employment. Despite support from her mentor and her department chair, she accepted another position, believing that the attitudes of the caregivers she had been working with would never change and they would not be held accountable for actions that resulted from their racial bias, whether conscious or unconscious. She also severed her friendship with Lisa. There was already enough stress in her life and she didn't need any more, especially from someone who was supposed to be her friend.

Why is it so hard to be friends with those who do not share our racial identity? As it turns out, making a friend of a different race is not as easy as just making the simple decision to do so. From a psychological perspective, it is hard for several reasons: first, how our brain forms prejudices; second, psychological factors; third, cultural encapsulation; fourth, personal choice; and fifth, demographic challenges.

OUR BRAINS ON DIVERSITY

Current research in neuropsychology offers promise for shedding light on individual and group preferences that extend beyond social structures, interpersonal factors, and identity-group preferences. The use of functional magnetic resonance imaging (fMRI), a neuroimaging procedure that allows us to track blood flow, has also enabled us to learn a great deal about how the brain functions. It has allowed researchers to make sense of certain behaviors related to race and racial attitudes.[6]

One hallmark of executive functioning, or the neurological skills related to mental control, is the ability to be able to stop inappropriate reactions to stimuli. For example, a toddler might be excused for yelling out, "Look, Mommy, her is a nigger!" as one toddler did, much to the chagrin of his mother, when he saw me at a mall in a predominantly white suburban neighborhood of a major US city. However, we would not excuse a teenager or adult who yelled out a similar response. We would hold that individual accountable for control of his executive functioning (unless that functioning was impaired). Even from someone who is impaired, however, such outbursts can cause intense psychological discomfort to those on the receiving end.

The use of the fMRI has led researchers to suggest that the executive function becomes depleted and needs to be refreshed when one has interracial contact, particularly when combating stereotypes and unconscious bias.[7] Research facilitated by Dr. Jennifer Richeson and her colleagues suggests that harboring racial bias limits our cognitive functioning, and during interracial contact our brain is working hard to overcome the social loadings of racism and bias. In other words, our brain has to work harder in cross-racial friendships than it does in same-race friendships.[8]

Current neuropsychology research further provides an explanation for the lack of cross-racial friendships. Behavioral neuroscience indicates that specific brain regions, particularly the amygdala, or emotional center, are active in initiating and maintaining racial bias. Our brain is wired to manage our emotions in such a way that if we encounter differences and do not know what to do about them, we go into the "fight or flight" mode. This is how it works: We get a visual signal that goes into the thalamus, where it is translated into brain language and then moves on to the visual cortex to be analyzed and interpreted. If the message is interpreted to be emotional, then it finds a home in the amygdala—the emotional center of the brain. When we get a visual signal that ignites fear, it bypasses the cortex and goes directly to the amygdala. We experience an "amygdala hijack," a term coined by psychologist and science journalist Daniel Goleman in his book *Emotional Intelligence*.[9] The emotional reaction of fear and experience of threat is immediate and overwhelming. In reality, the feelings are out of proportion with the actual stimulus.

When we encounter differences and we lack diversity skills, most brains respond via the amygdala hijack. We may claim to have no biases or may believe that any prejudices that we might have are under our control, but we all possess unconscious, hardwired processes that do not allow us to easily approach and befriend those who do not share our same racial identity.

The way that we are wired also makes it easier for us to perceive racial differences as a threat. Our nervous system reacts differently to stressful situations that we perceive as challenges versus those we perceive as threats. Although both situations incite a physiological response, challenges incite a sequence that sends more blood to our system, whereas threats restrict our blood flow.[10] Challenges enhance our physical and cognitive performance. It is why people challenge themselves by competing in triathlons, climbing Mount Everest, or even just trying to clock ten thousand steps a day on a Fitbit. It is why the American quiz show *Jeopardy*, where contestants are presented with clues in the form of answers and must phrase their responses in the form of a question, has been on television since 1964. Each year, more than seventy thousand people take the very difficult online test just to be able to be one of three thousand who get to audition for the show.[11] Challenges are emotionally draining but very rewarding.

Threats, on the other hand, break down muscle tissue and halt our digestive processes in order for us to face them. Over time these responses wear down muscles, including the heart, and damage the immune system. Lacking the experience of socializing and making friends across racial lines, coupled with our proclivity toward being with those who share our racial identity, leads to perceiving cross-racial friends as a potential threat to avoid or perhaps, at best, a challenge that must be mastered. As a potential threat, or even a challenge to master, establishing cross-racial friendship is simply not easy.

We also know that our cognitive processes are wired to draw us to those who are most like us. People are tribal, and whereas in-group favoritism can be perceived as a form of everyday discrimination, it is simply the result of human nature. Most individuals do not have friends across racial lines simply because they prefer to be with others like themselves.

In some typical, mostly unconscious ways, we make decisions that interfere with how we make choices about who to socialize with and that prejudice us toward those who share our racial-group identity. Pattern recognition and emotional tagging are normally reliable decision-making processes that are part of our evolutionary advantage as humans. However, in certain circumstances, like managing differences, both of these processes predispose us to choose friends of the same racial group.

Pattern recognition is a complex process that integrates information from as many as thirty different parts of our brain. When we are faced with a new situation, we make assumptions based on our prior experiences and judgments.[12] Cross-racial friendships are shaped and influenced by social, historical, and political context. Focus group participants from ages eighteen to sixty-five agreed that the way they were raised influenced whether or not they crossed racial lines in making friends. Some quickly made the assumption that the color of one's skin foreshadows the kind of values one holds and practices. When we extend that assumption to people who are of a different race, it is easy to draw the conclusion that a friendship is not possible.

Emotional tagging is the process by which emotional information attaches itself to the thoughts and experiences stored in our memories.[13] Emotional tags associated with race become rooted in our socialization process during childhood and remain catalogued in our brain. We are socially loaded with stereotypes and assumptions about racial groups from a variety of sources, positive and negative. Emotionally tagged stereotypes offer an explanation for why children have less difficulty making friends from many different races and it becomes more complicated to do so as an adult. As we get older, our brains are loaded with a lot more stereotypes and unconscious biases that take work to mitigate. We may experience ourselves as being inclusive but we have to work with our primitive brain to act in egalitarian ways rather than from stereotypes and unconscious biases.

Positive emotional tags about race also cause people to overestimate the number of cross-racial friends they actually have, as well as the depth of those relationships. A focus group participant states that he is "pretty sure that I am about twelve different people's black best friend and I have all of these white people who once knew me in high school as friends . . . Most likely I probably just sat next to them at lunch one day."

PSYCHOLOGICAL FACTORS

As a result of how our brains form prejudices and process differences, we have to work harder to move toward others who are different from us. This does not mean we are predestined not to like those who are different from us. It simply means that we have a *preference* for those who are most like us. Implicit stereotypes and biases can be revealed and reduced with awareness and intention.[14] It is very much like erasing an old tape and recording new information over it or realigning a car's tires. As a result of how our brain processes information, we have to work at moving outside of our natural preferences to obtain and maintain cross-racial friendships.

We also do not have friends across racial lines because we are lazy. Not lazy as in slovenly, but lazy in the sense that we choose not to make the extra effort it takes to cross racial lines to achieve friendship and understanding. Going for tolerance is so much easier. We do not have to move out of our comfort zones or take in new perspectives or change in any way. It takes a lot of motivation and work to form a friendship that is optional.

We are also scared to make friends across racial lines because we do not want to risk hurting other people's feelings and opening ourselves to criticism or rejection. When it comes to race issues, we often feel like we are walking on eggshells. No one likes feeling this way, so we remain racial isolationists and never develop the communication skills and emotional resilience necessary for crossing racial lines in friendship without fear.

We also do not have friends across racial lines because we are insecure. We want to believe in our inherent goodness and act out of our core identity as humans. Differences are met with fear and treated as a threat. When we are fearful, our best selves do not surface.

CULTURAL ENCAPSULATION

Standard measures of segregation, such as evenness of distribution, exposure to potential contact, concentration of physical space, and clustering of identity groups, show that American cities are more integrated today than they have been since 1910, but spatial racism still exists.[15] Spatial racism is a pattern of housing development in which racially and economically segregated suburbs or gentrified areas of cities are created.[16] Simply put, we still live in neighborhoods with others who share our race. Considerable research has demonstrated that the degree of intersectionality and the opportunity for contact between social positions (class, age, and education level) either constrain or facilitate social relations between racial/ethnic groups. The opportunity for contact further depends on whether or not members of smaller groups live near or work with one another.[17]

Although racial diversity has increased in the workforce, coworkers experience limited contact with one another outside the work environment. The resulting cultural encapsulation from living apart and having limited contact with others of different races outside of work settings may lead to ethnocentrism and limited understanding of another's worldview and explains why it is challenging to make cross-racial friends. Despite increased opportunity to live and work in mixed-race settings, Americans remain racially segregated in their friendship patterns.

PERSONAL CHOICE

Making and maintaining friendships is enough work without adding racial differences into the mix. Americans lead busier and busier lives. Modern communications provide countless ways to keep us informed and thus ever occupied with projects, deadlines, and goals. Time is at a premium and precious leisure time is generally spent with people we can easily relate to and who share a common understanding of what it means to have fun, relax, and enjoy life. When friendships are complicated by differences in how one views and experiences the world, or when one's race evokes or solicits different reactions from the environment, it interrupts the natural flow we expect from a friendship. When we cross racial lines in friendship, it does indeed take work. As a result, many people choose, consciously or unconsciously, not to have friends who cross racial lines. In friendship with whites, many people of color, consciously or unconsciously, choose not to make the effort to be fully authentic and become "safe friends."

This safety facilitates a more comfortable interaction and what researchers have termed the "facade of liking."[18]

DEMOGRAPHIC CHALLENGES

Just on sheer numbers alone, until at least midcentury there will be about two whites for every person of color in the United States. Add to this our geographic segregation, and people of color end up being "*the* friend" for many whites. A young African American male relates that he is the first black friend of many of his white college friends. He says that when he goes to their weddings, he never has to be introduced. People come up to him and say, "You must be Victor!"

"How did they know that?" he jokingly asks.

There's a story of a town in which people generally went about without shoes that was also home to one of the largest shoe factories in the world. When the townspeople were repeatedly asked about getting shoes to protect their feet, their standard response was, "Yes, why don't we?" And then they continued to go about their lives shoeless.

The United States has the widest and richest population diversity in the world, yet, like shoeless people surrounded by a large shoe factory, we continue to not fully take advantage of our racial diversity in support of the creation of an informed, inclusive citizenry. Nor do we utilize that same environment as a natural laboratory for managing the dynamics of our racial differences with ease and competence. Sadly, we remain "as separate as fingers" and monoracial in our everyday lived experience, and we will remain a society that settles for tolerance as the standard for race relations, a standard that has persisted for over a century, preventing us from being "one as the hand toward mutual progress." But in a global society, Americans cannot afford to have tolerance as the high bar.

Improving US race relations requires more than a financial solution or a leveling of the playing field toward job creation, better educational systems for those who are disadvantaged, health equity, and prison reform. The root causes of bias, prejudice, and discrimination can thrive even despite these advancements. Real progress will be made when we own and manage our biases and are accountable for our learned tendencies. Only then, collectively, being "one as the hand," will we mark progress toward a fuller democracy.

Chapter 3

TWO-BUTTON CHOICE: ACQUAINTANCE OR LOVER

On a beautiful summer day in 1968, my sister and I were busy writing out the lyrics of our favorite songs as we heard them being played on the radio. We had discovered on those lazy summer days that if you listened to the radio long enough, your favorite tune would play at least two or three times in a four-to-five-hour cycle. We would wait until we heard "our jam" and, ready with pen and notebook, rush to write out the words. It certainly wasn't demanding work for fifteen- and sixteen-year-olds without summer jobs, but in those days, absent Google, it was the only way to get the lyrics of our favorite songs. We loved doing it. Yet, after a few hours on a reasonably productive day of completing all the words to Sly and the Family Stone's "Dance to the Music," we decided to move on to something even more exciting, like cruising around the city.

My sister called her friend Greg, who had just gotten his driver's license and had access to his parents' car. He came over with one of his friends, Ryan, and we began our destination-free journey. The drive into Cleveland from Huntsburg, Ohio, was a straight shot down Route 322, Mayfield Road, from which we could easily make a left just at the end of the hill and cross over County Line Road to the East Side suburb of Gates Mills, where my friend Joan lived. We decided to make a stop and invite her to continue cruising with us.

It took just the ring of the doorbell and the question, "You doing anything? Come, go out with us," for Joan to enthusiastically jump in the car, now occupied by two black teenage boys, two black teenage girls, and her. Joan sat in the backseat, nestled between me and Ryan. We stopped at the giant slide right near the interstate highway, a summertime attraction for little and big kids during the summer months. With only enough money for one or two slides, we were done in a half hour. We decided to show Joan the old house where my sister and I spent our childhood years and headed to the Glenville neighborhood, a part of the city where just two weeks later, race riots would result in seven deaths, many more critically injured, and the Glenville community destroyed. Since we spent our days listening for our favorite songs rather than the news and because we found our parents' conversation about anything political boring, we were unaware of the racial unrest brewing. I only knew Glenville as my old neighborhood, which was often called "the ghetto," a term that didn't seem particularly offensive to me because of the fond memories I had of a close-knit community that provided us with a sense of belonging.

We were a group of sheltered, protected, naive teenagers out joyriding when, at a traffic light, we heard loud cursing and ranting coming from the car idling next to us, filled with young adult black men. The conversation went something like this:

"Brotha, you got that bitch hanging out with you!"

"You don't know shit. And what do you care?" Greg bravely responded. I had never heard him use the word "shit," and he stated it more as a mild peep rather than putting a heavy accent on the word to make it a strong definitive statement.

"It ain't got nutting to do which you," my sister Simone joined in, itching to start something and adopting Ebonics. I wasn't quite sure where she picked up the black American English, since she went to Cardinal High School, where there were few black students.

"That white bitch does," they retorted.

I looked at Joan, examining her whiteness, seeing it as a racial classification for the first time. It then dawned on me that they thought Joan was Ryan's girlfriend. When we picked Joan up, I noticed her older brother watching her get in the car. It briefly occurred to me that he might not like her hanging out with a bunch of black kids, but that he was probably cool enough not to say anything.

"I think they are talking about you," I said to Joan, sensing she didn't have a clue what was going on.

She didn't. "Really?" She eyed me incredulously and could barely speak. "They're being racist against me? What did I do?"

The light turned green and Greg quickly sped off. I don't recall feeling fear, and when we talk about it all these years later, Joan doesn't recall being afraid either. In fact, we remember laughing about it all the way back to Gates Mills. Joan, to this day, talks about that encounter as if it were a badge of courage she received for outstanding racial-equality work.

Many contend that the fear of socializing across racial lines is rooted in the traditional taboo against interracial dating and marriage. On the interpersonal level, we tend to skip the possibility of cross-racial friendships. It is as if there is a two-button choice for crossing racial lines—the forced-choice categories being either acquaintance or lover. Our survey data shows that most individuals welcome cross-racial relationships as coworkers or professional colleagues and accept those who fall in love, recognizing that love is something over which we have little control, especially when we live and work in diverse settings. Many even applaud intimate interracial relationships as symbolic of a color-blind society. But having cross-racial friends? Nope. You either know the person of a different race superficially in your acquaintance as coworkers or neighbors, or you are in the throes of intimacy. There is no in-between.

Negative attitudes toward interracial dating have changed over the years, and more people are either much more tolerant of, or remain neutral about, interracial couples than ever before. The large majority (92 percent) of respondents to our national friendship survey approved of interracial marriage.[1] Not surprisingly, the minority of those in our study who reported having no friends that cross racial lines disapproved of interracial marriage. Somewhat surprisingly, a similar minority held true for every category among those who had friends that crossed racial lines; whether they reported having one friend or eight or more cross-racial friends, there were those who expressed disapproval of interracial marriage. In other words, having cross-racial friends does not necessarily translate into approval of interracial marriage.

Although race as a biological construct remains meaningless, as a sociopolitical construct, race is fraught with emotional triggers. From an early age, children begin to process the negative stereotypes and perceptions of other racial groups and learned misinformation about race.[2] They become conscious of and often disturbed by contradictions between what parents, teachers, and other influential adults tell them about the value of racial diversity and how they see it lived out.

Many parents drive home the message of not dating across racial lines born out of this negative perception early in their children's lives. Andrew, a professional black man in one focus group, candidly expressed his concerns about the possibility of his young son dating a white woman. "I'll tell him that it is all right for now to be friends, but after a time, if he is still looking at little white Suzy over here, he's going to know that he needs to be talking to Shaneequa." Apparently, any black Shaneequa, in his mind, would cause a lot less hassle in his life than any white Suzy.

In another focus group, a forty-year-old Asian Indian female stated:

I told my children not to marry a white person because history would come into the marriage. I am going to teach them the beauty of the Hindu culture. It is not racism. I will promote having more Indian friends because you can't control who you fall in love with. If his circle of friends were more Indian/Hindu, he would be more likely to marry a Hindu woman.

Santiago, an attorney, shared with me his anxiety about having "the talk" with his teenage daughter, who was starting to date. "The talk" goes something like this: "Honey, we know that you are a good person and you can do anything and achieve anything you want in this life. We are proud of being Puerto Rican, but we need you to know that some people will find it a problem when Johnny says that he wants to take you to homecoming. Now, we like Johnny and don't have a problem with you and Johnny together, but just so that you are aware . . . do Johnny's parents know you are Puerto Rican?" In his eyes as a Latino parent, not to have armored his daughter with "the talk" would have amounted to negligence.

This message about racial-friendship boundaries transmitted by parents of color to their children predates "the talk" currently given to black and brown children about police brutality. In a study on children and race commissioned by *Anderson Cooper 360°*, students reported discouragement of interracial dating from their parents, and from their friends, with reactions ranging from wariness to outright forbiddance.[3] The study points to the fact that these attitudes are generational; however, the message parents give their children about interracial dating is a strong one. The architect of the *AC360°* study, child psychologist Dr. Melanie Killen, says parents of both white and black kids have significant anxiety about the prospect of interracial dating. Killen contends that parental disapproval can have a profound negative effect on their children's friendships and racial attitudes as a whole.[4]

Maria, a parent of two strikingly beautiful African American women, has been giving her daughters "the talk" since they were teens, and considers it an ongoing conversation. In her opinion, it would be naive not to anticipate problems with interracial dating. She recalls being encouraged to date those of her same race as a young adult. Friends were always quick to match her with the other few black men in her class.

"Friends would tell me, so-and-so is nice. Maybe I didn't like those guys. Maybe I wanted more of a selection." Maria believes that "the talk" may have been modified over the years, but it persists.

Laurie, also African American, tells me that "the talk" among black parents and one that she has with her young adult daughter is now focused on how to attract and maintain a relationship with a black man. There are a number of black women in her social network who are very anxious about their sons' choice of a dating partner and worry that they will not choose black women. Laurie says "the talk" has shifted focus and is now about lessons for young black women on how to take care of a black man like a white woman would.

"What does that mean?" I ask.

"Not being competitive, argumentative over nonsensical things, providing a safe space," Laurie explains. Twitter posts by black men underscore that Laurie's approach is warranted. Many black men claim they have turned to white women because black women often act like they do not want to be bothered with them, put a lot of pressure on them to achieve, have a number of requirements for what they want in a man, and do not offer enough emotional support.[5] Posts calling black women uncoachable in this regard set off a Twitter storm.[6]

"The talk" happens among white parents as well. Perhaps not quite as directly, but it happens.

Maria recalls when her daughter Solange began dating a white student in high school. "I gave her 'the talk' and I could tell that his mother had given him one as well. She might have been a bit more subtle about it but I knew she was thinking about it. From that point on, she never allowed her son to visit at our house. She told me that she thought she 'would have more control of it' if they came to her house."

Mary Ellen, a focus group participant, revealed that her father "was not a prejudiced person, but the message was clear: 'Do not bring a black boy into this house.' The preference was strong—if he were Catholic, and especially Catholic and Slovenian, then there would be a big wedding."

This ever-present taboo trickles down into the norms by which we can and are willing to establish cross-racial friendships. Although most people approve of interracial relationships, and millennials seem to not give them a second thought, some highly educated and accomplished women of color still sizzle when they see men of color with white women. They resist vehemently when I urge them to widen their pool of candidates for potential mates to include white men. White men are still accused of getting themselves a "jungle bunny" when they cross the racial line with women of color. During a diversity training session, a white man in his late twenties, who is married to a black woman, stated that he is constantly expected to justify his choice of a life partner; his wife has had the same experience.

Rare is the parent who asks his or her child, "Why do you have only white friends?" or, "Why are all your friends black?" Most likely, the question is the opposite for white parents, if the child has more than a token black friend: "Why do you have so many black friends?" Or for the black parent: "Where are your black friends? Why do you have to hang around with so many white kids?" Further, parents rarely if ever work to encourage their children to have a diverse group of friends in order to support their personal and professional development. They may want them to have diverse experiences, but it is okay if their children's friends look "just like us."

Parents often do not role-model having a diverse group of friends for their children. Many are excellent role models for respecting diversity and cultural differences, but not for having diverse groups of friends.

Even when we grow up in welcoming, inclusive homes, it is easy to have our comfort levels threatened. This discomfort usually increases in adolescence. Aaron, a thirtysomething African American man, recalls growing up in Columbus, Ohio, and having an equal share of black and white friends. "It was never an issue for me. Yet other black friends assume that if you have white friends, you don't want black friends."

Pamala, a Chicago mother of two biracial children, states that it is easier to be "more relaxed in the parental structure when you are younger—sleeping over, trading clothes, et cetera. It is much harder as you grow up, when you really have to be cool to socialize." I interpret this to mean that (just as the research tells us) when you are young, you are not quite so discerning about who your friends are—being in close proximity or drawn to the same game or toy does the trick. I can be friends with you because you live next door or down the street, or because you have the coolest technology for gamers. But as we get older, if our differences and all the meanings attached to those differences are in the forefront, then I would rather travel across the city to socialize with someone like me, and get my own cool technology game.

Pam, a white mother of three who lives in a small, predominantly white township just outside Cleveland, has made some progress in dealing with racial discomfort developed when she was a child, but she struggles with how to "teach" her children about racial diversity. "How do I introduce my children to that when they are not around it? I can only tell them how I feel. When I grew up, [my parents] didn't even talk about it."

Not talking about "it" led to a high degree of discomfort with racial differences, I am sure, for Pam and countless other white Americans. It rarely occurs to Pam that she is living in a neighborhood that lacks diversity and, because of that, will have to "work hard" to help her kids experience racial differences outside of what the media presents. She, like most others, makes the assumption that to live in a decent, crime-free neighborhood, where the property values increase and the school system is excellent, means that it has to be an all-white neighborhood. Yet Pam strongly agrees that having the competency to navigate an increasingly multiracial world successfully is something that she wants for her children.

Parents of color struggle with the dilemma posed by raising their children in predominantly white neighborhoods, often chosen for the school systems. As a result, they have to make a special effort to allow their children to form friendships with those of their same race. Those who have the financial means secure coveted spots in organizations like Jack and Jill, dedicated to strengthening future African American leaders through leadership development, volunteer service, philanthropic giving, and civic duty.[7] An intentional and happy by-product of such organizations is that children and young adults get to meet and socialize with "their own kind."

Beverly Daniel Tatum's book *"Why Are All the Black Kids Sitting To-gether in the Cafeteria?"*, a best seller in 1997 and reissued in 2017 for the twentieth anniversary, reflects the question often asked by educators and white parents.[8] The title gives a clue to the fact that the book is about the psychology of racism and the racial-identity development process. Although the book lays out a strong case for how racism is connected to how children respond to others and the world, it saddens me that even twenty years after the book's publication, the answer to the question posed in the title is so rooted in the dynamics of racism. Maybe the question we should be asking is, "What are all the parents teaching their children about race?"

Parents are role models in the area of relationships. If kids never see their parents with different-race friends, no matter what is *said* about appreciating and valuing racial diversity, they will not go out of their way to develop friendships across racial lines. This fact is true for people of color as well as whites.

The remark was made after a casual conversation between two wedding guests who had known each other for less than five minutes. She approached me during the cocktail reception following the ceremony to comment on how much she liked the purple color of my dress. I admired her floral print shoes. We chatted about how the day's perfect weather made the outdoor ceremony at Cylburn Arboretum in Baltimore even more celebratory. She had traveled from nearby Arlington, taking the train because she planned to try at least two of the signature cocktails named after the couple's two dogs and two horses. We had traveled from Boston by air and were staying in one of the block of hotel rooms reserved for the wedding guests. She was a friend of the groom's parents, having known Jeremy since he was a toddler. I was a friend of the bride's parents, having once been a faculty member at the same university where Rhoni's father was formerly a dean.

After the introductory chitchat, there was a long pause as we both stood looking out over the assembled wedding guests. The pause provided the perfect opportunity to say how nice it was to have chatted and excused myself to go after the server with the Parmesan cheese asparagus appetizers, which I wished I had taken more of. But then she blurted out exactly what I was thinking. "Well, this is the most diverse wedding I have ever attended." I turned to her and chuckled. As a diversity professional, my attention is automatically programmed to scan for diversity in my environment, but I was pleasantly surprised that Laurie, my new white friend of five minutes, was having the same experience.

As a Chinese American and Jewish American couple, Jeremy and Rhoni became part of the 17 percent of couples in interracial marriages.[9] With the dismantling of legal and social barriers to crossing racial lines, the number of Americans entering interracial marriages will accelerate and increase. Sheryll Cashin, author of *Loving: Interracial Intimacy in America and the Threat to White Supremacy*, believes that "interracial intimacy is poised to explode," in part as a result of media "de-whitening" and representing a fuller expression of cultures.[10]

At the risk of oversimplifying the issue, I believe that interracial couples support us all in moving toward a shared American experience that is critical to improving race relations and building a truly inclusive society. We had a taste of that shared experience during those five hours at Rhoni and Jeremy's wedding.

Whites, blacks, Asians, and Hispanics shared in the beauty and joy of the Jewish wedding traditions. The lavender yarmulke that my husband donned along with other male guests, as if planned, perfectly matched his shirt and tie. Rabbi Douglas Heifetz seamlessly guided us through the ceremony, allowing us to engage in a very intimate way and making us all feel like family. Die-hard meat lovers, like my husband, consumed a lot of incredibly delicious vegetarian Asian, Italian, and Mexican dishes.

Dancing is a major feature at most weddings. No Jewish wedding is complete without the bride and groom getting hoisted in the air on chairs by (hopefully) strong and trusted family and friends. And nothing is more lively and festive than seeing folks representing different races, generations, socioeconomic classes, and sexual orientations dance the hora.

When Rich and Kennee told me about their daughter's engagement, they shared how much they really liked Jeremy and his parents. "They are just like us," was how Kennee described Heng and Anne. I understood that "like us" referenced values, attitudes, and work ethics, as well as the dreams and goals they had for their children.

We witnessed in Rhoni and Jeremy not only the ability to disencumber oneself of society's racial baggage but also evidence of the inherent right each of us has to fulfill our human potential by loving. It is how we love, not our historical relationship to America, that dictates our ability to grasp the richness of the American experience.

As we move past the fiftieth anniversary of the 1967 US Supreme Court decision *Loving v. Virginia*, which struck down all antimiscegenation laws remaining in sixteen states at the time, we are reminded that interracial marriages still come with many challenges. Interracial marriages have a slightly higher rate of divorce than same-race marriages.[11] Maintaining and nurturing interracial marriage is accompanied by the added burden of the married couple having racial-identity development processes not in sync with each other, which is not an issue in same-race marriage. Similar to the challenge experienced in a marriage between individuals of different generations, the adult developmental tasks that need to be mastered in the various stages are not in sync, which makes it challenging to find common ground as the relationship matures. If a thirty-nine-year-old woman marries someone who is twenty-three years older than she and desires to have children before her generativity stage ends, it causes tension. Her partner is reaching blissful contentment in the integrity stage, a time in life when everything finally comes together. Together, they have some work to do to align their life journey. Similarly, if a person of color marries a white person at a time in her or his life when race is not salient, and after some years of racial-identity development begins to experience race as an essential aspect of his or her identity, the couple has some work to do to align their life journey together. Two cases illustrate this point.

The fact that Lucas was Puerto Rican and his wife, Caitlin, was Irish and German mattered very little, if at all, when they married.[12] At that time, their deep love, strong religious faith, and commitment to supporting the young-adult ministry in the church that had brought them together provided a strong foundation. Neither questioned whether there was enough support to sustain the marriage. Yet, fifteen years and two children later, the foundation of love, religion, and ministry, although still present, was being lived from two separate realities.

To Caitlin and sometimes even to Lucas, it seemed that almost overnight he became irritated by the American-sounding names of his children, the seemingly bland meals the family ate, and even the contemporary artwork that hung on the walls in their home, which he had helped decorate. His children knew very little Spanish, and displayed annoyance at family gatherings when their cousins shared stories among themselves in Spanish. The kids were starting to display a preference for spending holidays with Caitlin's family rather than his. He noted that he began to think of Caitlin as white. He recalled talking about his wife to a colleague and describing her as "really white." At an out-of-state work conference, he found himself feeling at home and relaxed with a group of colleagues he had known for only twenty-four hours. At first he thought it was because they were all human resources professionals, but then he noted that everyone in the group was Hispanic. He found himself complimenting the looks of one of the women and contrasting her dark hair and caramel complexion with his wife's light hair and skin. The fact that the woman was Puerto Rican, he decided, made her more attractive. For the first time in over fifteen years he found himself attracted to another woman, and only later realized that he had been unconsciously flirting with her, or at least flirting with the idea of being married to someone who shared his race.

By the time Lucas sought counseling he was deep into the affair and even deeper into the anxiety and depression resulting from his emotional confusion. He no longer recognized himself as a person of integrity, a faithful husband and dutiful father, which had been the bedrock of his adult life. It took just a few therapy sessions to discover that his racial-identity development process was at work, whereby Lucas had reached psychological resolution as a Puerto Rican man. He needed his race to be an integral part of every aspect of himself.

Over the course of two years and with the continued support of a therapist, he made some very tough decisions in support of stabilizing his mental health. He ended the affair and later his marriage. He did his best to provide an explanation for his behavior as a means of keeping the lines of communication open with his former wife. He worked on his relationships with his children and was able to provide them with a sense of belonging in the culture that was now so important to him. He worked on forgiving himself for the pain he had caused his family.

Elaine met the man who became her husband, Tom, while in college.[13] They shared a love for mathematics and all things *Star Trek*. It came as no surprise when the close friends announced their engagement and married shortly after graduation. For many who knew them, the fact that they were both math nerds was more remarkable than the fact that they were an interracial couple. Elaine was black and Tom was white. Their families accepted the cross-racial relationship without concern and delighted in the fact that they had both found someone to love them.

Not long into their marriage, Elaine and Tom fell into a typical suburban lifestyle. Elaine worked in a professional association and was quickly promoted to chief financial officer. Tom was a comptroller for a large medical-device company. They raised three sons who were making good choices about their futures. Life was good. Except that Elaine felt empty.

She explained to her therapist that she knew and felt loved by her husband, children, and others in her family. She even felt accomplished as a professional and complete as a wife and mother. Yet there was something missing at her core. The anxiety was manifesting itself in rapid weight gain. She thought with all of the talk about diversity and inclusion in her workplace that it might have something to do with race. The conversation made her nervous, and she assumed and was all but told that as a black senior executive she was expected to represent minorities, especially blacks, yet she didn't have a clue as to what that really meant. She wondered what her coworkers thought of her as Tom had accompanied her to many an organizational function. Her husband was sympathetic but didn't feel equipped to talk with her about it and in secret felt a bit ashamed that his whiteness might be the source of her pain. She was embarrassed to talk about race with her children, and felt guilty that she provided them with little to no guidance on how to navigate racism. Up until this point she didn't feel that she had disowned her blackness. It was just that race was a passive aspect of her world. She always considered herself and Tom to be race-neutral. Now she was deeply troubled that she might have her head in the sand and that her passiveness might have caused some unintentional consequences for others. Did Tom see her as an exception to her race rather than the norm? Would he have married her if he experienced her as black? Did her sons experience the microaggressions she had heard about in the workshops? Did they see her as supportive? Had she colluded with her white colleagues to get promotions?

All of these questions swirled in her head, disrupting her thoughts at home and at work and interrupting her sleep. The fact that she had no answers for them haunted her. She was irritable, especially with Tom, over little things that never seemed to bother her before. He chided her for being overprotective with the kids and wondered if she was trying to delay their independence as teens. Most of all, she was unaccustomed to being so self-absorbed, and didn't like herself as a result. Through a year of focused work with a therapist on racial-identity development that at times included having her husband and sons join her for sessions, she came to a heightened awareness and pride in her black identity without sacrificing her marriage. In fact, Tom seemed to appreciate her confidence and newfound race esteem, and she felt closer to her children as they shared with her their own pride and challenges as biracial children.

As a psychologist I know that, on an individual level, when someone's personal history has been marked by abuse and neglect that interrupts the person's developmental progress, it takes a great deal of time to heal the wounds and form a relationship with those perceived to be responsible for the abuse. Often these people find it difficult or impossible to love until the unfinished work of their past has been psychologically completed. This seems to have been the case with both Lucas and Elaine.

Similarly, for many people of color, on a societal level, this is the case with their relationship with America. We as racial minorities focus on how far we still have to go to be able to feel included in America, while whites focus on how far we as Americans have come and find it hard to believe that race is still an issue for people of color. There is truth in both of these realities.

As a result, today, even more so than in the past, we have an opportunity to create a reality for America that we can all share—a reality in which parents erase the adolescent taboo of crossing racial lines of friendships and encourage friendships among different races beyond childhood. Contemporary scholarship bears this out. Children who believed it was wrong not to invite a black friend to sleep over only because their parents would feel uncomfortable with age believe their parents' discomfort is a legitimate basis for not inviting a different-race friend to a dance.[14] Parent disapproval plays a large role in justifying racial exclusion.

Although the fear of socializing across racial lines stems from the long-held taboo against interracial dating and marriage, a deeper analysis suggests that it is also a result of how power and wealth are distributed in America. The perception remains that white people will inherently do better academically and professionally than people of color.

Jason Johnson, a political science professor, MSNBC commentator, and politics editor for the news site The Root, states it this way:

> People of different races—you know, black people, white people, Asian people—have been jumping out of each other's beds for hundreds of years . . . but being friends and being able to go get a drink together and inviting somebody to your house, that's what hasn't changed in this country in the last thirty years, and I think that's a conversation that needs to be had a lot more often than some of the things we focus on. Once things like job competition, scholarships, and heading off to graduate school come into play and a friend that you have known since age twelve looks at you funny because you get into Harvard and he didn't, that's when the separating begins.[15]

Work-based competition further fosters racial division. Stricter enforcement of equal employment opportunity laws occurred during the Obama administration, accompanied by heated debate over whether or not it was justified.[16] Was the Equal Employment Opportunity Commission straying from its mission of protecting employees from discrimination, or was it working to punish large companies with class action suits designed to detect systematic violations and bring them to light? A rational case could be made for either side of this argument; however, the debate has residual impact on people of color, who report increased incidents of unconscious bias and microaggressions in the workplace, undermining opportunities to extend workplace relationships socially.

In a *Cornell Law Review* article, "Work Identity," legal scholars Devon Carbado and Mitu Gulati explore the kinds of work people of color often feel pressured to do to avoid negative assumptions about their identities.[17] People of color often have to work twice as hard as whites to earn the respect of white employers and other white coworkers. They strive to demonstrate industriousness, intelligence, moral fortitude, responsibility, and piety to overcome stereotypes of being lazy, unintelligent, immoral, shiftless, and lascivious.[18] Having to "perform" in this way interferes with bringing an authentic self to work. I know many people of color who share my experience of encountering a white coworker outside of the work environment when socializing with members of our same race and have them comment that "for the first time I saw you as black."

It was a comment I found confusing at first, and sometimes even tossed it back on them as their racial insensitivity. Over time, I put this comment in context and coupled it with the fact that many other black professionals also had similar comments made to them, realizing that I probably wasn't showing my "blackness" as much at work. I now accept the fact that often work environments require an assimilation process for access and success. It forces those who are different from the prototype to adopt the look and behavior of the prototype. In my case, however, it is an impossible task to become a white male.

Asians have long been dubbed the "model minority" and continue to pay a price for this label. In the fields of science and medicine they are overrepresented, and as a result not afforded the same supports provided for other minority groups. Affirmative action practices tend to work against Asian Americans. Studies demonstrate that Asians belong to communities that highly support education and work extremely hard to achieve and do well.[19] The results are that top universities tend to admit blacks and Hispanics with lower scores who are underrepresented because of the history of discrimination. When other numbers of admission selections go to legacy students, talented athletes, and wealthy donors, Asians find themselves in competition for limited spots with other high achievers.[20]

This competition extends to the workplace, where Asians are almost invisible in executive-level positions despite their achievements.[21] Asians often find themselves working to repudiate stereotypes about being docile, timid, and lacking in political and intellectual courage.[22] This makes it particularly challenging to turn workplace relationships into cross-racial friendships.

Ellis Cose, author, columnist, and contributing editor for *Newsweek*, states in his book *The Envy of the World* that although the obstacles for black Americans are not so daunting as in previous times, black Americans are still at a decided disadvantage. Cose describes the difference as "stepping into the ring with both hands lashed behind your back and stepping in with one hand swinging free."[23] If that description is indeed true for black Americans and other Americans of color (and I believe it is), then in our world of increasing racial diversity, most white Americans go into the ring blind, and others without their glasses on, not realizing or accepting the fact that whites will no longer be the majority race by midcentury. At the same time, decades of discrimination have rendered some people of color defining their existence from the framework of racism and reacting to whites as continual oppressors and white supremacists. This same history has positioned white Americans to repeatedly rest comfortably on the soft pillow of privilege, normalizing access and opportunity as rights afforded to them because of their status as members of the "predominant culture" in the United States. Many white Americans are angry that the rights issuing from white privilege have been challenged and have turned that anger onto those perceived to be "the other."

This presents a disorienting and complicated backdrop for friendship based on mutual respect, affection, and positive regard. It means that to have such a friendship across racial lines requires a considerable amount of work. It means that I either like the other person just enough to be able to work successfully with them to forward a shared agenda, or fall in love with them with the kind of powerful love that weathers all of the predictable hard times to follow. Unless we are willing to secure, maintain, and nurture cross-racial friendships, the two-button choice will persist.

Chapter 4

SAME TREATMENT DOES NOT MEAN EQUAL TREATMENT

By definition, the notion of friendship supports relaxation, intimacy, and comfort between and among individuals. Kimili, a thirty-six-year-old black female, says she finds it difficult to have white friends, particularly because a friend is someone with whom you can "just feel like you're at home." Her friend Myla, also black, underscores the concept by stating that friends are people in whose homes you can "do a 'number two' in their bathroom and don't have to worry about it." For some reason, Myla has never experienced this level of comfort with white folks.

Consistent with my research over more than two decades, those who have friends across racial lines report having a different kind of relationship with cross-racial friends than with same-race friends. It is a qualitative difference that people admit they cannot always clearly articulate, but it is there nonetheless.

Laurie, who is black, came to this realization after planning a get-together and noting that she had not invited any of her white friends. "It was a time in my life when I needed some emotional support and decided to invite folks over for brunch. It was what I called 'poor girls' therapy.' It occurred to me that I didn't ask any of my white friends, yet some of these black women that I invited I didn't really know as well." She states that she is "emotionally close" with her white friends but does not socialize with them in the same way she does with friends who share her race.

Maria, who is also black, describes her close friendship with Anna, who is Asian. She recalls that Anna approached her in the small, predominantly white town where they both lived and introduced herself by saying, "As one person of color to another, I want to introduce myself." They hit it off and continued to become close friends as they raised their children in a majority-white town in Massachusetts. Maria tells me that their friendship deepened on a "universal level" when Anna's cherished thirteen-year-old daughter died of liver cancer and her beloved husband passed away eleven months later. The tragedy brought them even closer as Maria worked to be there in any way possible to support her friend.

Because of the visibility of racial differences and all of the negative social loadings attending on race, perhaps it is just a matter of individuals of different races spending consistent time together before a friendship blossoms. Do cross-racial friendships just take more time to develop and nurture? Studies show that in organizations, homogeneous groups reach consensus faster, but diverse groups are more creative and lead to innovation.[1] Could it be true that cross-racial friendships take longer to develop but impart greater benefit to our personal and professional growth over the long haul?

Imani, a black focus group participant in her twenties, puts it this way: "I have white friends, Asian friends, Indian friends, and starting out in the friendship there might have been a conversation that I would have with my African American friends that I wouldn't necessarily have with my white friends, but over the course of time, as that trust started to build, the conversation pretty much became the same with all of my friends."

Yet the majority of focus group participants over the years have admitted that getting to a deeper level and building that trust does not always happen. "It never goes deeper, you never have that conversation with people because you may not be comfortable digging too deep into that relationship," Melinda states. She admits that after attending a historically black college, she lost touch with friends of different races, never to regain the kind of comfort that would have allowed the friendships to deepen.

"It is trust that leads you to have a more effective company or school system or whatever it is . . . because once you trust your colleague, you can trust that you could say something that might come across offensive at first until you really get to a deeper understanding," says Aaron, who is black. "You understand that that person didn't have a malicious intent and you don't want to jump and become overly sensitive because you understand the person has a good heart . . . but it takes a lot to develop that sense of trust with anybody." He continues, "I think, just as a nation, we're kind of closed off to thinking about going across racial lines in friendship because you have to open yourself up to be vulnerable and that's another hurdle you have to think about."

Jean and Jacquie met in graduate school in Ohio thirty-five years ago and have sustained a deep friendship since that time. For the past thirty years Jean has lived in London. They have worked to maintain their friendship by squeezing in visits during Jean's trips to visit family or when Jacquie travels to London for business or professional conferences. They also made a commitment to Skype once a month at a minimum. Jean, who is white, finds the current racial dynamics in America leaving her "almost speechless."

"I can talk about racial issues with Jacquie but don't always. I am very sensitive to the fact that there's no way I can fully share in the depth of that. For example, she has two teenage male grandsons and we would be much more likely to talk about the parenting and the philosophy of parenting boys. We talk about it in that way openly. But when she begins to talk about her worries with the way young black men are being treated, to me, that's different. At that point, I become a listener. I stay in the listening mode when we start talking racial dynamics, always thinking about Jacquie as all of who she is and her race is a part of that. With Jacquie, I would certainly say, 'Look, I don't know what to say here,' and she and I could and would talk about that."

In his extensive research on social capital, Robert Putnam, Harvard professor and author of *Bowling Alone* and more recently *Our Kids: The American Dream in Crisis*, notes that diverse communities trust each other less.[2] Making meaning out of this phenomenon is complicated. He suggests that neither *contact theory* (diversity eliminates in-group/out-group distinction) nor *conflict theory* (diversity strengthens in-group solidarity) reflects the social reality in contemporary America, so he introduces *constrict theory*. Constrict theory suggests that living in diverse settings causes people to "hunker down" and "pull in like a turtle."

If diversity makes us like turtles, I believe it is because we lack the skill sets to come out of our shells. If Putnam and his colleagues' findings have validity (and I believe they reflect a reality that exists) and if diversity breeds mistrust (mistrust that stems from past experience or direct data), I am not convinced that that is necessarily a bad thing. It is simply a reflection of our tribal nature and an indicator that we are on the right track to connecting with others who are different. Because connections with those who are different from us further our personal growth and allow us to reach our full capacity as human beings, we must commit to moving forward in the relationship and work to turn mistrust into trust.

My sister Nancy has worked in retail management most of her professional life. At one time, she worked for a company in which she was the only black employee in her local office. There was another woman named Nancy in that office. The receptionist often had to ask clients who came to the office to see "Nancy" which one they meant. My sister told me that more times than she could count, the person (always white) would lean over the desk and whisper, "The black one." This became a joke in the office, and the Nancys affectionately became "black Nancy" and "white Nancy." If a person whispered, "The black one," the receptionist would yell out, "Black Nancy!" to the great chagrin of the client.

I imagine that in whispering the word "black," the client thought he or she was being more racially sensitive, or "color-blind." However, whispering "black" as if the term were derogatory implies that there is something wrong with being black. When a person tries to be color-blind, it generally leads to the opposite effect. The people in my sister's office were comfortable enough with each other that race was no more than a neutral identifier.

It starts with some basic skills on communicating across differences— for example, how we identify race. What we call one another does include an element of political correctness. Politics is about the use of power; indeed, what I am called (individually or in my group-membership identity) depends on who is claiming the power to identify me. If I decide that I want to be called Deborah and not Debbie, then that is my choice. Similarly, if Asians want to be called Asians and not Orientals, it is certainly within their power to identify themselves as such. Now, I grant you, for novice students of the racial-identification lexicon, this might all be a bit confusing: "Is it black or African American? I know it's not Negro." "Are they Hispanics or Latinos or Latinas?" "Native Americans or American Indians?" "Why are they offended when I say 'colored people' but they say 'people of color'? What's the difference?"

Since most of us don't have the lexicon memorized or carry around a laminated copy in our wallets, here is a simple key to remember what to call people. What we call people is about respect. If my racial-group-membership identity is African American or black and you prefer to call me Negro because you are fond of that term and what it evokes, then it will be considered disrespectful. If you don't know whether I prefer the term "black" or "African American," simply ask. It is a legitimate question, and I am the insensitive one if I call you out for asking.

I do not think that respectful group identification is really all that difficult to master. After all, as Steve, my friend and colleague, is insightful enough to point out, how many times do we actually refer to one another in terms of our racial-group membership? We don't walk up to each other and say, "Hi, Debbie, my African American friend."

If I am at a meeting and a colleague that I have been working with for a week suddenly begins to call me Barbara instead of Deborah because the only other person in the room who is black is Barbara, I might just politely correct him. If he continues to make the same mistake over and over again, I may choose not to be so polite the next time I correct him. If he tells me not to be so sensitive because we "all look alike," I might choose to take the cover off the elephant in the room and name it as racism.

A few of my white friends were not attuned to, and didn't understand the sensitivity surrounding, President Trump's repeated description of black neighborhoods as "war zones" or Hispanics as "bad hombres."[3] People of color are all too familiar with being seen by whites first and foremost in terms of their race—and not in a good way. Race is often viewed by whites in a very stereotypical manner, perhaps even causing them to remark that you are a credit to your race because your accomplishments resemble their own. They would be surprised and confused if you were to return the "compliment" by calling them a credit to their own race.

In my search for an academic position a few years after I completed my doctorate, I once had a department chair tell me that although I was indeed the best candidate for the position, the most qualified, and that I had interviewed extremely well, the department members were "hoping to get a true diversity candidate and did not feel that I was black enough since I came from such a charmed background." Apparently, a stable family background was not associated with being black. If I were raised along with my six siblings by a single mother who was drug addicted and had to work my way through college while helping to financially support my family, now *that* might have made the department members see me as a "true diversity candidate." The fact that my family background resembled theirs negated their perception of me as black. What race did it make me? Who knows?

That comment made to me in 1991 was not dissimilar in its thinking from Trump's June 5, 2013 (4:05 a.m.) tweet:

Sadly, the overwhelming amount of violent crime in our major cities is committed by blacks and Hispanics—a tough subject—must be discussed.

This is not only inaccurate, but cements a racial stereotype in the minds of millions of Americans struggling to make meaning of the deep racial divide. Perhaps harder to understand for some white Americans is the implicit stereotype embedded in the appointment of Dr. Ben Carson as secretary of the Department of Housing and Urban Development (HUD) despite the fact that, brilliant neurosurgeon though he is, he has never managed an organization even remotely close to the size and financial scope of HUD. Implicit stereotypes are powerful enough to be outside of one's consciousness. Because the stereotype of HUD links government housing, poverty, and blacks together, just being black qualified Carson to lead HUD. Even though Carson's only qualification for leading national policy and programs to address America's housing needs is that he once lived in an economically unstable neighborhood, the appointment of a black man to HUD is deemed not only acceptable but desirable. In conversations with white friends who voted for Trump, they come to understand how this kind of free association as an implicit stereotype is actually indicative of racial bias. People of color are so attuned to sensing an implicit racial stereotype, they can almost smell its stink as easily as if it were sour milk.

This point brings me to my next example. I have had many white friends over the years who have said to me at some point in our relationship, "Debbie, I don't think of you as black." There are two aspects to uncovering the elephant in this statement—intention and impact. Undoubtedly, the people who have said this to me have been good friends who have known me for many years. Their intentions, I am sure, were not anywhere in the racist, evil category when they said it. I am relatively sure that in most cases they were trying to give me a "compliment." The impact on me, however, is profound. I will admit I am sensitive about this. I wonder what they do see if they do not see black. I wonder what being black means to them. I am whirled back into the world of trying to resolve my own racial-identity issues and being too white for some of my black friends and too black for some of my white friends. I immediately feel as if I have been punched in the stomach. Sometimes I want to crawl into a hole, and sometimes I want to punch back. "Gee, she really is sensitive," you might be thinking (if you are white), or, "I've been there. I know exactly what you are saying" (if you are a person of color). How do I know this? Inevitably, when I share this example in training sessions, whites support the intention side and offer me all kinds of ways to understand what my white friend was lovingly trying to say. People of color, particularly other blacks, support the impact side and are eager to have the floor and share their own "I don't think of you as" stories.

Let's move to the other side of the racial fence for a minute, before I come back to unraveling intention and impact. When white people "get it" or "got woke," they are often claimed by people of color as "one of us." The implication here is that when a white person is sensitive to racial microaggressions or insults based on race, then he or she isn't *really* white. Being white is synonymous with oppressor or entitlement as a member of the dominant race.

My good friend and former pastor Michael Barth is a white Catholic priest, a masterful liturgist and preacher who now heads his religious order, Missionary Servants of the Most Holy Trinity, in the DC area. He has an amazing gift of being able to minister successfully to a diverse community of people—blacks, whites, and Hispanics; old, middle-aged, and teen; GEDs and PhDs; urban and suburban; ex-convicts and those who have never even received a parking ticket. He not only lived in an all-black community for most of his adult life but also fully embraced the culture and its people. On one occasion, when he was pastor of St. Agnes–Our Lady of Fatima parish in Cleveland, Father Mike and the former head of his religious order, another white man, joined our family and members of our youth group for dinner at our home. I insisted that we set the table with the good china used for special occasions. "We don't need to use the china, Debbie," Paul, my godson, chastised me. "Ain't nobody here white but you."

Although I laughed endlessly when he made the remark, I had to resist the urge to go academic on him. By my count, there were two white persons in the house that day—Father Mike and Father Austin. By Paul's count, there was just me. What I desperately want to communicate to Paul and the many who think like him is that they are doing the same thing that people do when they say, "Debbie, I don't think of you as black."

"Not exactly," my friends who are people of color might be quick to tell me. What whites think about blacks are stereotyped representations perpetuated by the media and a product of their proven racism. When whites say to me, "Debbie, I don't think of you as black," it is because they find it hard to relate positive qualities or intellectual rigor to blacks. What blacks and other racial groups think about whites is based on direct and indirect experiences of being discriminated against. When we think of Father Mike as not being white, it is because our experience of him as a white man is very different from our experiences with all the other white men we have encountered. I can't argue that these statements aren't true, at least in part. What I would want to do, however, is examine the assumptions behind them and check out how the persons (white or black) think before I dump them into a basket of racial stereotypes.

It underscores another fact when I hear these statements: whites don't really know many people of color as friends, and people of color don't really know many whites as friends.

I have met my share of whites who buy into stereotypical thinking, and I have met a whole lot more who do not. I have also met my share of people of color who hold stereotyped views about whites based on a belief that whites are the sole beneficiaries of structural racism (they are all rich; they all have good credit; they all have clean houses; they all have health insurance, good jobs, educational advantages, and if they don't, it was because of choice or stupidity or both). I have also met a whole lot more people of color who are far more realistic in their views.

In mixed-race settings, we need to release the stereotypical views that may have seeped into our consciousness, and we need to learn the skills that will enable us to deal with the elephant in the living room. It is important to take the time to make meaning out of the intention and to unbundle the effects of the impact.

When a white friend tells me, "I don't see you as black," I ask her to explain to me what she means by that. Even my closest white friends become uncomfortable with that question. When they get past their discomfort, they usually say something like they do not experience me being anything like all the racist portrayals in the media, or they tell me that I don't resemble what their parents might have said black people were like. Or they admit they're ashamed to be thinking of blacks as poor, uneducated, crafty, and pugnacious, and they acknowledge that they're unclear about where all that comes from. I express to them the impact on me of hearing such a statement. And I talk about my personal struggle with racial identity, about what it was like to grow up both black and Catholic (not Baptist), and black and Jamaican-Panamanian (not from the South). I talk about my experiences in an all-white religious community where there was no room for me to be black and how I worked to reclaim my black identity. I also talk to them about the joys of being black. It is an important, extended dialogue that takes time and some skill to understand, but it builds the kind of trust necessary for sustaining cross-racial friendships.

It does not take a group of social scientists to tell us that we choose our friends because we have something in common with them. It is natural to assume that those who resemble each other on a physical level would begin the process of friendship selection there. We also choose our friends because of common interests. So it is reasonable to argue that we do not easily enter into cross-racial friendships initially because of the visible assessment, but over time and given the choice of a same-race friend without anything in common and a different-race friend with a lot in common, we would choose the different-race friend. Not exactly.

Studies that examine the precursors of relationship suggest that it is much harder than we think to assess interest among interracial dyads.[4] Individuals tend to engage in what is called "defensive distancing" when it comes to the development of cross-racial friendships: What if they don't like me because I am Asian (or black, or Latin, or Native American . . .)? What if they think I am racist? What happens if I say the wrong thing? To avoid this potentially embarrassing situation, they wait for signals, often amplified, from the other person that it is okay to go forward. It's a lot of work to even get the friendship started.

Once started, in its initial stage, cross-racial friendships continue to have challenges. There's a dance that gets played out due to divergent impression-management goals that each holds for the relationship.[5] In cross-racial dyads, because of historical underpinnings, whites desire to be liked. They want to be liked by the potential friend of another race and seen as color-blind. In order to gain acceptance they often overcorrect their behavior.

While in high school, my niece Mercedes went to a church retreat with her white friend Colleen. She laughs. "I knew there were questions and discussion. 'Is she black?' 'We haven't had one in ten years.' 'Hope she's okay with it.' They were extra nice to me. You could tell they were trying to make me feel comfortable."

People of color in cross-racial dyads desire to be acknowledged for their competencies and overcompensate by demonstrating their experience and intelligence. They want to feel respected. They want to be empowered in the relationship and considered equal partners. Jamain, a twenty-five-year-old African American man, states that he doesn't "feel comfortable with whites. They don't understand me. I have to speak two different languages, one at work and one at home. All that extra energy. I've got to repeat everything four or five times. I'd rather stay home. It is like I have to put on a show. I am generally quiet around whites because if I were to show my true colors . . ."

Whites desire to be liked in the friendship and people of color want to be respected. That should be pretty simple. Again, not so. Research tells us that these divergent impression-management goals—to be liked and to be respected—set off an opposing interaction.[6] Whites tend to take an assimilation approach and ignore power and social privilege by downplaying differences. This approach results in people of color feeling disrespected. "We are all alike. . . . We all bleed the same way. . . . I don't see color. You are just like *me*!" This kind of thinking makes people of color smile politely and then run to the nearest exit.

People of color tend to adopt an integration approach that disregards similarities and highlights differences. "You just don't get it and can never understand. . . . That doesn't represent me. . . . That is not my experience." This approach results in whites feeling they are not liked and frustrated that their efforts have been rejected even though they were never slave owners and were acting with good intentions. Nobody wins.

We know from the seminal work on stereotype threat by Claude Steele and his colleagues that elements in a setting can undermine a person's sense of belonging.[7] Cues such as greater attention given to actions of women and underrepresented minorities, the number of other people in the setting with the same racial identity, the number of people with power who share your identity, how a setting is organized by identity, the setting's degree of inclusiveness, and "integration concerns"—all of these are active in everyday life and act as small barriers to crossing racial lines in friendship.[8]

Linda Tropp, a social psychologist and professor at the University of Massachusetts, Amherst, has an impressive and extensive body of work that focuses on how people's experiences as group members influence their interpretations of each other, especially those relationships that differ in status and power. Our conversation about her research in the context of cross-racial friendships is a lively one. She tells me about the great deal of care and concern whites have when talking about race. Often it stems from not feeling comfortable about how to navigate the socially imposed taboo around the subject of race. As a result, people set up certain contact strategies to help them figure out what to expect and what to avoid. In some of her research, she has focused on how people can approach cross-racial interactions as learning opportunities.[9] By envisioning cross-racial interactions as opportunities for learning, making mistakes is allowed, and practice and experience lead to greater efficacy.[10] What she has learned from years of extensive research is that the more contact people have with those of a different race, the less anxious they feel about interacting in racially diverse settings. People need to feel confident and efficacious in managing cross-racial interactions; otherwise they may try to avoid them. Helping others to gain confidence and reduce anxiety in cross-racial interactions is key, as is helping them understand implicit bias.

Mahzarin Banaji, an Indian American social psychologist at Harvard, studies human thinking and feeling as it unfolds in social contexts. Her focus is primarily on mental systems that operate in implicit or unconscious mode. After the Implicit Association Test (IAT) was introduced into the scientific literature, Banaji, along with Anthony Greenwald and

Brian Nosek, developed Project Implicit to create awareness about our unconscious biases.[11] The IAT has been taken by millions of individuals across the globe.

Banaji is interested in the unconscious nature of assessments of self and others that reflect feelings and knowledge (often unintended) about social-group membership that underlie the us/them distinction. Taking the IAT and hearing Dr. Banaji present her research heightens one's awareness of the pervasiveness of unconscious bias in everyday life. My untested hypothesis (empirically at least) is that we could interrupt the involuntary process of unconscious biases by more and frequent interactions with friends across racial lines. Although further study on the correlation between reducing implicit bias and cross-racial friendships is warranted, studies point toward the influence of cross-racial friendships in improving racial attitudes.[12]

Other research on implicit bias has suggested that to rid oneself of stereotypes that interfere with fostering cross-racial friendships, an individual must train his or her brain by providing contradictory stimuli.[13] Exposure to other races, particularly in friendship, can be a powerful way to reduce bias and change cultural beliefs.[14]

However, this throws another metaphorical wrench into the acquisition of cross-racial friends. If we need friends of a different race in order to reduce bias and challenge cultural assumptions, how do we get around those biases and assumptions in order to form an interracial friendship in the first place? The first step to getting past the awkward dance of being liked or respected is to simply "do you" in all of its authenticity. "Doing you" in all your glory requires suspending the pre-analysis of the relationship as one where race will be a barrier. If you find someone interesting because of their personal style, similar interests, or intellectual prowess, then approach the individual as you would any other new relationship. If you find yourself interested in the individual simply because they are of a different race and you find that race fascinating or exotic, then slow yourself down before you make your move. You may label that interesting person of a different race as your friend, but that individual may think differently as a result of the fact that they end up being "*the* friend" for many whites.

Entering a cross-racial friendship is a lot of emotional work for both parties. Whites report feeling like they have to be cautious, especially at the beginning of the relationship, to avoid being deemed a racist as a result of some unconscious bias they didn't know they possessed. My friend Donna, a healthcare administrator who is white, says that "you have to have a sense of personal security to maintain a mixed-race friendship." Having a friend of a different race requires that "you have a certain degree of cultural competence and resiliency, so that any possible racism can be pointed out to you."

People of color report feeling like they often have to educate their white friends on the impact of race in everyday situations. Although many older people of color report that they are tired of "educating whites" about the race experience, younger adults and teens of color consider it just part of living in the real world. "Okay, school's in session," is what thirty-one-year-old Lawrence thinks when racial issues come up with his white friends.

Whites are not the only ones who have to do a lot of pre-work for cross-racial friendships to happen naturally. People of color have to acknowledge and work on their own biases against whites. Nikia, a focus group participant, reports that she was so oversocialized to think of whites as being biased or prejudiced against blacks that it almost derailed her success in the work world.

> Coming from an HBCU [historically black college or university] as a business major, you're really conditioned and coached, maybe sometimes overcoached, about racism, if you're deciding to go into corporate America. I believe I was so overcoached that when I got my first job, I was prejudging white people's motives. I would call my boss and tell him that I thought individuals were doing things to me because I was African American. He told me that I was just being oversensitive. So a lot of times you can get too much coaching and put on too much armor against whites.

Getting and maintaining friendships is enough work without complicating it with "the race thing." We often underestimate the amount of emotional intelligence and degree of cultural competence required for cross-racial interactions. Organizations invest in training their employee base in learning these skill sets to foster high-performing and inclusive work environments. They realize that treating everyone the same does not translate to equal treatment. The rationale for learning diversity competencies is strong when there are shared tasks among coworkers to achieve the mission of the organization or to reach a business objective. Employees are also compensated for and evaluated on their ability to work in diverse teams. Not so with a friendship.

———

Kimili, who was introduced at the beginning of this chapter, talks about inviting a newly made white friend in college to a fashion show. "I wanted to warn her about possibly being the only white person there. It's weird, because after that night of the fashion show, our friendship wasn't as close anymore." People who have friends of a different race often feel obligated or duty-bound to warn them when they will be the "only one" of their race at a function. There is a sense that they might not be treated the same as everyone else. They also know that the treatment we might receive from others is not necessarily the treatment they will get.

My own experience with cross-racial friends constantly puts me in a position to assess the degree of emotional safety I might experience in predominantly white establishments and white neighborhoods. Once when Joan's dad decided to treat us to lunch and took us to a restaurant in Little Italy, I panicked. Cleveland's historic Little Italy is known for its fabulous bakeries, unique gifts, art galleries, and enthusiastic celebrations of the Feast of the Assumption, a Catholic holy day that commemorates the day Mary, the Mother of God, was assumed body and soul into heaven, with a parade and festival. It also is perceived as a community that is not welcoming to blacks. This perception is grounded in its history, particularly a racially motivated shooting in Little Italy during the time of the 1966 Hough riots.[15]

Most Cleveland residents who are black and of baby boomer age can recall their parents avoiding the drive down Mayfield Road through Little Italy and, as kids, receiving instructions to duck in the backseat of the car during that portion of the drive if the route could not be avoided. So when Mr. Agresta wanted to take us to Little Italy for lunch, even though it was many years after the 1966 murder, I held my breath. I worried that Joan's feisty, undisciplined advocacy wrapped in white naiveté would get us into trouble if anyone dared to do or say anything to me that was inappropriate. Ultimately, I knew that it would be all right precisely because I was with Mr. Agresta, someone well-known to the Italian community as a respected businessman, and it was.

Not being aware of my Little Italy experience, my niece Mercedes shared with me that when she and her friend Colleen, who is white, went to homecoming senior year, the group wanted to go to Little Italy. She and her date were uncomfortable with the choice of the location. She called Colleen and told her that she wasn't going to Little Italy. Colleen did not understand why. She explained to Colleen the history of Little Italy and the black community, a history that had obviously remained alive some forty years later. Ultimately, Mercedes decided that because she was going with her friend Colleen she would be okay and that just having the opportunity with Colleen to assert herself and speak about her discomfort helped to make her comfortable in her choice to go.

Little Italy today is a gentrified cultural hub that remains predominantly, if not exclusively, white. Millennials and Generation Z individuals of color freely participate in its many activities. In recent years, I browsed the Art Walk with my friend Donna, who is white. The fear remains. And not because Donna could probably do little in an effort to physically protect me if anything happened, but because there are some whites who still harbor racist beliefs and Donna could not readily change those beliefs.

The sixty-fifth annual Columbus Day Parade took place on October 9, 2017, in Little Italy, beginning on Murray Hill Road from the intersection of Cornell Road and marching down Mayfield Road past Holy Rosary Church. It occurred amid heated debate about the significance of the day and whether or not it should be renamed "Indigenous Peoples' Day."[16] The evening news covered the parade and particularly (perhaps intentionally) featured angry whites speaking in defense of the day as "their history" and disparaging those efforts to "change history." Comments in news articles on the parade evidenced the deep divide on this topic, where facts are scarce and emotions are abundant.

This is another reason that I, along with many of my black and brown friends, still avoid visiting Little Italy and miss out on the opportunity for some of the finest, authentic Italian dining in the city, in addition to some good shopping. Most of my white friends are cognizant of this avoidance and try to reassure me that although my fears are understandable, the vast majority of whites in Little Italy are not racist. I believe them. Yet going there myself doesn't seem worth the risk for nonessential items. I do, however, appreciate gifts from the shops and will indulge in takeout food delivered by my white friends anytime.

Our unwillingness to cross racial lines in friendship is clearly understandable. It is a lot of work and requires us to embrace multiple realities while remaining curious instead of staying in the comfort of certainty. It means that we have to constantly challenge our assumptions about the reality we experience while working to have a collective understanding of that reality that embraces different perspectives. It is hard work. Why would anyone want to have friends across racial lines, given that it is clearly burdensome to try to develop the competencies necessary in order to have cross-racial friends?

We need these competencies, and we need them not only to support more productive workforces—we need them to survive as fully functioning human beings. That statement may seem a bit extreme. If you are saying, "Are you telling me that to be personally fully functioning, I have to have friends of different races?" then I have to say yes. I believe that the benefits derived from cross-racial and cross-cultural experiences support us in being fully ourselves. As a result of these friendships I become racially resilient, an invaluable skill that is necessary for navigating our increasingly multicultural world. Racially resilient individuals are folks who stay engaged during racial clashes and don't give up until they are familiar with the script of multicultural living. That work is best done among friends.

Racially resilient friends have the ability to encourage others to take the first steps toward achieving racial equality on a structural level. Racial-equality legal scholar Daria Roithmayr convincingly argues that "racial inequality reproduces itself automatically from generation to generation, in the everyday choices that people make about their lives." She declares that "choices like whether to refer a friend (or the friend of a friend) for a job"[17] become self-reinforcing and cumulative. She posits that a "lock-in" model to racial inequality exists. Roithmayr derived the model from economist Brian Arthur's theory that an early development model in technology gets fixed, or locked in, for extended periods even after there is a superior alternative.[18] Roithmayr's lock-in model of racial inequality focuses on a perpetuated economic structure in America where, during the Jim Crow era and now in its wake, racial discrimination leads to financial profits. This unfair advantage that happened early in America's history is present in the racial gap of family wealth distribution, homeowners associations, labor unions, political parties, school districts, and other groups that have created monopolies by excluding racial groups. From Roithmayr's perspective, these material differences will continue to persist, making racial equality next to impossible to achieve.

Same-race friendships and monoracial social networks do become self-reinforcing structural processes that perpetuate racial inequality. However, those processes do not have to be locked in. Interpersonally, cross-racial friendships unlock the cycle that perpetuates racial inequality. On a societal level, cross-racial friendships, in practice and in witness, help us to reframe our understanding of these persistent racial gaps in wealth, education, housing, and employment and to recognize that same treatment does not mean equal treatment. It is an honorable start toward racial equity.

Chapter 5

WHAT'S IN A RACE?

I didn't know that I was black until I was in the first grade. Call me a slow learner, but race was not particularly figural in our racially encapsulated household and neighborhood. My entire family was the same skin color, without the varying shades of brown that are sometimes represented in black families. Our entire neighborhood was black. I attended St. Thomas Aquinas Elementary School in Cleveland, which was racially mixed at the time. In kindergarten I probably experienced so much separation anxiety from my mom that my severe navel-gazing kept me from noticing different skin colors. By first grade I was adjusted enough to observe differences. I was especially enraptured by Kitty Ribar's blue glasses, their pointed frames beaded with rhinestones. Returning from school that day I was greeted by my mom, who was ironing at the time. With excitement I told her about Kitty's glasses and announced that I wanted glasses just like Kitty Ribar's. Her reply: "Oh, honey, colored people don't look good in blue glasses."

My attention was suddenly diverted from the coveted blue glasses to the concept of "colored people." What were colored people? I asked my mom that question and she stopped ironing long enough to look with bewilderment and confusion at the strange child she had birthed standing before her. Like most good moms do when confronted with a complex topic from an inquisitive child when there is ironing to finish and dinner to get on the table, she ignored my question and told me to get out of my school clothes, put on my play clothes, and help set the table.

Absent my mother's input on the subject of the nature of colored people, the next day I did my own experiment at school while waiting in the bathroom line. I took my arm and matched it to the arms of my classmates until Sister Ruth told me to stop. Sure enough, some people were brown, some were tan, some were pinkish, and some were cream. Some even had tiny tan spots all over their arms. I concluded that this was what was meant by colored people.

―――――

Until the 1980s, the racial-identity development process was excluded from textbooks and courses in developmental psychology. Many pages were devoted to other subjects, and many classroom hours were spent on the topics of physical, cognitive, social, and personality development during all life stages. Nothing was ever said about what you think about and how you acknowledged your skin color and how this affects your growing-up process. For most people of color, however, skipping this particular topic was not an option. School was always in session in everyday life.

Racial-identity development is characterized by the psychological connection one has with one's race. Because of its physical visibility, its meaning must be confronted. This developmental process involves cognitive, emotional, and behavioral components. When the identity-resolution process is a healthy one, race functions in a protective capacity and provides a sense of belonging and group identity for those who share that same race, allowing one to experience racial identity as distinct from other identity roles.

Early research on racial-identity development proposed a stage process, which assumed that one completed the developmental tasks associated with one stage of racial-identity development before progressing on to the next.[1] For example, in stage one, called *pre-encounter*, as a person of color I would define my race as juxtaposed against the majority or dominant culture. I would know myself as a black person only because I was not white. Furthermore, I would define blackness in relationship to whiteness. Somewhere along my developmental journey, typically as a teenager or young adult, I would have an experience that would cause me to rethink blackness apart from whiteness. For example, I might be introduced through reading or attendance at an event to an idea that challenged my previously held notions of whites as superior or dominant and begin to perceive blackness outside the context of whiteness. This experience is characterized as stage two of the developmental process, called the *encounter* experience. As these self-revelations deepened, I would become more and more immersed in my race and thus experience the third phase of racial-identity development, called *immersion*. In this stage, a person might have his hair in a natural style of an afro and wear a dashiki and other African garb. As one matured in other areas of human development, the final stage, that of *integration*, would be achieved. In the integration phase, I experience race as part of my full self. In this stage, the style of clothing I would choose to wear might be less representative of race and I might freely seek out and participate in multiracial settings without regard to race. For example, the same individual who as a graduate student wore an afro and dashiki becomes a professor in a predominantly white university, and while retaining racial pride, racial identity is less visible in his clothing and hairstyle.

Whites were thought to experience a similar stage-process of racial-identity development; however, the stages were characterized differently: stage one involved *being unaware of self as a racial being*. In this stage, race is only conceptualized as "other" and white as a race is conceptualized as a "not" (not black, not Asian, not Latino, not Native American). Stage two, similar to the racial-development process for people of color, is characterized as an *encounter* experience. However, the encounter is experienced as an acute awareness that whiteness represents dominance in society. As this awareness deepens through multiple encounter experiences, the *identification* of whiteness with inequitable power and oppression might lead the individual to openly disavow whiteness. In stage four, *integration*, whites are able to achieve racial-identity resolution by the rejection of whiteness as oppressor and acceptance of "self" outside that context of white oppression.

For example, as a young child and teenager, living in a white community and attending a white school, a white person might have few or no interactions with other races and thus be unaware of her own race as white (stage one). Attending college, she might have a Mexican American roommate, who opens her eyes to racism and bias (stage two). Learning more and experiencing more through interactions in multiracial settings, she is faced with the realization that her whiteness represents privilege (stage three) and she works to eradicate structural racism in her choices of where she lives, works, and how she participates in the democratic process as an informed citizen (stage four).[2]

Later, applied research suggested that the process of racial-identity development did not occur in stages but rather manifested in various statuses, with stage process as one type of status.[3]

Although the statuses are depicted in a progressive manner, the lived experience dictated a number of ways that racial identity could reach resolution. The process could be linear, in that one's entire life could be lived in one status. For example, I might have a lifelong experience of myself as black-identified and remain immersed in that black identity throughout my entire life, living in a predominantly black neighborhood, working in and supporting black-owned businesses, and socializing primarily with other black people.

The racial-identity resolution process might be manifested in a stage-wise process, as originally considered to be the only form of racial-identity resolution, with whites and people of color progressing through the developmental stages in a manner that moved from unawareness of self as a racial being to awareness of one's racial identity to full integration of race into the "self."

The racial-identity process might be spiral or cyclical in that I go through all of the statuses at various points in my life experience and then circle back and repeat the developmental tasks at later life stages.

Racial-identity resolution has also been experienced as multifaceted in that depending on circumstances in my environment, I may choose to manifest different aspects of my racial identity. For example, I may present as linear with my family of origin, who all share the same racial identity; at work I might manifest a more neutral racial identity, expressing more of my professional identity than my racial identity. Socially, longtime friends may have seen me as expressing the various statuses of awakening, identification, multiracial, and transracial in the period that they have known me.

The jury is still out on how we come to terms with our racial identities. What we do know is that the process is complex and perhaps related to developmental tasks over the life span. For most whites, the concept of a racial identity rarely surfaces in their daily lives. Thus, one's group-membership identity as a white person remains somewhat stable during the course of a lifetime. The face of that white identity does not change in professional or social settings. Many people of color find that a healthy resolution of the racial-identity process demands that they have many faces—professional, social, political, and spiritual. For example, how one expresses one's racial identity may depend on context. As one black man put it, "I can hardly wait to get home from corporate America and be a black man again." This statement implies that there is a different "black self" expressed while at work than at home. It gives witness to the concept of double consciousness, the challenge of having one unified identity, described by W. E. B. Du Bois in his 1903 publication *The Souls of Black Folk*.[4] Whites can be white at home, at work, and at play, not having to adjust their racial identity.

Instead of stages, current scholarship considers racial-identity development as characterized by five statuses aligned with the principles of Gestalt psychological theory.[5] From this perspective, two separate processes for people of color and whites are not necessary, as the sum of our multiple identities are understood as greater than any single identity. These racial-identity statuses are described in the paragraphs that follow.

UNAWARENESS/NEUTRALITY RACIAL-IDENTITY STATUS

The status of unawareness/neutrality describes a state of unawareness of self as racial, or low importance given to race matters in one's life (i.e., race neutrality). From a Gestalt perspective, the individual focuses on that aspect of identity that is prominent or uppermost at the time. For example, I might be more cognizant of my identity as a woman when I am speaking in front of an audience that is predominantly male. I would generally identify as a black woman, but in this particular context, race recedes to the background along with other aspects of identity, such as my profession, age, sexual orientation, and family relationship. Like the familiar figure/ground image of the vase, in which the same image can appear as either a vase or two faces depending on how you look at it, race becomes the background and is only brought to the foreground when it is brought to attention.

In a more permanent expression of an unaware or neutral status, race as an aspect of one's identity recedes to the background. I identify myself as a person who happens to be black. Or as a psychologist, or a mother, or a middle-aged woman, or a New Yorker . . . my race is not in the foreground of my identity.

In cross-racial friendships it is possible for both parties to put race in the background and to give it little, if any, attention. This typically happens in global settings in countries without the same racial history that has been so integral to race identity in the United States.

For example, Marcos, a twenty-six-year-old Panamanian visiting in the United States, looks at me with a confusion that is not attributed to the fact that English is his second language. He is trying to understand my question about cross-racial friendships. Having visited Panama several times and having relatives there, I know there are white-skin Panamanians and black-skin Panamanians. Again, Marcos is confused when I point this out. I ask if there is a problem with black Panamanians being friends with white Panamanians. He looks at me as if I eat babies for breakfast. Without the same history of systemic racism as exists in the United States, he doesn't grasp my meaning, and it is a very short interview. Arguably, there are those who would name the lack of Afro-Panamanians in leadership roles as a form of discrimination, and that colorism (light skin versus dark skin) does exist in the country, but for the most part, everyday people on the street describe racism in Panama as being nothing like that in the United States.[6] Like during my brief interview with Marcos, they would express confusion in response to an inquiry about "cross-racial friendship," underscoring that these relationships in the US are wrapped in deep social context.

Yurima, who is Venezuelan, gives a similar response to my inquiry on cross-racial friendships in Venezuela.

"We are a more mixed than pure race," she tells me of Venezuelans. She describes her father as Spanish and her mother as "mulatto" and other members of her family as blond Corsicans.

"We never have racial issues, just social class. People can't tell if I am black or white or Indian. We have never had segregation like in the US. Social class does separate us. You can be blond and poor."

Working in the United States, she experiences race differently. "Here it is not like they don't accept you. They [whites] just don't integrate you. They are not your friends."

AWAKENING RACIAL-IDENTITY STATUS

The awakening status describes a state of awareness as a racial person. Currently living in a predominantly white neighborhood, I find my racial awareness acutely heightened whenever I see another African American in the grocery store or at my place of worship. For the most part, I go about my day with race as an embedded aspect of my identity until I "bump up" against the figural aspect of race in another person. As with the vase and two faces image, race becomes the figure in the foreground and other aspects of my identity recede to the background. Here is another example:

"I grew up in a predominantly white neighborhood," Michael shares in a focus group, "so when I went to college it was really my first time that I was around other Asians. I was scared to death of other Asians, to tell you the truth. What has really been my ultimate goal, has always been, and more so when I was younger, is assimilation. I wanted to assimilate in society. I wanted to be like the rest of the neighborhood, which was white. So, I resisted anything that would look Asian at all. It was only when I went to college that I had more experiences with people of more diverse backgrounds. That's when I met friends of Asian backgrounds and different backgrounds. So it's a little bit of a flip side for me; it's the fear of Asians, I guess, and of being Asian."

During this status, cross-racial friendships can be and are more prominent. As Michael recounts, only having friends of the same race would mean that he had not assimilated in a society where the dominant race is white. In healthy friendships, friends are perceived as social equals. Being socially equal can be interpreted as synonymous with being racially equal. As long as racial differences are not openly discussed and white friends emphasize that the different-race friends are "just like them," cross-racial friendships can be maintained.

IDENTIFICATION RACIAL-IDENTITY STATUS

The racial-identity status of identification describes a strong connection with one's race apart from racism and/or a rejection of privilege based on race. How one identifies and expresses his or her race in this status is very critical to meaningful relationships, particularly in cross-racial interactions. Regardless of the environment where racism exists, I am able to organize my racial identity as intact and whole and remain fully functioning. For example, a black student who is actively working to change the criminal justice system's disproportionate incarceration of black males might operate from a clear sense of self as a racial being apart from any stereotypes of blacks as criminals. In doing so, the black student's racial-identity status would demonstrate the status of identification. Similarly, a white student whose application is rejected from the Ivy League school of her choice, but who does not attribute that rejection to reverse discrimination, would demonstrate this status as racial-identity resolution.

Cross-racial friendships where both individuals demonstrate this racial-identity status of strong racial identification hold promise for closing the racial divide. Here is an example from an interview with Detra, a black professional woman who works in a college setting.

> My closest friend is a white male with whom I am in communication on a regular basis. (He lives in Connecticut, so we talk on the phone at least once a week and communicate by email almost daily.) He and I met in the workplace, around the time of the LA riots, immediately following a staff meeting. In fact, I was a bit surprised that he actually approached me because as a new staff member he had described himself as rather politically conservative and, based on some of his right-wing comments, I thought that his approach would be quite separatist. When we worked together, I was the only African American on staff, so I was certain that he and I would spend little if any non-work-related time together. However, as time progressed, he sought me out more for social reasons. In his own words, he expressed that he found me "intriguing," "different," and all of the typical "you don't meet my stereotypes of a black woman" stuff. Ironically, following that somewhat ignorant icebreaker, we became fast friends. I had thought to myself, "At least he's honest." When he said to me that I was "intriguing," I actually knew what he meant but pressed him to talk more about it. In essence, this strange white man had latched on to me because I obviously came across as somewhat sage or, for lack of better words, a "good" black. To date, he and I have great debates about everything in life from race to politics. However, *most* of our conversations are about race. In fact, we share our divergent views openly and freely, almost to the point of inflicting pain upon one another. Although there are many cultural differences between us, what really drives our friendship are the sincere attempts at honesty between us. He and I create for one another a space to talk openly, across racial taboos and about our deep frustrations about race. Our friendship is a beautiful one, though, because we both fight and love vigorously.

MULTICULTURAL RACIAL-IDENTITY STATUS

Similarly, the multicultural racial-identity status offers the foundation for bridging the racial divide. The multiracial status describes an integration of race in one's life with the expression of multicultural attitudes. The individual acts with authenticity, honestly shares thoughts and feelings, and experiences meaningful contact with others while challenging any level of system that supports inequality, oppression, and social injustice.[7]

An example of this status is the cross-racial friendship, richly rooted in civil rights, that was shared by Olympic medalists Tommie Smith and John Carlos, who were black, and Peter Norman, who was white. Their friendship was forged out of their shared experience of being ostracized after the controversial "salute seen around the world" by American runners Smith and Carlos at the 1968 Olympics. Australian runner Peter Norman was the quintessential upstander. An upstander is a person who has chosen to make a difference in the world by speaking out against injustice and creating positive change.[8] As John Carlos stated, "Although he [Norman] did not raise a fist, he lent a hand."[9]

At the awards ceremony, Smith and Carlos had planned to do something to call attention to racist practices in the United States and within the Olympics and sports in general. Their mentor at San Jose State University, Professor Harry Edwards, a sociologist and organizer of the Olympic Project for Human Rights (OPHR), had planned the unsuccessful boycott of black athletes to the Olympics but told them that "there were many ways to boycott the Olympics."[10] They decided they would both wear black gloves. John would wear beads to symbolize those who had been lynched and Carlos would wear his jacket unzipped as an expression of support for blue-collar workers. All three actions were in violation of the Olympics dress code. They also wore OPHR buttons, which had been distributed to other American athletes who wanted to demonstrate their support.

Right before the awards ceremony, Carlos realized that he had left his gloves back in the village. Norman suggested that they each wear one glove and asked, "Hey, mate, you got another one of those?" referring to the OPHR button. Neither Carlos nor Smith had one. A member of the Harvard row team gave Norman his button. "I proudly wore it on the stand."[11]

On the dais after the awarding of the medals, during the playing of "The Star-Spangled Banner," Smith held his gloved hand up as a cry for freedom. Carlos followed that action with his gloved hand. Norman maintained a fixed stare, proudly wearing his OPHR button in solidarity, as Australia had its own appalling record for discrimination against its own indigenous people. All three were banned for life from the Olympics as a result of this action, and they all faced deep public disdain for their protest; only decades later were they recognized as civil rights activists.

The three men stayed in touch over the years and continued to support each other through personal trials as well as celebrate their achievements and successes. Smith always referred to Norman as his close friend, and Carlos referred to him as his brother. Smith and Carlos were pallbearers at Norman's funeral in 2006.[12]

At San Jose State University there is now a statue depicting both Smith and Carlos in salute. Norman is not depicted in the statue, as the sculptor Rigo23 intentionally left the space empty so that future visitors could envision themselves as upstanders in that space.[13]

TRANSRACIAL RACIAL-IDENTITY STATUS

The transracial status, in addition to the behavioral characteristics of the multiracial status, is characterized by a high level of fluidity and intentionality about one's actions. The individual experiences race in its full integration of the many dimensions of diversity and the multiple identities that characterize us as human beings.

In an individual or a personal context, diversity refers to the differences among people with respect to race, ethnicity, culture, gender, gender expression, age, class, mental and physical abilities, sexual orientation, religion, education level, job role and function, and personality traits. It embraces the many ways in which we are similar to and different from other human beings. As an individual, I am like some people and unlike others. I am unique, yet I am a member of the human race and share other humans' genetic and emotional constitution. That is the paradox of diversity. We are unique, and we are the same.

Traditional approaches to understanding differences emerged from a dominance model. This model says that yes, we are all alike, yet some of our inherent differences are considered better than others. Males are better than females, white skin is better than dark skin, able bodies are better than disabled bodies, young is better than old, heterosexual orientation is better than gay or lesbian orientation . . . and the list could go on for every existing dimension of difference.

You are perhaps reading this and thinking how illogical it even sounds to think that way. Yet we tend to see differences in a hierarchical manner. That is how the brain works in an efficient and organized manner. It is part of our evolutionary advantage as humans. Unfortunately, this kind of thought process leads us to treat differences as independent variables—as if you could go about your day only choosing to use one aspect of your identity. For example, entering a room that is exclusively filled with people of your gender, your race, your mental abilities, or your age simply is not possible.

Current scholarship treats differences from a relational perspective and takes into account the intersectionality of our differences. Two major forces are the impetus for changing the meaning of identity in the twenty-first century—globalization and an intellectual/political shift in how language and culture is experienced.[14] The free flow of goods, services, capital, and information across seamless national borders challenges the notion of stable identities. In addition, identity is now constructed through language and social practices that make it more contextual, multiple, malleable, and evolving.[15]

Thus, we, as humans, are a complex intersection of the many dimensions of diversity that make us unique and yet like other people. Such thinking supports an understanding of the complex interactions of social relations and fosters the skills necessary to navigate our increasingly multicultural world. I cannot separate my gender from my race or my ethnicity, or my mental from my physical abilities, or my age from my sexual orientation. I am a wonderfully made complex set of variables that makes me uniquely me.

I tested out this hypothesis by distributing a forced-choice survey question: "Which part of your identity is *most* important to you?" The choices were race, gender, age, sexual orientation, class, ethnicity/nationality, mental/physical ability, and religion. Forty-four percent of the respondents chose mental/physical ability; 29 percent chose religion; 15 percent gender; 8 percent race; and 4 percent ethnicity/nationality.

No one chose age, sexual orientation, or class. All found it challenging to choose one aspect.[16]

Cross-racial friendships support us in our developmental process to more effectively master the expression of our multiple and intersecting identities in a holistic manner. In other words, I do not experience myself or others in terms of a fixed, inflexible identity. Healthy racial-identity resolution is a complex process that researchers suggest is foundational to one's psychological wellness and influences how one navigates career choices, community and political participation, cultural activities, and relationship commitments.[17] As children, having more diverse friends leads to greater social competence and increased acceptance of different cultures.[18] As adolescents, having cross-racial friends is associated with greater academic success, higher educational aspirations, and leadership.[19] In adults, having cross-racial friends demonstrates reduced prejudice and discrimination, changed perceptions about racism, and a strong belief in the possibility of lessening the racial divide.[20]

The transracial-identity status may evoke images of flower children and idealistic hippies from the 1960s, but it is much more grounded and timely than one would imagine. A transracial identity is the fruit of a healthy and well-developed cross-racial friendship that moves us to believe and act in a collective capacity, allows us to understand and manage the complexities of life, encourages us to share resources in the wisest and most effective manner, and allows us to remain curious and hopeful about the current reality and to maintain a state of responsiveness to the world in all its diversity. That is a lot of benefit.

When I think of a transracial-identity status, I think about my friend Rita, who, along with Joan, is one of my oldest and most enduring white friends from my high school years. Rita often appears a bit dumbfounded when I bring up racial issues. It is not because she is naive, race-neutral, or lacks an understanding of her social privilege as a white woman. It is truly because she experiences race as a nonissue. "Nonissue" should not be interpreted as not important or not significant. Rita cringes when I talk about racist practices and is baffled that race alters how people think and act in various situations or determines one's behavior. Race is just not a determinant in her life choices. Other things, like finance, safety, values, ability, and time, may factor into a decision but never race. Honestly, I used to think racial stereotypes were just a bit more hidden in her, just waiting for the moment to erupt like a pressure cooker on a timer. I've even subtly tested her with prompts and triggers known to uncover subtle racial tendencies. "Why are you thinking about buying a condo in that neighborhood?" I ask, referring to a city development where she really wants to live. "What are your concerns about the neighborhood?" I ask, trying to tease out the obvious racial diversity in that neighborhood. Nope. She doesn't bite, and I know she is oblivious to the fact that others (including blacks and Hispanics) would take into account the racial diversity in the area and equate that diversity with more crime and decreasing housing value. It is not that Rita doesn't consider these factors. It is just that they are not connected to race. Sure, she has unconscious biases just as every human being who is alive does, but race in her mind is not synonymous with the stereotypes that have been socially loaded into our psyche.

I would like to flatter myself and think it is all due to the fact that Rita and I have been friends for over fifty years and our cross-racial friendship has influenced her worldview, but frankly it is probably largely because Rita's own racial-identity resolution process reflects a transracial status that enables her to seek out and maintain with ease cross-racial friendships.

I reimagine the world of my elementary school years: Kitty Ribar, Carlos Roland, Judy Schwelgien, Maria Mabini, Gayle Starling, Michael Easler, Deborah Harris, and Zoe Maxwell were all in the same classroom. White, black, Asian, Latino—all there together. I dream of a world that would have treated us all the same, skin color notwithstanding, and in my vision we become adults whose racial-identity resolution process, regardless of its status, would put up no barriers based on race that would prevent us from being friends again as adults. It would be a world of "colored people," all of whom looked good in blue glasses.

Chapter 6

GENTLE (AND NOT SO GENTLE) BUMPING

Friendships, like people, have a developmental pattern. In early childhood, we form our friendships based on geography. We become friends with others in the neighborhood, with the kids of our parents' friends, or often with kids from our faith communities. In late childhood, friendships are based on sharing particular activities and interests—sports, learning the same musical instrument, school subjects, membership in the same clubs. In adolescence, friendships are based on emotional support and serve as a testing ground for new values and working out our identity. In adulthood, friendships are based on shared values, attitudes, and expectations. In later adulthood, friendships provide considerable stability and life satisfaction.

Very few people would doubt the value friendships add to our lives. Outside of family, friends provide the primary vehicle for support. Some people, however, might question the benefit that cross-racial friendships provide, especially as the differences among racial groups become more pronounced. Whites and people of color, as racial groups, are discovering racial identity at different developmental stages in their life cycles. Many whites find themselves in adulthood struggling for the first time to figure out what race and whiteness mean as an integral part of their full identity.[1] Whereas the majority of people of color are immersed in race as something that is essential to and inextricable from their existence and, as a result, have integrated racial identity with other aspects of their developmental process from early childhood.

The value of cross-racial friendships is that they provide both people of color and whites with a vehicle for maximum self-expression. Our chances of being fully authentic are increased by bumping up against differences. Bumping up against differences, particularly racial differences, helps us define who we are, individually and collectively.[2] When whites and people of color "bump," they experience themselves as racial beings as each partner in a friendship interacts to form a healthy and equal relationship. Inevitably, they must confront and address racism and the inequities it creates; otherwise, it seeps into the friendship. In cross-racial friendships, achieving maximum self-expression and the full expression of our collective American identity require gentle bumping.

For many people, however, any kind of bumping experience—even gentle bumping—evokes resistance. Thirty-five-year-old Yvette, a black focus group participant, believes that "whites have to be pushed to move into other cultures." She may have a point. But resistance to cross-racial socializing is not limited to whites. Larry, an African American financial planner, recalls a bad experience in his elementary school. Over thirty years later he vividly remembers when he was eleven and a teacher used the rhyme "Eeny, meeny, miny, moe, catch a nigger by his toe," to choose which student would go to the board. Since that time, he reports that he "keeps [whites] at an arm's length until they prove themselves to me."

There are many individuals, including some whites, who believe that cross-racial interactions should not be gentle. They believe that whites need a decent emotional punch to reach profound insights about white privilege, dismantling racist institutional structures, and erasing the social loadings that perpetuate racism. Without doing this identity work, whites enter cross-racial friendships unconsciously (or consciously) trying to preserve the status quo. Change-management research supports the assertion that it often takes a significant emotional event to move people out of their comfort zones. Early diversity training sessions were intended to do just that. Simulated and experiential exercises were specifically designed to shake up white people and awaken them emotionally to their active role in racism.[3] Like provocative talk shows that attempt to get resolution on a controversial subject in one hour, these sessions may have enlightened white participants about the nature of racism but often left them frustrated and angry about having their emotions manipulated. Just because of their skin color, they were perceived to not only be the perpetrators but the beneficiaries of racism. And as with provocative talk shows, ending with pleas to tune in tomorrow for yet another controversial subject, there were no lasting effects on attitudes or behavior as a result of this kind of training.

Change-management theory also tells us that resistance is a natural response to many human experiences. We resist doing necessary things that we don't like to do and often put off doing them. Sometimes it is easier to buy more underwear than to do laundry. We also resist, on some level, things that we like to do. We just overcome that resistance. I don't like getting up at 4:00 a.m. to go to the airport to arrive on time for a flight to Hawaii, but I will do it because the benefits of getting there are worth it to me (and to those on my work team who encourage me to take vacation rather than working all the time and nagging them to work more). For those committed to bridging the racial divide, overcoming resistance to crossing racial lines is necessary.

From the perspective of Gestalt psychology, resistance is merely information about the resister's thinking and values. When perceived through this lens, resistance is a useful tool for facilitating change. In cross-racial interactions, listening to each other's life stories helps us understand resistance but is not enough to build healthy friendships. We have to understand the dynamics of difference—stereotypes, privilege, unconscious bias—and how they play out in cross-racial interactions.

Racial stereotypes abound in our society and are circulated within our families, educational systems, work environments, media, and faith communities. These stereotypes serve as barriers by maintaining and creating resistances to these friendships. American comedian, rapper, and actor Nick Cannon sparked an internet debate by wearing "white face" to promote his new album, *White People Party Music*, using a number of stereotypes about the white lifestyle, such as kissing their pets, frequenting farmers' markets, and playing beer pong.[4]

Particularly negative stereotypes are attributed to poor whites, especially those from the Appalachian regions. In his 2016 memoir *Hillbilly Elegy*, J. D. Vance offers a compassionate understanding of Appalachian values and attitudes from a sociological perspective and through the insights gained from examining his upbringing through the lens of his current privileged position as an attorney and a venture capitalist. He examines the stereotypes of individuals from the region as nonworkers, addicts, ignorant, and tribal people who have been branded "hillbilly."[5]

In one example from the book, where he examines the underpinnings of a stereotype about white Appalachians, the author, perhaps unwittingly, reinforces another stereotype about blacks and inherent racism among Appalachians. He writes, "My dad, for example, has never disparaged hard work, but he mistrusts some of the most obvious paths to upward mobility. When he found out that I had decided to go to Yale Law, he asked whether on my applications, I had 'pretended to be black or liberal.' This is how low the cultural expectations of working-class white Americans have fallen."[6] While evaluating the cultural expectations of the white working class, the author failed to acknowledge the falsehood of the stereotype that to be black or liberal is inherently society's rock bottom. Of course, not all readers will have this interpretation for this statement, as it could also mean that Ivy League colleges favor blacks and liberals, and by doing so are being politically correct. This interpretation implies that blacks could not be qualified to get into an Ivy League and that white liberals who believe they are qualified believe so in sympathy or ignorance. Either interpretation echoes an often heard objection to being friends with whites, as illustrated by one black focus group participant: "They [whites] always think they are better than you, even poor white trash."

One could legitimately argue that the stereotypes that have plagued people of color for decades have influenced laws, policies, and practices that have greatly hindered them and in some cases threatened their quality of life. This fact underscores that whites enjoy racial social privilege, a major barrier to fostering cross-racial friendships.

Privilege is what enables you to receive unearned rights, rewards, benefits, access, opportunities, and advantages simply because of your group identity and without regard to achievement. Racial privilege is afforded on a systems level but oozes into cross-racial relationships because it is often experienced unconsciously. It is similar to driving the same route to the same destination every day. The route becomes so familiar that we become oblivious to the stops and turns. We often get to our destination with little or no memory of the journey. This accounts for why whites are generally oblivious of their privileged status unless approached with acute awareness and acted upon with intention. Just as fish in water do not need to understand wetness, when whites experience social privilege stemming from their whiteness, they neither understand what it means to be white without privilege nor experience a need to understand it.

In cross-racial interactions, it requires awareness and attention to recognize and acknowledge that there is disparate treatment for people of color in education, healthcare, employment, and within the criminal justice system. My friends Joan and Rita find it hard to grasp this concept, as they are acutely aware of my personal and professional achievements. On measures of wealth, education, career, I have accomplished more "societal success milestones" than they have. They would definitively declare that I held more privilege. Putting aside individual choices about our careers (Joan and Rita are both elementary school principals) and personal lifestyle choices, I believe my journey to success was more challenging than theirs could ever have been, even if we had mapped out the same career path. That is because having social privilege just makes life easier. Think about returning a rental car and seeing the sign DO NOT BACK UP TO AVOID SEVERE TIRE DAMAGE. You see the spikes and are not sure if they will lie down or not, so to be certain, you have to find a way to navigate the car around the spikes. Privilege is the assurance that every time you ride over the spikes they will lie down and if they don't, the rental car company will pay for the damage.

When we have a conversation about white privilege, Joan listens and nods her head but is a bit skeptical that I have experienced these roadblocks. How could that be? She knows my supportive family, my academic abilities, my work ethic, a formula for success in her mind. We went to the same high school and college, had worshiped at the same churches, traveled the same streets on the East Side of Cleveland, ate at the same restaurants, and shopped at the same stores. It was hard to understand. Our lives were similar in so many ways outside of race.

Rita is more emotionally confused. She tells me that she feels bad that these "things have happened to me" and she didn't even know about it. It makes her sad. She doesn't know what to do with the sadness.

I understand the cognitive and emotional confusion that Joan and Rita experience, as I have had similar cognitive and emotional confusion when I "woke up" regarding my privilege in comparison with my LGBT friends. The process of privilege works the same way regardless of the diversity dimension. It allows us to be ignorant about how the world operates from that identity. It allows us to minimize the experience of those not in positions of privilege by further reinforcing the discrimination. By doing this, we are able to hold on to the belief that there really are level playing fields and that the metaphorical car-rental spikes do lie down for everyone. It allows us to believe that successful individuals (for example,

Barack Obama, Oprah Winfrey, Sonia Sotomayor, Jay-Z, Ursula Burns, Sean "P. Diddy" Combs, Jennifer Lopez) are indicative of a postracial society rather than examples of individuals who have achieved despite institutional racism.

With Joan and Rita, I change the conversation from privilege to what we want to order for dinner, knowing that we have bumped enough for the day and that bumping needs to be gentle.

What does it mean to be white in a society where race is only attached to people of color? It makes it easy for whites, as a member of the dominant race, to conceptualize themselves as the norm. It is very much like a computer system in which the default value is already set. White European Americans are pretty much the default value in this country. American cultural norms have been rooted in an amalgamation of European backgrounds and ancestry. History, education, corporate policies and procedures, and leadership in this country have all been determined and influenced by white culture. Thus, it is easier for white Americans to never be made aware of "whiteness," or struggle with being different from the norm, or find limited representation of themselves within the world. I hear and witness this often in my professional and personal lives. White often means a *not*. I'm not black. I'm not Asian. I'm not Hispanic. I'm not Native American Indian. *I am American.*

Many whites run like the wind or quickly change the subject when the consciousness of being white is raised. It is changed so quickly that you can forget that the entire civil rights movement ever happened. Since the 1960s, spurred by the urgency of managing race relations, many white social psychologists, sociologists, and social justice advocates began to research white identity in the hopes of raising their own and other whites' racial literacy.[7] They were joined by the black psychologist Janet Helms, who outlined a widely circulated model of white racial-identity development in classrooms, texts, and workshops.[8] Much of her work and that of other white-identity researchers is devoted to an understanding of racism, power, and privilege, where whiteness is associated with racism, oppression, and elitism. Today's research and work around white identity still has this focus, which is why so many white people avoid the topic or quickly change the subject when it is brought to their attention.

In the past, while enjoying the privilege of being the majority race, understanding and being conscious of one's white identity was not a necessity for white Americans. This has changed over the past decade. Many whites now have a new consciousness but still struggle to understand white identity both on an institutional and a personal level.[9] Eight years of having a black president and a First Family who looked like only 13 percent of the American population stirred even the least race-conscious white person to think about racial identity. The uprising of out and proud white nationalists, members of the alt-right, and neo-Nazis caused many white Americans to feel the need to defend themselves and emphasize that these groups did not represent all white people. Protests against the removal of Confederate statues that are meant to honor Confederate leaders, soldiers, or the eleven Confederate states made curious historians of many Americans. Many whites had made the assumption that these monuments represented "our history" and "our culture." They recently learned that many of the monuments were actually erected between 1900 and 1950 as states enacted Jim Crow laws to disenfranchise African Americans and formally segregate society.[10]

Among those who had that insight was Mitchell Landrieu, the former mayor of New Orleans, who is white. It was only through his conversation with his friend, jazz musician, composer, and educator Wynton Marsalis, who is black, that he came to the understanding of the impact of the statues on black Americans. They shared their story in an interview for the National Geographic Channel's *America Inside-Out* with Katie Couric.[11]

"What about these statues, man? Especially that statue of [Robert E.] Lee. No reason to have a statue of him; he didn't win anything," Marsalis recalls saying to Landrieu in a 2014 conversation. He continues to explain to Couric, "The issue is that this is a symbol of a defeated general. I always wanted it to be removed. I used to dream about it being blown up. Of course, I wasn't going to do anything, but I would dream about it, like in high school. It was always on my mind."

After this conversation with Marsalis, Landrieu said, "That was the first time that I actually put myself in somebody else's shoes and then I started researching it. Some were put up well after the Civil War ended by the Daughters of the Confederacy. The people that lost decided to put these statues up to send a message to people just like Wynton, that you're lesser than, and even though we lost the war, and the United States won, we're not coming along. And that's why Robert E. Lee's arms are folded and he's looking north. It's an affront to the idea of what America was supposed to be postwar."

Landrieu acknowledges the impact of the Charlottesville riots on his thinking about the statues, but he credits this conversation with his longtime friend Marsalis for his decision to call for the removal of the Lee statue.[12]

My family personally experienced the impact of a symbol of the Confederacy when, as a teen, I moved with them from inner-city Cleveland to a rural area thirty miles outside the city. Our neighbors were angry that blacks had moved not only into town but right next door to them. They immediately erected a barbed-wire fence that stretched the length of our adjoining properties. On each post of the fence, they placed NO TRESPASSING signs. They also flew a Confederate flag. My sister Simone would go to the fence and boldly play a very poor rendition of Taps on her trumpet (she was just starting to learn how to play) as they took the flag down each evening.

My parents, although angry themselves, continued to provide us with security and love, meanwhile teaching us the valuable life lesson of how to fight racism with dignity. They did everything they needed to do legally and publicly to secure the safety of our family. Politely, yet assertively, they responded to every ploy the community used to get us to move; zoning laws that were suddenly unearthed stating that our land was too narrow for building; school officials who thought my sisters, brother, and I would be better served if we attended another school district where there were already black children (they would graciously see that arrangements could be made); even our Great Dane was cited, for some now-forgotten reason.

Through the course of all these challenges, my parents led us to believe that they were in charge not only of our family and its space but also the world. They had a great deal of courage and believed strongly that they had a right to live where they pleased. I asked, "Why do these people, who don't even know us, dislike us so much?" My mom's response was that people work hard throughout their lives to earn money to buy a nice home. She told me our neighbors had worked really hard to buy their dream home. She had heard from someone that the family had moved all the way from Euclid, a suburb outside Cleveland, because blacks were moving into Euclid. Shortly after their move, we came and moved right next door to them. She got pleasure out of that irony. "We're everywhere!" she told me. "Where did they think they could move?" She equated their beliefs with pure ignorance. As an adolescent, I was confused about their "ignorance" and fearful of it.

On a 2017 Facing History and Ourselves civil rights study tour to Alabama, we visited Old Live Oak Cemetery in Selma, where the seven-foot monument that honors Nathan Bedford Forrest resides. The monument names Forrest as "Defender of Selma, Wizard of the Saddle, Untutored Genius, the First with the Most." To be clear, Forrest served as the Grand Wizard of the Ku Klux Klan, and the monument was erected in 2000. Forrest is one of the three celebrated "heroes" of the Civil War along with Lee and Stonewall Jackson, having quickly risen to the rank of general despite having no military training. After the Forrest bust was stolen in 2012, considerable effort was made to restore the monument, and a second ceremonial unveiling of the new monument happened three years later.[13] Freshly placed Confederate flags line the monument and the wide section known as Confederate Circle. Looking at the monument surrounded by all the Confederate flags had a chilling effect on me, especially as I glanced at my black skin. It had a sobering effect on my white friends, who walked around the scene dismayed. Together we felt like a collective throw-up was under way, leaving our vomit as the putrid bouquet the monument deserved. One would not have to stretch one's imagination to speculate on the intended message for blacks when some whites in the twenty-first century erect monuments and place flags to commemorate a war that was fought and *lost* over the right to keep slaves. Mind-boggling.

The assumptions about the representative nature of these monuments are vigorously challenged by Americans across many racial groups, including whites.[14] The monuments debate has also served as another contemporary case where whites can examine their identity in the context of institutional racism.

The definition of institutional racism as "privilege plus power" is one that is still promoted today. By this definition only whites can be racist because (1) they have privilege and (2) they have power. The implications of this definition is that white privilege as a social relational process provides whites with an advantage that translates into power, although it is invisible to most of its white recipients while clearly visible to those who are victims of oppression.[15]

From this perspective, white identity resolution is then a process of shedding one's racist thinking and the entitlement that has been deeply internalized. It offers no other avenue for defining or coming to resolution about whiteness but through first embracing oneself as racist and then rejecting that aspect of one's identity. This framework for racism treats white identity as a fixed status attached to skin color that is inescapable and intrinsic to a white person's identity.

This framework fosters the notion that diversity is not a benefit to our country but rather that diversity spurs conflict, a belief held by many and often the subject of conservative media, which argues that unity and not diversity is America's strength.[16] From this perspective, unity is synonymous with assimilation and the understanding that there is a single brand for America equated with white standards. The term "political correctness" is placed on any action or behavior that seeks to deviate from these norms, and a resurgent white nationalist identity asserts its place among other racial-pride initiatives that celebrate and hold in high esteem their race.

Because the vast majority of white Americans who are not wearing white hoods or sporting swastikas are just coming of racial age in understanding "whiteness," they can easily buy into this thinking, not understanding how power and privilege have been tethered to whiteness and are the bedrock of racism. Without understanding the connection of race to power and privilege, whites run the risk of embracing this notion of an American identity as equated with whiteness.

It can get complicated, and I can understand why whites reject the conceptualization of whiteness as equated with being a racist. It is not the racial identity that most white people own or embrace.[17] Yet understanding racism as part of a developmental racial-identity process is necessary in order to achieve a healthy white identity resolution. Just as you cannot reach sexual maturity without going through puberty, you cannot reach racial maturity as a white person without understanding and rejecting racism in all of its forms and expressions.

However, rejecting racism is different from accepting oneself as a racist, especially as something you have no control over and cannot change. When whites are urged to own and accept being racist as part of their identity, it can be rightfully rejected if they have never engaged in personal racist actions or held racist beliefs. This does not mean that there isn't racial-identity work to be done. The work is acknowledging and accepting the fact that by sharing a white group identity they have social privilege and benefit from this privilege to the disadvantage of people of color. Many whites do acknowledge and accept this fact while demonstrating racial equity in their personal and professional lives. Those (both people of color and whites) who hold the belief that whiteness is equated with racism and that white people are inherently racist and white supremacists simply because they are members of that racial group may have a theoretical argument, but such a thesis is not pedagogically sound if we want to convince whites of its veracity, particularly when being called a racist does not match their lived experience or their values. Such an assertion only serves to deepen the racial divide.

To reach common ground we have to meet each other where we are in our journey to racial-identity resolution, which is notably different for whites and people of color. For example, "Negros" and "colored people" came to a new understanding of "blackness" in the 1950s and 1960s during the civil rights movement. This process demanded disavowing a subordinate identity defined by whites and shedding the labels of being a marginalized, oppressed, victimized people. Clearly, we are a people who have experienced marginalization, oppression, and victimization, and that experience is a part of our current and past history, but it does not define our racial identity. Black Americans are a people of deep racial consciousness and high race esteem rooted in agility, creativity, wonder, and stamina. Black Americans evolved to this identity as their own psychological work and not because whites simply changed their minds and decided that black people were now a cool group of people. Whites have to find a way to claim their white identity as apart from that of oppressor, just as people of color have sought ways and continue to define their identity outside of victimization and marginalization. That is *their* work, and people of color cannot do that work for whites. In the words of James Baldwin in his 1962 essay "Letter from a Region in My Mind": "White people in this country will have quite enough to do in learning how to accept and love themselves and each other, and when they have achieved this—which will not be tomorrow and may very well be never—the Negro problem will no longer exist, for it will no longer be needed."[18]

Cross-racial friendships underscore the racial-resolution work that needs to be achieved for healthy race relations. Whites and people of color have independent and interdependent work in this regard. Independently we work to define our racial-group identities outside of racism and together we have to work to create that more perfect union as a nation. The difference in our racial-identity resolution work is what makes crossing racial lines in friendships so challenging and so rewarding. When we bump, we learn and grow. When we don't bump, we stay divided.

Language represents our limited thinking and words create small worlds. We have outgrown the terminology we need to explain the intersectionality of racial identity, power, and privilege. Whites are human beings who collectively share a history in the United States of racist practices and discrimination and are a people who play a central role in sustaining this structure. Yes, whites must actively work to end racial injustices and raise their consciousness about white privilege. But whites must also work just as hard to affirm an identity of whiteness apart from racial oppression and white supremacy that supports a positive white identity rooted in racial equality. Yes, people of color must name, acknowledge, and aggressively advocate against racial discrimination and all forms of contemporary racial bias while still holding themselves accountable for decisions and actions that affect their future. We can work to eradicate racism, but without a clear vision for how racial equality operates on an interpersonal level we have just created a void destined to be filled with old destructive patterns of tribal behavior.

Institutional racism exists. Yet we do not relate to individuals as institutions. In order to cross racial lines in friendships, we have to move past the certainty that every white person uses social privilege in ways that are destructive and damaging, or that whites are so fragile and lack racial stamina (defined as white fragility) that the only meaningful relationship they can have with a person of color is to be an accountable ally to the racism and discrimination that they as white people continue to perpetuate. Conceptualizing whites as being both the bearers of white fragility and white privilege gives them the impossible and conflicting task of being the healer of the wounds they continually inflict. We also have to move past the certainty that people of color have as their core identity that of being marginalized, oppressed, and victimized by the racist practices that exist in this country. This kind of thinking sets up an unhealthy dynamic in which whites cleanse collective guilt through relationships with people of color and people of color extract their self-worth from whites.

It goes without saying, and has been part of the civil rights movement since its inception, that both whites and people of color need to work together and in concert to eradicate racism. Racism is an ugly phenomenon that exists like a messy blob in our environment, threatening our existence and eroding our capacity to develop and grow. Racism does not define who whites are as human beings. Racism does not define who people of color are as human beings. Race, more than ever today, is a social-political construct.[19] We are one race, the human race, with diverse racial expressions of our humanity. In that diversity, we reach out to each other with the hope of connection. The connection of core speaking and witnessing to another's core allows both to experience their full humanity. These authentic connections are necessary for any kind of systemic change and for the elimination of institutional racism, and to, in the words of the preamble to the US Constitution, "establish justice, insure domestic tranquility, provide for the common defense, promote the general welfare, and secure the blessings of liberty to ourselves and our posterity." Diversity is truly America's strength.

To unravel the tangled web of racism is indeed quite a task. Any behavioral change process requires that persons or systems first experience a high enough degree of dissatisfaction with the current state to want to change. Then they have to have some kind of vision or mental image of what the desired state might look like. And then they have to possess the skill sets necessary to make that change happen. This is how resistance to change gets broken down.

I believe that as a nation we have done a lot of visioning about what a world would look like without racial boundaries. Martin Luther King's "I Have a Dream" speech is frequently quoted and supported in theory by people of color and whites. We do well with visioning. Based on our research, most of us are satisfied with the current monoracial environments we have created, and most of us lack the necessary skills to interact successfully across racial lines. As a result, we spend most of our energies resisting cross-racial interactions. In order to move forward, we start with managing resistance.

Understanding is a first step to managing resistance. Understanding is facilitated by recognizing areas of common ground. Research by Linda Tropp of the University of Massachusetts, Amherst, focused on the effects of mentioning race in a conversation and the degree of comfort experienced by racial groups as a result of bringing up this taboo topic among strangers. Results from these studies showed that whites were *less* interested in continuing the conversation when race was mentioned, while people of color became *more* interested in conversing with a white person who mentioned race.[20] In conversations about race, whites do not always feel confident that they can navigate the topic, while people of color, for whom race is integral to life, are eager to discuss it. Then how do we find common ground to facilitate understanding?

When facilitating workshops on racial bias and interracial relations, Dr. Tropp tries to have whites think about entering into race discussions as learning opportunities, similar to learning a new language or learning to play tennis, both of which take practice. "People need to feel efficacious and confident that they can manage cross-racial interactions," she says. Addressing people's anxiety about race, she believes, is as important as addressing implicit bias. "When whites are aware of how they feel during these interactions, it is a first step. They might not like what we are feeling. But it is helpful to understand that racial anxiety is natural and that is why they want to avoid it."

Her studies with teachers across the nation suggest that the more racially and ethnically diverse teachers' friendship networks are, the greater confidence they reported in the classroom with racially diverse students. Among white teachers, there is a correlation between having greater numbers of nonwhite friends and greater feelings of confidence about interacting with diverse students, and managing diverse classrooms, and a greater willingness to address race-related issues with students.[21]

Knowing how to bump requires emotional resilience when we make mistakes. It requires courage to own our personal and professional incompetence. Dee, a black college administrator, discusses her relationship with white friends in a way that illustrates this point:

I'm not their first "real black friend," so the incessant need to test the racial waters is not a priority. However, in those cases, connection is, on the surface, less political, but there is always, at least on my part, an awareness that racial differences exist. For example, going into a restaurant or other public place with a white male friend still gets stares or odd looks from others. I am aware of that, and now that I've pointed it out to the white men in my life, so are they. These kinds of "awarenesses" are often shocking to them, but like everything else, we analyze and discuss.

The other day, one of my white men (I jokingly call them that) told me he wanted to get the black church experience, so he wanted to go to church with me. I said, "You don't realize how fortunate you are to have me. . . . If it weren't for me, you'd just be curious like the rest of them." We laughed our knowing laugh. We both know that, although we care about one another, our friendship is as much about a "diversity experience" as it is about love. However, we realize that society did this to us, so we keep loving and keep coping.

Others, like Dee, state that their friendships with people who are racially different from them often include intense discussions about race. Faye, an African American woman, has been friends for many years with Donna, who is white. They both enjoy dancing and often go to black clubs. Faye describes Donna as a sister, but like sisters, they have disagreements, particularly when it comes to racial matters. Because Donna's world has included blacks for so long, she will render an opinion on a racial subject. Faye believes her own experience is "valid because I am black and grew up with this attitude" and has witnessed it among her black friends. "I thought it odd that [Donna] thought she knew more about being black than I did." Yet she reports no discomfort as a result of their disagreements. Faye believes Donna retains her white identity despite her many black friends, and Faye is able to retain her black identity while socializing in Donna's world.

For many blacks, the common ground is easily recognized with other people of color. James, a thirty-year-old black man, states, "I can relate more to Hispanics than to whites. They have the same mind-set. It is also easier for me with Jewish people because we have a shared history of discrimination."

Elizabeth, a young white woman, says that her experiences growing up as one of a few whites in a predominantly black school has often put her in the role of the "human racial translator." In high school, she had a friend who introduced her to a new girl who was black.

> When Dacia got to me, she said, "This is Liz, don't mess with her; she is the blackest white girl you will ever meet." Upon hearing this, I looked up from my work so confused on what that meant. I mean, I never purposely "acted black" or "dressed black" like some white girls did; I always just acted like myself. I am sure I was influenced by my environment some, but being or acting "black" was never a conscious act. After hearing this, I sat back and assessed what I knew about African Americans and I found that I knew a lot more than many white girls would know. . . . When I went to college, I found my experiences were helpful in the big picture of life. I made lots of friends of all colors and walks of life, and thought I felt most comfortable around African American people.

Later, she reports, in many late-night talks with racially mixed groups of friends, an African American friend, Robyn, taught her she should "be proud of what color I am and who I am and where I came from because that is what made me who I am today."

For most people, the work environment has provided them with the opportunity to cross racial lines. Some report that because of their work environment, they are more open to people of different races. A thirty-five-year-old black computer analyst, Aaron believes this to be true. "Workplace has become the only place to learn about races. I work in a white setting. We have roundtable discussions and people look at me and say, 'What do you think?'" Aaron feels the learning is bidirectional— whites learn about him as a black man and he learns about them as whites.

Neisha, an African American woman, has been in corporate America all her professional life. Here she has made friendships that cross racial lines.

> They consist of Latino and white. One of the most significant ones is a white female that I met in 1982. We have supported each other with children, parents, siblings, ex-husbands, and deaths. We have traveled

together to transport her daughter to spend her shared time with [the friend's] ex-husband. I was able to lend her emotional support/encouragement during the time her current husband was fired . . . the death of her sister, the drug problem with her daughter, and the divorce of her son. I gave a character witness interview for her. Every city [five] that they have relocated to over the years, I have visited and spent the weekend at their home. Last year I attended her husband's retirement ceremony to witness both of them getting pinned with honors. She was very supportive to me when I was facing the trials and tribulations of my son, a near-death experience with my daughter, and, most recently, the death of my dad.

Sustaining long-term friendships, even for same-race friendships, is tough. As Neisha discovered, it requires focusing on common life experiences. Getting beyond the fear of making mistakes in cross-racial groups and learning to live with some emotional discomfort are bumps on the road to meaningful cross-racial friendships. Marlene, a fortysomething white Jewish woman, states, "I have frequently fallen into the trap of assuming that because I have a friendship with one black female, for example, all black females will want a similar relationship. I just bumped up against that again in my new job. I have an African American woman who reports to me. Fortunately, a trusted friend and colleague cautioned me about the way I was talking about our pending relationship and caused me to reconsider my approach."

Marlene now knows that the path she needs to embark on is a journey of learning about her own history—white history. "Not revisionist versions, but real history." She tells me, "I can forget that this is a journey that will only be finished when I am dead. I can't let my fear of being called a racist get in the way of being as authentic as possible in those relationships I do have, bearing in mind that my intent and impact may not always be the same."

Ann, a fortysomething African American administrator in a university, relays the challenge of cross-racial friendships this way:

For me, personally, it has been challenging having friends of another race. I have a friend who was my next-door neighbor at one time. We were close then; however, she moved and I also moved, and now the friendship is more like an acquaintance. The challenges seemed to arise most often during social occasions. I wasn't comfortable with her family and friends and could sense that some of my family and friends weren't always comfortable with her. When she first moved, she called a lot about getting together, but I noticed that when my family and friends visited we were the only visitors. I wondered why we weren't invited to things that involved other family and friends anymore. We were invited to her son's bar mitzvah and I observed that we were the only African Americans there. We talk every now and then and occasionally get together, but it is more like an acquaintance relationship. I have other cross-racial acquaintances and colleagues, but we only socialize at work-related functions.

One can hope common ground can be found as a basis for cross-racial friendships in other ways beyond working side by side. One need not be the world's biggest risk-taker to gain a friend of a different race. Stephanie, a thirty-three-year-old black analyst, shares her experience of meeting her first white friend. "I grew up with all blacks and have always been a loner. It was through talking about the book *Memoirs of a Geisha* that I ended up bonding with a white woman who is now a good friend."

Crossing racial lines in friendships requires the courage of knowing oneself and having a vision of a world without racial boundaries. Knowing oneself is a developmental process. Good friends, especially those who cross racial lines, expand their self-boundaries in ways they could never have imagined on their own. Most of us are better humans than we believe ourselves to be. We learn that in these friendships.

Chapter 7

A NEW
GENERATION . . . A NEW
FORM OF RACISM

For the first time in our nation's history we have five generational co-horts, from ages seventy to sixteen, in the workforce, each with a differing understanding of the nature of work, different approaches to work, different work ethics, different learning styles, and different communication styles. As a cohort, each generational group is bound by a shared lived experience and time in history during their formative adolescent years. As a generational cohort, they grew up subject to the same significant events, paradigm shifts, innovations, technological advances, and economic and social conditions.[1]

Ask someone in the traditionalist generation about World War II, the polio vaccine, the space program, or the advent of color television, and you will get a history lesson. Ask a baby boomer about the Vietnam War, Beatlemania, Woodstock, Motown, or work life, and you will get a lecture on cultural experiences. Ask a Gen X-er about, the advent of videos, computers, and the massive layoffs, and you will get an education. Ask a millennial about political engagement, globalism, social media, and entrepreneurism, and you will be guided to the next big thing via technology. Ask a Gen Z-er about a new app, multiculturalism, social impact, and terrorism, and you will quickly appreciate the complexities of contemporary living.

Although these differences exist between the cohorts, a stark similarity exists in their attitudes toward race relations. The optimistic predictions of each generation harboring less negative racial attitudes toward each other until those negative attitudes were erased over time have faded.[2] Instead, studies suggest that for generations from traditionalists to Generation Z, tolerance may have increased but racism has not disappeared. With each generation, racism seems to have simply taken on a new form.

The overt, intentional forms of racism—cross burnings; lynchings; the denial of jobs, services, and memberships; and segregation—were prevalent during the traditionalist era. What it meant to be racist was clear. If you discriminated against nonwhite people by not hiring them in your business or refusing to serve them in a restaurant, terrorized them by burning a cross on their lawn, or persecuted them by hanging them from a tree, then you were a racist. If you didn't do those things, you were not a racist. You were not required to advocate or to condemn. If you didn't wear a white hood at night and were not a card-carrying member of the Ku Klux Klan, you were within your moral boundaries as an American. One could tolerate racism in the country or even hold racist beliefs and still not be considered a racist because that was the zeitgeist. As a result, there were clear boundaries for who you married and with whom you could safely socialize. Segregated schools and neighborhoods and racially discriminatory practices in the workplace that restricted diversity within the workforce eliminated or greatly reduced the geographic proximity necessary to foster cross-racial friendships. As a result, cross-racial friendships were rare and those that existed were often born out of social justice advocacy, religious beliefs, and a shared vision for racial equality.

Due to regulations and constrictions placed on racial discrimination as a result of civil rights laws formulated and enacted by the time baby boomers hit adulthood, overt racism became publicly abhorred and not tolerated by mainstream America. This value continues to be reinforced particularly after violence erupted in the college town of Charlottesville when hundreds of white supremacists, neo-Nazis, and their supporters descended on the town to protest the removal of a statue of the Confederate general Robert E. Lee. The results were tragic as one counterprotestor, Heather Heyer, was slain and nineteen more were injured. Following the August 12, 2017, rally, tens of thousands of demonstrators, emboldened and unnerved by the eruption of fatal violence in Virginia, surged into the streets and parks of Boston, Atlanta, Dallas, Portland, New York, and other major cities to denounce racism, white supremacy, and Nazism.[3] A 2017 NPR/PBS NewsHour/Marist Poll indicates that 94 percent of Americans disagree with the views of the

Ku Klux Klan, 86 percent disagree with views of the white supremacy movement, and 73 percent disagree with the views of white nationalists.[4]

However, covert, intentional racism—such as racial profiling, being ignored for service because of race, having a negative personality trait ascribed to an entire race, exclusionary hiring and mentoring practices, and gerrymandering—abounded during the 1960s and continue today. This form of racism, characteristic of the era in which baby boomers came into adulthood, allowed for the rise of racism as the belief that non-whites were not necessarily inferior but that whites were superior. In the area of Motown and Woodstock, it was fashionable for whites to have friends of a different race as long as they knew their place and stayed in their equal but separate spaces in America.

Whereas the concept of racism was clear for the traditionalists and baby boomer generations, it became muddy for Generation X. "Racism without racists," or color-blind racism, is a term scholars use to describe the kind of racism in which Generation X has navigated. In his book of the same title, sociology professor Eduardo Bonilla-Silva explains that this form of racism masks itself as nondiscriminatory, but underneath lies "a full-blown arsenal of arguments, phrases, and stories that whites use to account for and ultimately justify racial inequities."[5]

Covert unintentional racism also characterized this era. Examples of covert unintentional racism include patronizing remarks meant as a compliment ("He is a very articulate black man"), minimizing or dismissing racial differences ("I don't see you as black [or Asian, Hispanic, Native American . . .]"), and the endorsement of stereotypes (the majority of blacks and Hispanics are on welfare; they live in ghettos or poor neighborhoods due to lack of education). These attitudes are harder for the perpetrators to own and are psychologically confusing for their recipients. Thus, in friendships and in social situations when one's defenses are down—and usually one's thinking capacity, as well—slipups can happen. No one likes or wants this kind of stress in a social situation or in a friendship, which makes it safer for whites to only have friends who are white.

In this climate, our studies found that Generation X-ers did form friendships across racial lines, and those relationships tended to have more depth than earlier generations'. In other words, they shared experiences with people of other races, which increased closeness or intimacy and moved them beyond an acquaintance or coworker status. Examples on the depth index included socializing at each other's home, vacationing together, calling their friend for comfort or advice in times of emotional stress, witnessing a family argument, and borrowing money. Despite the level of depth in cross-racial friendships, respondents in the focus groups described a general reluctance to discuss any racially charged societal events, such as police shootings of unarmed black men and immigration reform, or to even have a casual discussion about racially themed movies.[6]

For millennials, who did not experience firsthand the era of intentional overt or intentional covert forms, racism goes beyond discrimination and destructive attitudes toward racial minorities to include whites. A Pew Research Center study reports that 58 percent of white millennials believed that discrimination against whites is just as big a problem as discrimination against blacks and other minorities.[7] However, black and Hispanic millennials, imbued with the Black Lives Matter movement, perceive racism in the classic definition of institutional racism as largely practiced by social institutions and organizations. Friendships across racial lines among millennials are common and expected. Yet there are qualifications.

Melanie, a thirty-one-year-old black woman, states it this way: "When I want to go quick and deep, I go with my black friends." Brice, a black man also thirty-one, echoes, "I'm one hundred percent with Melanie. I want to quickly go deep with the people that can sympathize with me." He then relates his frustration dating a black woman with "very white social circles," living in "a very white city—Seattle." His frustration stems from the fact that she appears to be constantly surprised at racist behaviors from whites. "I've engaged in my blackness in a deliberate way, and so it's interesting because even though she's a black woman that I am dating, you can't assume that you would get along because her experience is different than mine," he says. In other words, although the woman he is dating is black, he experiences her as culturally white.

Lauren, who is thirty-one and white, of Lebanese background, believes that millennials are trying to strive for racial balance rather than just "suppressing and oppressing" as with prior generations. Yet she acknowledges that there are a lot of individuals in her generation who "say they are open, but once you begin conversations on race, they back out. I think they are just trying to figure it out."

Caught in the nexus of diminishing overt racism and increasing covert racism without clear societal racial boundaries as previous generations had, millennials do have to figure it out. Many are doing so by drawing its meaning from their everyday life experience and drawing their own conclusions. An example comes from my meeting with Josh.

These days I spend a lot of time in Logan Airport going back and forth to meetings and especially going back and forth to Cleveland, which is my primary residence. Depending on traffic, I can make it to Logan in thirty-five minutes or in three hours, which means I opt for getting there early and end up hanging around the airport. I don't mind as it gives me time to read, write, answer emails, and return phone calls, and occasionally I treat myself to a good meal. This was one such occasion. I sat to enjoy my favorite Jasmine rice and shrimp dinner at Legal Seafood when a young white man at the next table starting making small chat (Did I need the outlet under the table to charge my phone? Was Boston home? Telling me he needed to download a movie for his long flight back to California). He then asked if I would mind telling him what I was reading. The book was Van Jones's *Beyond the Messy Truth: How We Came Apart, How We Come Together*. I told him that reading it infused me with a great deal of hope for the future of our country. He grunted.

Josh happens to be a nuclear/hadronic physicist specializing in precision measurements of fundamental quantities. I admit, I have no idea what that meant. I just knew he was very smart and also very nice. He asked what it was about Van Jones's book that gave me hope and shared that he was struggling to feel optimistic about America's future as well. I explained to him the reasons: Jones's candid and insightful letters to liberals and conservatives about honoring their traditions to reach common ground and the fact that he included specific actionable recommendations for coming together.[8]

Beyond what I had read in Jones's book, I was buoyed by the attitude of millennials and asked Josh if he was in that age group, as he appeared to be quite young. He admitted that he did fit into that generational age group. Josh became a nuclear physicist to understand the why of the universe so that he is better prepared to teach students. He is also very interested in advancing diversity and believes he can do that through teaching physics. Go figure.

His parents were both public school teachers and he was able to attend the school where his father was principal. It was a predominantly black high school where he had "the only one" experience and learned how racial dynamics work. He experienced those same dynamics in the Parable of Polygons, an online simulation game based on the work of Nobel Prize–winning game theorist Thomas Schelling and created by Vi Hart and Nicky Case.[9] The goal is to move the shapes around until they are "all happy." In the game there are equal triangles and squares. Although each shape "prefers to live in diverse crowds they are a bit 'shapist.'"[10] Although every polygon would be happy in a diverse environment, they also want to ensure that they live by at least a third of their same shape.

The game demonstrates the math behind segregation and illustrates how small individual bias leads to large collective bias and how the past haunts the present. It further demonstrates that if small biases, such as a desire to be with those who are just like you, can create a racial divide, then small antibiases can mitigate it.

This is where Josh sees an application to cross-racial friendships. He explains to me that the game demonstrates how cross-racial friendships can exist without closing the racial divide, because there are so few cross-racial friendships. But he tells me there is hope as he notes the fact that it only takes just a little bit to move the needle and change the dynamics. In other words, it doesn't take many people to come out of their racially segregated environments to tip the scales and create a critical mass of cross-racial friendships to close the racial divide. Josh is committed to doing that small thing and to inspire others to do that as well. Chatting with me at the airport, a black woman and stranger to him, and not being afraid of race is indicative of such a small thing that I found most inspiring.

In my interview with sociologist Edwardo Bonilla-Silva, he cautions that the optimism placed in millennials' enlightened racial ideology may be premature.[11] He points to the need to have longitudinal studies of millennials to determine their views on race in ten to fifteen years after they have completed some of the adult developmental tasks like getting married, having children, and choosing a neighborhood in which to live and where they are employed. Millennials, Bonilla-Silva believes, tend to "talk a better talk" about race than previous generations and tend to be more fluent on racial matters and more open to cross-racial interactions. However, he says that the real test will be whether or not their racial ideology will match their life choices, as this age period is generally a fluid life stage. "Being color-blind is like a balloon and it floats away with reality."[12]

This theory makes sense to me, but it doesn't kill my optimism that racial division could be lessened over time with each new generation. Generation Z (people born starting in the mid-1990s) echoed the extended notion of racism against whites as well as people of color, which also meant that there was an increased chance of races working together to eradicate it. Let me explain how.

Racism that can be targeted against people of color and whites was endorsed by a group of Generation Z focus group participants. They defined racism as "believing your race is superior to any other race" and strongly asserted that that belief could be held by anyone. Their understanding of racism was equated with personal prejudice versus institutional racism. Growing up witnessing a black president of the United States and immigration reform, and in a time of deep racial divide, they are acutely aware that no one race is clean of members who harbor personal aversion for another race.

Their understanding of race, like other aspects of their identity, is focused in the current reality and outside of historical context. Steven Becton, associate program director and director for urban education with Facing History and Ourselves, facilitates conversations around critical periods in US and world history with students, helping them to integrate history with complex topics of race and current events. His research focuses on creating a historical pedagogy as a catalyst for changing the current narrative on race. His hope is that by teaching students how systems of oppression work and about the psychological underpinnings of human behavior through disrupting historical narratives, navigating bias, and creating critical consciousness, Generation Z will be best positioned as fully engaged and informed citizens, without being locked in an ideology that tethers racism to whites, all the while helping students to understand the deep historical roots and influence of white supremacy and racism. Steve and I discuss how teaching history this way explains racism as an abuse of power rather than a product of white culture.[13] This kind of learning is transformative.

"I taught the Holocaust to poor black kids in Memphis," says Becton. You know what they say, 'I can't believe that white people did that to other white people.' Powerful. They wouldn't have learned that just from a lesson on civil rights. I taught them the Holocaust and how a system of oppression works. They learn that the first black men here in America didn't come as slaves. They came as free men who had indentured themselves to work on another man's land. When slavery became the way to build an economy, that's when racism was born. Race wasn't the issue in the beginning. So teaching history from this framework gives students the ability to take their power back and enhance their race esteem."

Because Generation Z individuals are more aware of their multiple and intersecting identities, it becomes important that the educators and adults in their lives value their evolving racial identity in ways that transform society to a less divided and more inclusive world. Richard Cohen, president of the Southern Poverty Law Center, addressing us as members of the Facing History and Ourselves Alabama Civil Rights Study Tour, stated, "Children are not observers of history but actors of history. It is our role to help them create agency for promoting equality."

All of the Generation Z focus group participants reported having a racially diverse group of friends. In fact, they appeared somewhat confused that a study of cross-racial friendships was even warranted. Their experience of self is one that rejects a notion of a single aspect of their identity, such as race defining what they thought and believed, how they experienced the world, and, most importantly, who they were. They have had little experience with the web 1.0 that had static pages and read-only capability with controlled content that one could either accept or reject. They are deeply infused with the web 2.0 (it was the primary way that they "hung out" with their friends), which is personal, interactive, connected, collaborative, and intersecting. Similarly, they have little or no experience with the Self 1.0 of previous generations, characterized by distinct dimensions of their humanity separate from each other and from those who do not share that group identity, to embracing the Self 2.0, which is layered, nuanced, relational, multifaceted, creative, and evolving. Perceiving and experiencing the world from this identity holds no boundaries on who they can be friends with and how they move through life.

As Generation Z may still be experimenting with different identities, it is all the more important that their parents, teachers, and mentors of influence, who represent previous generations, not pass on coping strategies for eradicating racism that though once very adaptive have now become maladaptive. For example, speaking with one voice as a race or not speaking at all when it came to racial expression or with responding to racial discrimination for traditionalists and baby boomers did send a unified message and communicated a brand for specific racial groups. What it meant to be a black Democrat, a Hispanic entrepreneur, an Asian mother, or a Native American tribal leader was clearly defined by one's racial identity. Most groups of people of color have terms that refer to persons whose demographic racial identity does not match their avowed psychological or racial identity. These are the folks whom racial groups deem as not being real. In the African American community, you are called an "Oreo." You are a "lemon" or "banana" if you are Asian, an "apple" if you are Native American Indian. Mexican Americans refer to the racially confused among them as a coconut or "Tio Tomás" (Mexican Uncle Tom), and Jewish people refer to a marginal member as a WASH (white Anglo-Saxon Hebrew). White adolescents who prefer to act more like African American teens are called "wiggers." There are probably many more racial terms of which I am not aware, as I have been told on several occasions that I myself am really not "black" when I move away from something that is considered culturally black regarding music, books, or leisure activities. Many people of color perceive and are especially sensitive to any hint of being called out for deviating from the expected and appropriate responses of that racial group.

Here's a case in point: A CNN panel, moderated by white anchor Brooke Baldwin, discussing President Trump's comments about the August 2017 neo-Nazis' and white nationalists' protest in Charlottesville went completely awry as black panelist Keith Boykin told Paris Dennard, a black Trump supporter and former director of Black Outreach for President George W. Bush, that he was "ashamed" that Dennard refused to say that Trump has not done enough to repudiate racism.

"I don't need you to pull my black card," Dennard responded. "I am well aware of my blackness and don't need you to classify me as being one. I understand what racism is—"

"Are you?" [Boykin interrupts]

"Keith, don't go there. . . . I know what it means to be a black man in this country. I experience racism on a regular basis by being a Trump supporter and a proud American who happens to be Republican. . . . I get racist comments about my family, about my mother, about my girl-friend, about my character mostly from black people if you really want to get down to it."[14]

This interchange emphasizes the importance of being seen as a member of one's racial group despite divergent views. It also stresses that a black identity is equated with experiencing racism.

A shared racial identity rooted in the same interpretation and expression of culture of race does not appear to be as important to members of Generation Z, who, due to technology, are not limited by geographic boundaries when it comes to making friends across racial lines and live out of multiple and intersecting identities.

There is no doubt that the internet has increased connections among diverse groups and provides people with an alternative way to communicate. Social media, particularly, serves as a bridging function by connecting people from different races and ethnic backgrounds, although it also serves a strong bonding function by reinforcing contacts with people of similar beliefs and interests.[15] Generation Z focus group participants uniformly believed that online communications helped them to make friends across racial lines.

Oscar notes, "I think our generation is very comfortable with online things so we can make online friends as well as friends in real life." Ben believes, "Online technology helps. I have a lot of friends that I've made online." However, he makes a distinction with the use of social media. "Social media doesn't help, because you can follow and unfollow as many people as you want and never be friends with them outside of that." All of the Generation Z focus group participants are savvy, aware that "there are pages that may be fake and people lie." Anni states, "Even with social media, I have to have a person in front of me to see if we can really be friends."

For Generation Z individuals it also means that race is not necessarily a barrier to friendship if racism, by their definition, can be experienced by anyone regardless of race. One would simply sort out that characteristic as you would any other interests or dislikes in choosing to make friends. In other words, you wouldn't rule out someone as a friend because that person was of a different race. More importantly, for moving toward racial equity, you wouldn't assume that someone is racist simply because of the color of their skin. There is a level of maturity and simple yet profound truth to this thinking that places Generation Z in stark contrast with previous generations whose leading identity is often race and who are quick to verbally deny membership to someone when there is disagreement about how race is lived and expressed.

A case in point, a powerful and provocative quote by a black woman was posted on a Facebook page by another black woman:

> White women have a unique form of currency. They are worshipped. They are both fire starters and fire extinguishers when it suits them to be. They are always given a platform and are afforded forgiveness even when they are egregiously wrong while Black women have to fight to be seen, heard and have our concerns addressed. And then we get belittled and criticized when we do.[16]

An active thread of comments evidenced replies in agreement from black women and men, and some in disagreement from white women who were then educated to the "lived experience of black women" by the woman who posted the quote. I was intrigued by the quote but was pressed for time, so I entered the conversation by simply responding with these five words: "I don't agree with this."

The reply came quickly from the poster: "And you're welcome not to. There are plenty of black white supremacists. They'll be happy to have your support."

She was able to make that assessment from a simple statement of disagreement. It made me laugh. After my chuckle, I shared the thread with other black women, many of whom didn't find the response about being a "black white supremacist" funny but, rather, found it appalling. They dismissed the comment while reinforcing that social media was not the forum for meaningful conversation.

I also became curious about what white women thought of the statement and the response I received by simply stating that I disagreed with it. As a black woman, I have certainly had experiences where the reality described in the quote played out to be true. For white men, white women are their mothers, sisters, and wives. As a result, most white men have had lessons on how to respond and treat white women but are clueless on what to do with women of color, especially strong women of color. In my opinion, this bond is also what allowed white women to disregard sexual harassment claims and vote in high percentages for Donald Trump, as they can relate to him as their father, husband, or brother and excuse or at least understand bad behavior rather than perceive it as criminal. As a white woman in a focus group stated, "He [Donald Trump] is no different than some of our fathers and uncles in what he says."

I have also experienced the opposite of the reality described in the quote. I have witnessed white women shut down and have to fight to be heard by white men and men of color. Alternatively, I have also experienced my voice being respected and acted upon on topics of serious consequences and minor consequences by whites and people of color. I have witnessed the same for white women. What I was hoping from the dialogue provoked by the statement about white women was a bit of an untangling of the process that sets up these dynamics. Perhaps too big of a hope for a Facebook thread.

The thread of responses to the assertion of powerful white women coddled by society was dismaying, particularly the responses of white women who agreed with the quote. A number of white women had swallowed this statement whole and even stated that they were "grateful for the insight."

I discussed the quote, the thread of responses, and the response I received calling me a "black white supremacist" with my white friend and colleague Eve. Eve tells me, "There's thinness in the description of white women that I don't trust. Really? She thinks that all white women are worshipped? And the poster calling you a 'black white supremacist'? It's dismissive. What can you say to that? There's no room to honestly engage and learn from one another. It makes for a lazy discourse, especially if no one is able to learn from and challenge ideas. How will this communication lead to any change?" Eve continues our conversation and lets me know that although the response was dismissive, she clearly understands the anger behind the quote as she imagines how difficult it must be in this moment in our history for African Americans. The awakening that is necessary for white women who voted for Trump to understand their part in sustaining sexual harassment in the workplace is the same wake-up call necessary for all of us in responding and taking appropriate action to racism. The more we can understand that the dynamics of "isms" (racism, sexism, classism, ageism, heterosexism, and ableism) are the same, the better we can collectively work to eradicate them. Eve understands that the anger expressed in the statement about white women is part of the process for racial healing and that we need to begin the conversation there.

Now that is a dialogue worth having. I am grateful that I can have that kind of conversation with white women friends like Eve. Her words of understanding are both grounding and empowering in a world of dichotomous thinking. It makes me less crazy, as it both honors the current nuanced dynamics of how white and black women are treated yet acknowledges the impact of the past on the current reality.

If you are white, it is challenging to imagine how friendships can be forged with blacks when it requires an acceptance of an identity as an oppressor and racist rather than the attribution of those labels stemming from behaviors that can be performed and words that can be spewed from anyone regardless of skin color. It is further challenging to be friends if you must accept and equate whiteness with white supremacy instead of part of our shared legacy that together we have an obligation to suppress regardless of skin color. It is also challenging if you must acknowledge and accept your white fragility before you can be friends with someone of color.

"White fragility" is a term coined by Robin DiAngelo in her 2011 article of the same title. As a sociologist, she describes being white and whiteness as a social process. It is equated with race privilege and perceived as external to the individual and expressed as a set of cultural practices. White fragility is "a response or 'condition' produced and reproduced by the continual social and material advantages of the white structural position."[17] Neighborhood segregation, white people's belief that their race represents all of human experience, racial arrogance, and the psychic freedom whites enjoy that allows them not to bear the "social burden of race" are factors that protect whites in society. Thus, white fragility manifests itself in white people's inability to even have discussions about racism without getting defensive or positioning themselves as being victimized.[18] From this perspective, the white racial-identity process is a struggle around owning whiteness as an oppressor and the beneficiary of racism. This struggle is one that causes white people to experience racial stress, and thus whites "withdraw, defend, cry, argue, minimize, ignore, and in other ways push back to regain our racial position and equilibrium."[19]

An example of the pushback characterized as white fragility is illustrated in the young adult novel (read by many not in that age category, including me), *The Hate U Give*. The novel is a Black Lives Matter–inspired, award-winning debut novel by Angie Thomas. It is the story of sixteen-year-old Starr's two worlds: her inner-city black neighborhood riddled with poverty and crime, and the suburban, predominantly white prep school that she attends. Consistent with data from Generation Z focus group participants, Starr "hangs out" with her friends, both in person and through social media, in this case Tumblr (Facebook has been taken over by baby boomers). They spend hours on Tumblr starting blogs and posting pictures. A thread in the story is a friend who unfollows her Tumblr account where Starr has reblogged pictures and "signed every petition out there" for Black Lives Matter. When her white friend Hailey stops texting her and unfollows her on Tumblr and "Black Twitter," Starr is disturbed but works to process it internally before she confronts Hailey months later. Here is the dialogue:

> " . . . You unfollowed me. Months ago. Why?"
>
> She doesn't say anything.
>
> I swallow. "Is it because of the Emmett Till picture?"
>
> "Oh my God," she says standing up. "Here we go again. I am not gonna stay here and let you accuse me of something, Starr—"
>
> "You don't text me anymore," I say. "You freaked out about that picture."
>
> "Do you hear her?" Hailey says to Maya. "Once again, calling me racist."
>
> "I'm not calling you anything. I'm asking a question and giving you examples."
>
> "You're insinuating!"
>
> "I never mentioned race."
>
> Silence comes between us.[20]

I have experienced this dynamic in action, and it is not limited to whites. We, as a people, are *all* racially fragile and do not like to talk about or discuss race—at least across races. In Attorney General Eric Holder's February 18, 2009, remarks at the Department of Justice's African American History Month program, he avowed that we are essentially a nation of cowards because we do not talk enough with each other about race.[21] Rather than leading us to a discussion about race with each other, this remark sparked a great deal of discussion about whether or not his description of us was true. It is easy to dwell on one word ("coward") of a powerful message in order to avoid, yet again, talking about a topic that is so prickly. Still, Holder's remarks served as another attempt to bring the race dialogue to a public space. We may not be cowards . . . but we are clearly scared as people to discuss this topic. We are scared to have the conversations because we lack the language, emotional resilience, group-dynamics skills, fortitude, thick skin, and solid experience with friends who cross racial lines to do so. We are scared because we are inherently good people who do not want to hurt other people's feelings and we want to act out of our best selves. When it comes to race issues, we often feel like we are skating on thin ice.

From the white-fragility perspective, talking about race and talking about racism are synonymous. White fragility equates minority race status with victimization and marginalization. People of color are victims and marginalized people rather than people who have experienced racism and marginalization. It sets up the dynamic where whites can claim the flip side as black entitlement.

Mirroring Peggy McIntosh's classic list of white-privilege examples, lists of black entitlements circulate in blog posts.[22] In McIntosh's 1988 autobiographical paper, she outlines twenty-six opportunities or advantages that were provided to her because of her white skin. McIntosh is careful to caution generalizing the lists to all white people and says we must see white privilege as "the up-side of oppression and discrimination.[23] Yet, from my days in graduate school, when I first saw the list disseminated as a working draft, people have been adding to it and using it as the playbook for whites and more as a cerebral exercise (how long can we make this list!) instead of using it for observation and self-exploration.

McIntosh's "invisible knapsack" of privilege has now become the springboard for counter lists of black entitlement and black privilege. These lists range from blacks using race as a badge of honor and feeling like whites owe blacks something to being able to blame poor grades on race and having cops second-guess the criminal behaviors of blacks.[24]

My point is not to present an analysis of white fragility, white privilege, or black entitlement but to note these dynamics as another reason why we don't like to talk about race with each other and another barrier to crossing racial lines in friendship.

We do not like to talk about race or racism because this dynamic makes us racially insecure. We struggle to truly believe in our inherent goodness and act out of our core identity as humans. Having friends who cross racial lines helps us to know whether or not the inability to talk about racism stems from deep emotional pain or paralysis that comes from awareness that this ugly evil exists in our world, or from resistance to giving up power and privilege. Not all white fragility comes from embracing social power and racial privilege. The source of fragility makes a difference in how we become more racially facile.

McIntosh says of the source of her paper on white privilege: "I compared my own circumstances with some of those of African American women I worked with."[25] This prompted her to work on herself to identify some of the "daily effects of white privilege." When you travel with friends of a different race, you get to experience the spikes of life lying down for whites just like the tire spikes when returning a rental car. You get to experience that they often don't go down for people of color.

Here is a mundane example that nevertheless makes the point. My friend Peggy, who is white, was my closest friend in graduate school. I admired a lot about Peggy. She was pretty, very witty, and, as they say in New England, "wicked smart." We remain friends today and on one occasion when I was in her hometown of Columbus, Ohio, for a speaking engagement, we got together for dinner. Seated at the table we were deeply engaged in conversation, and it was many minutes before we noted that no one had approached us to provide service. The restaurant was only about half full and there appeared to be enough wait staff. Distracted by our hunger pains, we began to scan the room to get someone's attention.

"Gee, we don't even have any bread," Peggy remarked, noting that all of the other tables were amply supplied. We took another look around the restaurant, both noting the racial composition of the room where I was the only black diner.

"It's because of you!" Peggy stared at me and joked. "This always happens when I am with you."

This remark caused side-splitting laughter and one that was so good for my soul. The probability might have been slight that we were not being served because I was the only black in the restaurant. There was no way to prove it, and we did not choose to spend our energy trying to do so. I loved the fact that the possibility of racism was noted and acknowledged by Peggy and that our friendship allowed us to talk freely and even share a laugh about racial dynamics. Cross-racial friendships with depth can diminish any white fragility. I don't become the beneficiary of her white privilege; rather, she gets a dose of racial inequity.

For people of color, "woke white friends," or allies who understand the dynamics of racism, can serve to eliminate any form of black entitlement. At one point in my academic career, I became convinced that a proposal I was championing faced resistance because of racism. As the only black professor in a psychology department of about twenty members, I was primed to expect it with every situation. It was a necessary coping strategy. There were many cases of microaggressions and unconscious bias that made my path to tenure challenging. It was especially rewarding that I had several white colleagues in the department who advocated for and with me during these times.

Certain that the proposal was being blocked by a few faculty members because of racism, I marched into my white friend Kathy's office to rail about the lack of acceptance by department members for my project, which I saw as clearly aligned with the mission of the university and, in its best form, was a revenue generator and, in its worst form, was budget neutral. Moving the project forward required a majority vote from the department members, and the few holdouts had no basis for their lack of support outside of racism. In fact, one of the professors had told me that he was voting against it simply because it was being put forth by me. I had already gotten several of my proposals passed when he had yet to get one passed. He thought this was not fair because he had been in the department much longer.

Kathy listened attentively and was familiar with my proposal and the process I was engaging in to gain acceptance. My closing argument ended with declaring that once again racism had reared its ugly head in our department.

Kathy continued to provide me with possible reasons why some department members might disagree with the proposal and suggested different metrics for success. I was not willing to give up on the idea that the evaluation of the proposal was tainted by racism, as the program would inevitably increase the number of students of color in the department and enhance my portfolio as a director and any perceived or real power attached to that position. I had received enthusiastic support from the dean, so it further reinforced my belief that members feared that the proposed program would brand the department as focused solely on racial minorities. Kathy was direct in her response: "Well, I'm white, and I'm your friend, and I am telling you that my thinking has nothing to do with race and more about the program design."

She was right. As a result of our conversation, and with more objectivity, I reviewed my proposal. I had not considered that limited resources would impact the quality and sustainability of the program. I also had not heavily weighted the financial stability of the partner organization that the program would be dependent upon. I lost sight of these details while focusing on the big-picture gains for increasing diversity and getting sidetracked by the real or perceived racism of some of the department members. It had become about winning and fighting against racism rather than forwarding a proposal for the good of the department and the university. Cross-racial friendships with depth can smack any signs of black entitlement out of you. Although the proposal ultimately passed by a slim majority, I ended up agreeing to cancel its implementation. It was the best decision for the department and the university and for me.

Labels were something that the Generation Z focus group participants completely rejected. Everyone in the racially diverse group (white, black, Asians, Hispanics), ages sixteen to nineteen, had friends of a different race. "It doesn't matter about the race; it matters about the person. If this person understands you, then race doesn't matter," nineteen-year-old Anni, who is white, replies to my questions about the differences in the relationships with friends of different races.

Oscar, who is eighteen and also white, agrees. "Some people you can talk with about anything, but other people may react differently. So, some friends can be a different race and understand what you are talking about."

Pearl is an eighteen-year-old black African who takes a leadership role in the focus group to explain their responses to this baby boomer (me) who is asking questions they perceive to have very simple answers: "When I'm with my friends, we talk about stuff. But those who are of a different race, we talk about other stuff."

I probe a bit more; "Are there some activities that you don't do with your friends of a different race?" The entire room goes silent and I wait patiently for their response. Pearl scans the room as if to get permission again to speak for the group. She leans forward to help me to understand what she is about to say.

"We just do something else then . . ." She pauses. "If that makes sense?"

It does. Friends are, well, friends.

If we were to close our eyes and then opened them to see an entire human race of the same color, the dynamics underlying racism would still exist. As tribal people we would find some other human characteristic to sort out and prioritize. The dynamics of difference—power, privilege, and bias—would remain. I know this because I have simulated this experience hundreds of times in workshops with diverse groups from all over the United States. The results were the same whether the group was composed of executives from Fortune 500 companies, educators in urban or suburban schools, nurses and caregivers in hospitals, social workers, university professors, or a gathering of two hundred nuns.

The Community Experience is an experiential exercise designed to simulate a "have and have not" situation that results from uneven distribution of resources. I created it in 1984 as a graduate student under the direction of my advisor and mentor, Dr. Sandra Shullman. She charged me with designing an experiential exercise to be used for a diversity retreat with the psychology graduate students and the department faculty at Kent State University. It was meant to heighten awareness about how culture influences our behavior and thinking and to support our work as future psychologists. I recall drafting the exercise in Sandy's office on a piece of paper. The exercise was based more on what we had known and observed about the world than from extensive academic scholarship. In fact, I don't recall referring to any journal articles or textbooks in making up the exercise. We didn't know if it would work. There was no need to worry. It worked.

Since that time the exercise has been used repeatedly in cultural competency workshops and remains a part of the curriculum for the Diversity Management Program at Cleveland State University. In 1997, the use of the exercise extended to corporations, nonprofit agencies, and faith-based institutions, facilitated primarily by diversity and organizational development professionals. I have personally facilitated the exercise over a hundred times and most recently conducted it with medical students and faculty at University of Massachusetts Medical School.

The design is simple. Resources are divided disproportionately to the number of participants in the workshop, who are divided into three unequal family groups. In the exercise the resources are chips, pretzels, sodas, paper plates, forks, napkins, and paper cups. There are three family groups: the Suns, the Moons, and the Stars. Participants self-select their family group with the number of slots in each group predetermined to match the exact number of participants. That forces the participants to choose only one group.

The family group with the fewest members gets the most resources, roughly half of the sodas, paper plates, forks, napkins, paper cups, and two bags of pretzels and two bags of chips. They are called the Suns. The group with the average number of members gets an adequate but insufficient amount of resources, roughly two-sixths of the sodas, paper plates, forks, napkins, paper cups, and one bag of chips and one bag of pretzels. They are called the Moons. And the group with the most people gets the least amount of resources, roughly one-sixth of the sodas, paper plates, napkins, and paper cups. They do not get any bags of chips or pretzels. They are called the Stars.

What is made clear in both the verbal and written instructions, which read, "The room and the persons in it now make up their total community," is that the group that you are in is your primary family group. "The resources necessary to support your family in the community are in the room. There is *enough for everybody collectively*." In other words, there are exactly enough resources for everyone to have what is required, but they will have to work together across family groups to achieve the goal.

It is predetermined that the defined minimum resources for each participant are one fork, one paper plate, one napkin, one paper cup, and one can of soda (or pop, if that is what it is called in that neck of the woods). In addition, each family group minimally needs one bag of chips and one bag of pretzels. A fair exchange rate is provided (one can of soda = three cups or six forks; one bag of chips = two plates or four napkins; one bag of chips = one bag of pretzels) and directives are provided for charitable distribution if members so wish to use that option. They may make charitable contributions or deviate from the accepted exchange rates but only if everyone in their family group agrees.

They are also given two goals to be achieved during a fixed time period. First, they must obtain for each individual in their family group the predetermined minimal resources necessary to remain in the community (one plate, cup, napkin, and fork for every member in the family group and one bag of chips and one bag of pretzels for the family group). Second, they must amass the greatest amount of resources as a family group to receive bonus opportunities (typically cash collected from each participant).

The family groups are positioned in the room so that the Suns occupy the front of the room, the Moons are in the middle space, and the Stars are somewhere crowded in the back space of the room. As participants have signed up for their family group, most assume that the group with the most members has the most power. At the start of the exercise, participants also assume that every group has been given an equal amount of resources, as the resources are not provided to the family groups until the directions are clear and they are positioned in their family groups.

It is only in the chaos experienced by the Stars when they attempt to get organized and wait for a leader to surface that they realize the other family groups are ready to begin exchanging resources. It doesn't take long for the Suns to see that they have hit the lottery, and they typically begin to stash all of their extra resources or at least put aside at least one item as a little extra to assure a win. The Moons work to strategize how they might get the few items that they need and many members make an effort to try to join with the Suns believing there is strength in numbers and that the Stars pose a threat.

The Suns sit and observe, rarely if ever moving from their position in the front of the room. Faced with a lot of demands from the Moons and the Stars, they start to draw up rules of engagement to impose on how others may interact with them if there is to be any hope for getting any of their resources. On at least two occasions, the Sun family group has provided resources to the Stars in exchange for one of their family members who they then charge with guarding their resources against potential Star thieves. And there have been Stars who have resorted to just stealing what they need from the Suns. They never feel guilty and are quite proud of their accomplishment when they pull this off.

Within minutes, the three family groups discover their status in the community is based on their resources. Within minutes, the family groups devise strategies for accumulating what they need. Within minutes, they begin to experience themselves as less than others or better than others based on their family group status.

The exercise focuses on social-class differences, and within minutes, the process of discrimination begins to erupt. People begin to place labels on family group status and behaviors associated with that status. The Suns are perceived as privileged, entitled, and inconsiderate, and no matter what the racial makeup of the group are perceived to be like white men. The Moons are perceived as not ambitious enough to aspire to be Suns and far too complacent. The Moons are generally taken care of by the Suns because they don't need too much and are generally respectful. No matter what the racial or gender makeup of the group, they are perceived to be like white women. The Stars are perceived as (1) disorganized, because they cannot get themselves together quickly enough with a winning strategy; (2) unethical, because they resort to stealing or cheating since they will tear up their napkins and plates in smaller pieces to provide something for everyone; and (3) lazy because many in the group just give up very soon, realizing that there is little hope for winning, and sit idly by watching the whole scenario play out. No matter what the racial makeup of the family group, the Stars are perceived to be racial minorities.

The debrief session following the end of the exercise is always quite animated. The Suns justify their behaviors and provide rationales for how they even "earned" the resources simply by signing their name to the group with the fewest numbers of participants. The Moons share stories about how they could have survived with just what they had and how frustrating it was to realize that the Suns had so much and the Stars had so little. The Stars are frustrated and angry; most notably they are angry at the Suns.

I have witnessed both white and black individuals in the workshop go from being openly disagreeable due to their different worldviews to closely aligned as the Suns with race absent from the dynamics.

After the simulated exercise is over, it usually takes several minutes for individuals to shake off their "roles." Most participants admit that they were freaked out by how they thought and behaved so differently than their perceived selves within the context of this experience. They also admit that the goal for trying to amass as many of the resources and win the prize motivated them not to choose an obvious simple solution— for each family group to pool their resources and then distribute them evenly to each person in the community.

Participants admit that the behaviors felt like role-playing, but their emotional states were experienced as very real. Suns felt entitled. Moons felt okay. Stars felt angry. They also acknowledged that their feeling toward the other family groups felt genuine. It was easy to see the parallels to the real world. Given what they knew about each of the family groups, they quickly formed beliefs or stereotypes. They quickly experienced how racism and discrimination are born out of capitalism.

The exercise is predictable because stereotypes follow a predictable pattern. They reflect how our brain attempts "to extract average tendencies from a complicated world, using both our own and others' observations to make inferences about the mind of others."[26] It's a predictable error that we all make for how we think about group behaviors. Research tells us that we will go for the general sense or gist of the group and apply that general sense to everyone. We will also tend to exaggerate that general sense and then believe that the differences are wider and more intense than what really exists.[27]

If we could make everyone in the world the same color and racial differences were nonexistent, the dynamics of the exercise would remain the same. With humans of all colors, our primitive brain has to work to not act out of greed, self-interest, and tribal self-protection.[28]

Another simulated exercise, Jane Elliot's widely known "Blue Eyes/ Brown Eyes," in which children are draped in brown and blue collars representing their eye colors and then either praised or shamed based on their eye color, demonstrates how arbitrary the conditions can be for simulating discrimination.[29] When Elliot first did the exercise with her third-grade class in Iowa the day after Dr. Martin Luther King's assassination, in 1968, wide publicity resulted. Many hailed her as a hero and many were concerned about the potential psychological harm she had caused the children by exposing them to the dynamics of racism.

As an anti-racism educator and diversity trainer, Jane Elliot continues to facilitate the exercise with people of all ages and in countries around the world. Academic research on whether or not the exercise actually reduces prejudice is inconclusive. Some studies show moderate impact with reducing long-term effects. Despite its moderate results reducing prejudice, what is certain is that the exercise demonstrates how easily prejudice can be formed and how arbitrary and illogical racism can be.[30] Racism is a learned, predictable attitude to societal conditions.

Because Generation Z individuals believe that anyone can be racist they also intuitively understand racism in its comparative form.[31] Previous generations are challenged to understand this juxtaposition. Ta-Nehisi Coates's *Atlantic* article, "The First White President," provides an example in reference to Donald Trump:

> The mind seizes trying to imagine a black man extolling the virtues of sexual assault on tape ("When you're a star, they let you do it"), fending off multiple accusations of such assaults, immersed in multiple lawsuits for allegedly fraudulent business dealings, exhorting his followers to violence, and then strolling into the White House. But that is the point of white supremacy—to ensure that that which all others achieve with maximal effort, white people (particularly white men) achieve with minimal qualification.[32]

By comparing Trump's campaign challenges to Barack Obama's, Coates provides a concrete example for understanding the socially sanctioned rights and privileges afforded to whites that are withheld from people of color. People of color are often perceived, evaluated, judged, and held accountable to different standards of behavior than whites.

That is what modern racism looks like. Authentic friendships that cross racial lines exist when friends of color can relate their experiences of racism and discrimination and not have their realities minimized or rejected by white friends. And white friends can give witness to privilege and not have their experiences met by their friends of color with blame, shame, or anger. These friendships provide a natural juxtaposition of how the world reacts to people of color and whites. Cross-racial friendships hold the possibility for changing the narrative and eradicating modern racism.

What we learn from a review of race relations and its impact on friendship patterns across the generations is that race remains an enduring and persistent hurdle in having friendships across racial lines. However, the experience of racism from traditionalists to Generation Z has changed from clearly defined, overt forms sanctioned by institutions to covert, subtle, and pervasive forms of behaviors and attitudes that can be exhibited by anyone. The range of these forms of racism coexists in society and influences our choice of friends.

Roenna, an eighteen-year-old African American in the focus group, states, "It's harder for older generations to cross racial lines, but older generations made it easier for us to cross racial lines. You made it okay for us to feel free to go ahead and make those friends. My mom won't . . . She's uncomfortable. . . . It's not something that she would do with a person of a different race. But she will encourage me to make friends."

I closed the Generation Z focus groups by asking what advice they would give their son or daughter about having friends of different race. Here are a few of their responses:

> "Cross-racial friendships can be really eye-opening and you can learn a lot about the world and other people. And you should hang out with people who make you feel good and encourage you to do good things. It doesn't matter about race." (Stephanie, Asian, 17)

> "Interracial friendships will help close the racial divide." (Liam, white, 17)

> "It is very important to have friends of a different race. It gives you an idea of what other people live through with different cultures." (Sofia, Hispanic, 18)

> "Cross-racial friendships are more fun and you have more things to talk about by having them." (Manuel, Hispanic, 18)

Generation Z is more racially diverse than previous generations, and subsequently their social networks are more likely to be more diverse than previous generations'. Gen Z-ers also seem to understand the dynamics of racism as opposed to perceiving racist behavior as belonging exclusively to a particular skin color. Is it possible that Generation Z offers promise for the day when friends experience the spirit and essence of humanity that transforms our society and moves us toward racial equality? We can only hope.

Chapter 8

DIFFICULT LAUGHS
MADE EASIER

"So race-based humor is sensitive terrain," host Trevor Noah said as he introduced "Lessons on How to Navigate Race-Based Humor" on the April 13, 2016, episode of *The Daily Show*. "But luckily, we have two correspondents who are experts at navigating it—Roy Wood Jr. and Jordan Klepper!" The camera turns to comedians Roy Wood Jr., who is black, and Jordan Klepper, who is white. They are seated news-anchor style, prepared to impart words of wisdom as role models for how racial humor can be used effectively between cross-racial friends.[1]

"Look, folks, it's true. Jokes involving race can be tricky," says Roy.

"But if you work together, listen, and keep an open mind, it can really pay off," replies Jordan.

"That's why Jordan and I work so well together on camera, because our friendship exists off camera. In fact, just a couple weeks ago, we were doing a stand-up gig at this college."

"Yeah. First time this guy's even been to college," Jordan retorts.

"That's not . . . true . . . I . . ." Roy stumbles, then chuckles. "Okay. Uh, I see." He turns to the audience. "Look, Jordan is playing with the idea of the undereducated black man, and it's okay, because we're friends. He's using stereotypes to create satire. It's a powerful weapon."

"Almost as powerful as Roy's unregistered handgun," Jordan responds.

"I don't have a gun. But I see what you're doing, and it's okay." Roy continues to go along with Jordan's attempt at humor, giving a strained laugh, and then instructs the audience: "When Jordan confronts me, it forces me to keep an open mind."

"And when Roy confronts me, it forces me to keep an open cash register." Jordan tosses his head back in laughter and then throws his hands up in the air. "Take it all! Go home and feed your nineteen kids!"

Jordan continues to laugh at his own jokes while Roy has obviously had enough and can no longer keep the open mind he just professed allowed him to accept Jordan's inept attempts at humor.

"What's your problem?!" Roy, now angry, unleashes.

Jordan sheepishly responds, "I'm only saying this because we're friends."

By the end of their testimonial on effectively navigating race-based humor, the blatant use of a series of racial stereotypes by Klepper leads Wood to declare that they are no longer friends. Klepper responds, "Wow, that's really heartbreaking. I can't believe I am losing my best friend *and* my favorite Uber driver."

The comedy sketch exaggerated the unintentional, unconscious bias of a white friend and highlighted the all-too-familiar negative impact on the friend of color. It demonstrated how laughter, known to be medicine for the soul, is often a difficult pill to swallow among friends across racial lines. Their advice to remember that "context is everything" and that race-based humor is easy among friends with "an open mind" rings hollow.

───────

The social benefits of humor and laughter in friendships are well documented and considered a barometer of a healthy relationship.[2] Laughter acts as a strong buffer against stress and has a number of physical and mental benefits. Physically, it boosts immunity, lowers stress hormones, decreases pain, relaxes muscles, and reduces heart disease. Mental benefits include easing anxiety and fear, adding joy and zest to life, improving mood, enhancing resilience, and relieving stress overall.[3]

Humor also provides us with a snapshot of social equality and social inequality. Shared experiences such as parenting, dating, eating and drinking excessively, sexual activity, and the ups and downs of marriage and relationships are often the subjects of humor that represent social equalities. Humor that focuses on economic conditions, health challenges, housing patterns, stereotypes, and discrimination resulting from one's social-group identity depicts patterns of social inequalities. Depending on the audience, these conditions discussed humorously can be experienced as either funny or toxic, with race-based humor considered among the most sensitive of humorous approaches. Race-based humor that contains stereotypes and surfaces hidden biases reinforces the racial divide and has us laughing at each other in our separate worlds.

I know this because many of my white friends have told me that whites in all-white company tell racially offensive jokes without a second thought. My racially sensitive white friends spend a great deal of energy "correcting" and "monitoring" these conversations. "In a same-race group, people are free to say racist things," my friend Donna, who is white, tells me. "Why would I want to say something offensive, if some of my best friends are a member of that race?" It must be frustrating, I imagine, for my white friends who are constantly challenging their own white friends' beliefs. I love them even more for their efforts on behalf of people of color. But it still doesn't make me completely comfortable, knowing that if I leave the room or happen to show up on time, instead of being stereotypically late for a party, that I might be stepping on some hidden racial slurs hastily shoved under the carpet.

Similarly, I have been in all-black or all-black-and-brown settings where racially insensitive jokes about white people have been freely and openly told. Many of these jokes are rooted in unearned rights, rewards, benefits, access, opportunities, and advantages afforded to whites simply because they are white and with little regard to any achievement. In other words, jokes by people of color tend to highlight our understanding of the dynamics created by white privilege. Here are a few examples:

"What is the scariest thing about a white man in prison? You know he did it."

"Why do white people have so many pets? Because they can't own people anymore."

"What do you say when you see a white man carrying a TV? Excuse me, sir, you dropped your receipt."

People of color find these jokes acceptable because they underscore a social condition that has disadvantaged them for generations.

Many of the jokes that are told in predominantly black and brown settings ridicule white people's perceived social ineptitude and overreliance on cognitive functioning. If we as people of color are honest in our analysis, we would recognize that these jokes are no more acceptable than those that characterize minority races in monolithic ways. It is no different than whites who joke about people of color's perceived lack of intelligence, pugnaciousness, or laziness. However, we rationalize that we get to tell them because these jokes are cathartic and therapeutic for us as a people, given the past history and current struggles with racism. To date, whites have not earned that luxury.

Racial humor in its best form is used as social commentary. Comics David Chappelle and Chris Rock are among the most proficient in using race to send poignant social messages. One of the Chappelle sketches that gives my husband and I deep belly laughs every time we watch is "The Niggar Family," about a white suburban family living in house number 8 (a not-so-subtle reference to Section 8 housing, government rental assistance provided to low-income households).[4] The family has an unfortunate last name that is so close to the word that most Americans find very offensive. With Niggar as the last name, Chappelle threads a string of stereotypes while taking ludicrous stabs at how blacks are often perceived by whites.

"Look, hon! My sister just had another baby. Look at this bundle of joy." He shows the picture to Mrs. Niggar, who replies, "She's got those Niggar lips."

"Is Tim still sleeping?" Mr. Niggar asks his wife about their son.

"Yes, I think so."

"That is one lazy Niggar."

The four-minute sketch continues with references to the Niggar son Tim being a good athlete, being well-spoken, and who will one day be Niggar rich. Later, Chappelle meets the Niggar family in a restaurant and tells them, "You're going to get the finest table that any Niggar will ever get in this restaurant."

Similarly, in one of his comedy sketches, Chris Rock aptly notes: "Racism everywhere. Who's the maddest people? White people."

In his HBO special *Bigger & Blacker*, Rock offers arguably one of the best explanations of white privilege: "There's a white, one-legged busboy in here right now that won't change places with my black ass. He's going, 'Nah, man, don't wanna switch. I wanna ride this white thing out. See where it takes me.' That's right, because when you're white, the sky's the limit."[5]

The "white thing" extends social privilege to white comics who are able to use race-based humor in ways that many people of color find crosses the line from humorous to offensive. Lisa Lampanelli and Amy Schumer are two comics who claim their use of racial humor is done with good intentions. Both consider themselves to be equal opportunity offenders.

"Playing with race is a thing we are not supposed to do, which is what makes it so fun for comics," Schumer wrote. "You can call it a 'blind spot for racism' or 'lazy' but you are wrong. It is a joke and it is funny. I know because people laugh at it."[6]

Here are jokes from each comic. You can decide for yourself if they're funny or not.

From Amy Schumer:

"I used to date Hispanic guys, but now I prefer consensual."

"Nothing works one hundred percent of the time, except Mexicans."

From Lisa Lampanelli:

"What do you call a black woman who's had seven abortions? A crime fighter!"

"How many Hispanics does it take to clean a bathroom? None! That's a nigger's job!"

When I ask the following questions of friends, students, and coworkers using the "woman and man on the street" survey approach, this is what I find: Q: Who thinks David Chappelle and Chris Rock are very funny? A: Most people of color and many white people. Q: Who thinks Lisa Lampanelli and Amy Schumer are very funny? A: White people.

I wonder if Lisa and Amy have any friends who cross racial lines?

Among friends of the same race, humor triggers positive feelings and deepens the emotional connection between them. For friends across racial lines, humor is a sign of a shared worldview and a deep understanding of each friend's culture, which is essential for advancing positive race relations. Our inability to share race-based jokes among friends of color accentuates our separate and unequal worlds and underscores the challenge we face improving contemporary race relations. The paucity of Americans with friends of different races suggests that the path to improving race relations for most of us is very narrow. Given such limited contact across races, it is no wonder that we know so little about other races' lived experiences and, as a result, experience humor very differently.

Who Wants to Be a Millionaire, the international game show that offers cash prizes for correct answers to increasingly difficult, random questions, presents an interesting case example of racial encapsulation. In one particular episode, the contestant, a thirtysomething white man, has almost effortlessly breezed through the initial rounds to the final question. He stands a chance of winning a million dollars, but without any lifelines left to support him in his quest for victory, he has to go it alone. I'm watching the show with my husband, Mike, and when he yells, "Here it comes," he yells, "the black question! They are going to give him a question about black people that will be so easy . . . and he won't get it right!"

I laugh hysterically, almost missing the show's finale. Mike has this theory that the producers of the game show capitalize on the impact of America's racial segregation and intentionally create questions about multicultural issues for the million-dollar prize. Rather than asking the number of bones in a giraffe's neck, they simply have to ask the question, "Who was the first African American general in the US military?" Knowing that Benjamin O. Davis (and not Colin Powell, the obvious trick choice) was the first African American general in the US military wins you a million dollars.

As with many black Americans, I recall this information simply from immersion in post-civil-rights black culture, where it remains a common cultural practice to celebrate "firsts." Growing up, and well into my adult years, it was not unusual to see pictures of "firsts" lining the hallways in hundreds of predominantly black elementary schools, black churches, and even black-owned businesses. As a result, the probability of knowing Benjamin Davis as the correct answer over, say, knowing the number of bones in a giraffe's neck, would likely be much higher for blacks, just as other racial minority groups, women, and LGBT individuals would be more likely to recall "firsts" associated with their respective identity groups.

It may be that my husband's theory is totally wrong and the questioning strategy employed by producers of the game show *Who Wants to Be a Millionaire* is completely race-neutral. They just might use racially specific questions randomly, knowing they are harder to answer because we are racially encapsulated. We live in racially segregated neighborhoods; attend racially segregated churches, mosques, and synagogues; and socialize in separate worlds. As a result, you can bet a million dollars that we don't know enough about each other's race, and this limited contact makes it hard to understand what is funny and what is not funny. The insider message, "I guess you had to be there," applies when understanding race-based humor. We are not "there" in each other's world.

In this post–civil rights era, where overt forms of racism are outlawed, contemporary forms of racism such as implicit stereotypes and unconscious bias are hard to identify and difficult to measure. We are all horrified when someone burns a cross on the lawn of a family of color who has just moved into the neighborhood (overt racism). Yet, we judge that neighborhood as being either a "good" or "bad" neighborhood by its racial makeup (implicit stereotypes and unconscious bias). We have created what journalist and political commentator Chris Hayes calls, in his book of the same title, "a colony in a nation," rooted in the ideology of the first "law and order" president, Richard Nixon, with whites living in a nation with all of its rights and privileges and people of color living in a colony that undermines full citizenship, particularly by the US justice system.[7] In our separate, unequal worlds, everyday verbal and nonverbal communication among friends of different races often comes with covert, unintentional slights, snubs, or insults, resulting in "racism without racists."[8]

On a societal level, using humor to confront the reality of a racially divided nation borders on the unacceptable. An exception to this standard is when the humor highlights a race-based misunderstanding associated with the use of language. In these situations, when the parties take time to unpack the meaning, it not only leads to effective communication but a stronger bond between the friends. A quote from a focus group participant illustrates this point:

> I learned the term "minute" to be defined as a long period of time from a black friend. For example, "I haven't done that in a minute" would mean it has been a long time since I have done that, whereas normally this particular word would mean a short period of time. I used this term at work with another white coworker and a Hispanic coworker. They were both confused, and my Hispanic coworker asked, "I thought you said you hadn't done that in a while?" The white coworker thought that I had recently done it. It was a humorous situation.

Television programs like *Black-ish*, a sitcom about an American upper-middle-class family composed of an advertising executive father, physician mother, and four children, may have achieved the right formula for effective race-based humor. Unlike the Huxtables of *The Cosby Show* in the 1980s and '90s, which showcased American family life in a relatively race-neutral manner, the Johnson family of *Black-ish* deals with each family member's racial-identity developmental process in contemporary society.

The show takes its script from discussions of current events like the Black Lives Matter activist movement against violence and systemic racism toward black people. The name of the show, *Black-ish*, as well as its characters, exemplifies the complexity of what it means to be black in America across generations.

One particular episode (February 24, 2016) blew up social media with posts and tweets and blogs after its premiere.[9] In the episode, the Johnson family, like many real-life families, gathers around their television to watch a news report about the murder of yet another unarmed black man by police officers. In response, the grandfather quotes from Malcolm X and the grandmother encourages the teenage son, who wants to actively participate in the movement. Her encouragement comes with lessons learned from her own activism in the 1960s, and she tells him to be disruptive but respectful, especially toward police officers. His father and grandfather opine and go deeper into the complexity of how the teenage son should respond to the police. They warn him that respecting the police and doing what is asked still may not save his life. His mother's anxiety heightens at the very thought of her son's participation, and her nervousness is visible as she attempts to explain the situation in a hopeful tone to his younger siblings.

The few comedic moments in the show are tastefully done. For example, as the teenage son quotes from Ta-Nehisi Coates's *Between the World and Me*, his father takes credit for saying much of what is being said in the book many times over, many years before Coates, and is completely frustrated by his son's awe and admiration of Coates's writings. It is a scene that parents of teenage children of all races can identify with, as their children give more credence to outsider influence than to their own belabored parenting. The scene demonstrates universal aspects of parenting while addressing a polarizing topic.

The episode is wrapped in a strong political context and presents the various sides of the Black Lives Matter movement through the Johnson family members. What makes *Black-ish* different from other sitcoms with racial themes that address current events through the lens of its characters is the psychological integrity with which the characters are presented. It allows them to be experienced by viewers as actual black human beings rather than stereotypical tropes of how blacks think and behave.

The various statuses of racial-identity development are manifested through the presentation of the intergenerational Johnson family's interactions with their white coworkers and friends. The racial-identity development process, as the psychological connection one has with the construct of race, is woven into each of the characters' profiles. *Black-ish* creates situations where the characters illustrate racial fluidity.[10] Andrew "Dre" Johnson Sr., an advertising executive married to a physician, wonders if all their success has resulted in cultural assimilation, as evidenced by the low valence given to race as an aspect of their identity by his four children. Episodes highlight an awakening by various characters—family members, coworkers, and neighbors—to an awareness of themselves as racial beings interacting in a racially diverse world. Dre is acutely aware of race as a critical component of his personhood. His racial-identity struggle and his many attempts to imbue his four children with a strong black identity form the central plot of the show. This struggle is playfully and creatively developed as he parents his race-neutral children and works in a predominantly white, racially incompetent organization. His racial-identity status is juxtaposed against that of his wife, who is appropriately named Rainbow. She experiences race as an integral part of her intersecting identities (wife, mother, woman, and physician) and does not give race as much importance as her husband. Their struggles play out in parenting the four children under the watchful eye and outspokenness of Dre's parents, who define their racial identity in relationship to a dominant white culture. The race-based humor in *Black-ish* is the interplay of the developmental and complex process of racial identity, which is what makes it funny as well as informative for its viewers.

Despite the tarnished reputation of the show's producer and star, *The Cosby Show* provided the foundation on which *Black-ish* could have these deeper conversations about race and explore racial identity as something more than a demographic category that one gets to check off on numerous forms. Through *The Cosby Show*, viewers experienced a black family who had achieved the American dream and became accustomed to a black family outside of that characterized by the 1965 Moynihan Report, an analysis that depicted the deterioration of the Negro family as the root cause of racial inequality.[11] The Huxtables were considered an example of *the* American family, with perhaps only their affluent economic status rather than their race being atypical. For its humor, *The Cosby Show*'s episodes drew upon the trials and tribulations, joys and celebrations of American family life, which gave it a universal appeal. The humor itself was not race-based.

Through the humor of *Black-ish*, viewers experience race as a social-group identity distinct from other identity roles and racial identity as a fluid construct.[12] In doing so, *Black-ish* presents race-based humor with a success not achieved by other racially themed sitcoms like *Cristela* (Latino), *Fresh Off the Boat* (Taiwanese), or *Dr. Ken* (Korean).[13]

Similarly, late-night television viewers have sometimes found race-based humor too heavy and off-putting, as evidenced by the cancellation of Comedy Central's *The Nightly Show with Larry Wilmore*. As a comedian and writer, Wilmore' is widely known as punchy, political, and unabashedly steeped in black culture. His controversial remarks as host of the 2016 White House Correspondents' Dinner chilled the room the entire night and became the subject of the event's negative reviews the following week. "Welcome to Negro Night," was Wilmore's opening line, "or as Fox News will report, 'Two thugs disrupt elegant dinner in DC,'" referring to himself and President Obama.

Reportedly, Comedy Central president Kent Alterman stated that *The Nightly Show with Larry Wilmore* "hadn't resonated" with the viewers. Their goal to "provide viewers with a distinct point of view and comedic take on the day's news from a perspective largely missing in the current late-night landscape" was not realized.[14] Others would argue that the audience just wasn't prepared to accept the twisted perceptions about race and could not deal with the discomfort evoked by his satire.

Carefully scripted dialogues can result in race-based humor that uplifts rather than offends, as the humor in *Black-ish* demonstrates. But conversations among friends are not scripted, and as a result, race-based jokes are generally off-limits in cross-racial friendships. Permission is granted when the friend of color makes the joke rather than the white friend. A response from a white friend might sound like any of the following statements:

"I'm glad you said it [race-based humor] rather than me."

"You can get away with saying that [race-based humor], but if I said that [race-based humor] . . ."

"Oh, no, you didn't go there [race-based humor] . . ."

"Why is it she can get away with saying that [race-based humor] and I can't?"

Friends who cross racial lines provide you with a living laboratory to understand the complexities of race relations. With trust as a foundation and emotional resilience as a back-up, you can experiment and test out your assumptions: "I think this joke [or situation] was so funny. What do you think?" "I find this funny because . . . What's your take on it?"

A general rule of thumb is to ask yourself, Does it add insult to injury or does it deepen your understanding of another person's race? Does it deepen the bond of the friendship or does it strain the relationship? Just to be clear . . . signs that you are straining the relationship when you are saying something inappropriate include: irritation with anything you say immediately following the statement, shifting or rolling eyes while you are speaking, and deflecting comments like "whatever;" all are indicators that you need to stop and reboot.

Once I was bemoaning the fact that I had been called for jury duty at a time when my work schedule was already unbearably busy. Complaining that morning before I left to fulfill my civic duty, my husband advised me, "To every question they ask, just put your fist in the air and answer, 'Black Lives Matter!' That's sure to get you thrown out."

Later that afternoon I showed up unexpectedly for our regularly scheduled senior staff meeting. "I thought you had jury duty?" my colleagues asked.

"I got dismissed," I gleefully told them. I actually was dismissed because as a psychologist my views on drunk driving would have prejudiced my assessment of the case.

I shared with the team what my husband had suggested I do in order to get out of jury duty. It was met with uproarious laughter from the all-white senior leaders of the organization. Then my boss paused, shaking his head to indicate his disapproval of the perceived double standard. "Now, if I had said that I would have been jumped all over."

"Well, you've got to admit that it is funny," I told him. "And yes, funny depends on who says it and to whom you are saying it."

Context does matter. Intention does matter. Impact matters even more.

Considerable research has explored the alignment of intention and impact in communication and particularly with race-based humor.[15] Sociologist, Dr. Raúl Pérez, who studies race-based humor, remarked in an interview with me that if conditions were equal among the races, then sharing a joke across racial lines would simply be a joke.[16] However, because conditions are unequal in American society, racial humor is harmful because it reconfirms cultural scripts about who is undeserving or considered less than whites. Here are a few examples of what some consider funny:

"Why doesn't Mexico have an Olympic team? Because everybody who can run, jump, and swim is already in the US."

"How can you tell when the Mexicans have moved into your neighborhood? The blacks get car insurance."

"Why weren't there any blacks in *The Flintstones*? Because they were still monkeys."

"What's long, black, and smelly? The unemployment line."

"What's the difference between a Jew and a pizza? A pizza doesn't scream when you put it in the oven!"

Publicly, most civil individuals would not consider any of these jokes even remotely humorous. Privately, in some social settings, individuals in focus groups have admitted that they find these jokes funny and believe that society has become too politically correct. What is funny is context-dependent, which explains why individuals with friends across racial lines never find these kinds of jokes funny.

Although race-based humor is particularly sensitive, we need not shy away from crossing this boundary with others whose race is different than our own. Refraining from humor rooted in race only deepens our racial encapsulation and limits our ability to be fully authentic. Here are some tips for safely using race-based humor:

Who tells the joke is important. When race is peppered into humor, intention does not always mitigate its impact. Ask any white politician who jokes about "CPT" ("colored-people time") when coming late to a function and attempting to relate to a diverse audience, how well it went over. When Chris Rock asserts that "White men can make C's in college and land in the White House," it is funny because he is directly impacted by that remark. If MSNBC journalist Chris Matthews makes the same statement, it isn't funny because he is a beneficiary of that remark.

What is being said is important. If the impact feels like a punch in the stomach rather than a good belly laugh, it isn't funny. Even if people of color or the targeted group are laughing in the moment, know that it is being permanently registered as a faux pas. As one focus group participant stated, "If they can express their ignorance about race to my face like that, the joke's on them. They just showed me that they don't know the first thing about who I am."

Where the joke is being told is important. Knowing your audience is critical, especially those that are multiracial. Some comedians reportedly will no longer perform on college campuses because they perceive college students as too politically correct and unable to take a joke. Sociologist Raúl Pérez counters: "People challenging a joke doesn't mean that they don't have a sense of humor. They are challenging you on something they think is an issue or a problem. They don't find it funny not because they don't have a sense of humor but because it is harmful."[16] In other words, students are critically informed about social injustices. Most care deeply about racial inequality, and when comedians ask them to put aside their critical ability for a moment for the sake of a racist joke, that humor only adds insult to injury.

Why the joke is being told is important. According to developmental psychologist Erik Erikson, we mature when we successfully resolve crises that are distinctly social in nature. Among these tasks are being able to establish a sense of trust in others, develop a sense of identity in society, and help the next generation prepare for the future. If the race-based humor is rooted in the resolution of these developmental tasks, then we are deepening relationships and creating a better society.

In general, all the good intentions in the world will not lessen the impact of negatively experienced words or behavior. Language can represent unconscious biases, and words can create worlds saturated with everyday racism. When stereotypes, unconscious biases, faulty heuristics, and fixed mental boxes are embedded in humor, it results in difficult laughs. Appropriate race-based humor, stemming from a shared understanding of another's reality as experienced by cross-racial friends, offers us the possibility of a new tomorrow and a diminishing racial divide.

Chapter 9

WHAT WE DO WITH OUR LEISURE TIME

My former neighborhood in Cleveland Heights, Ohio, prides itself on its racial diversity. Seventy years ago, when a housing development was established there, a racial covenant prevented blacks, Jews, and Italians from moving into the neighborhood. These covenants were legally used for segregation purposes and prohibited a buyer of property from reselling, leasing, or transferring property to a given race.[1]

From 1990 until 2006, I lived comfortably and happily across the street from the Maiers, a friendly and supportive Jewish family. My next-door neighbors were the Fragassis, a family of Italian heritage, who remain good friends today. I often think about the fact that until around the 1970s our three families would not have been able to live in the neighborhood.

We often socialized together with Phil and Kristen Fragassi, sometimes in racially mixed settings, sometimes in predominantly white or predominantly black settings—so the race thing is hardly an issue between us. For years, my sister Felicia got a group of friends together to celebrate New Year's Eve. She and my brother-in-law love this holiday, so she spent some time searching out the best hotel party—for black people. One year, she invited Phil and Kristen and they agreed to come. Unfortunately, Phil's duties as a physician prevented them from actually attending. However, during the evening, I found myself imagining what the event would be like for white folks. What if Phil and Kristen had come? Would the energy have been different? Would the topics of conversation have changed because whites were present?

I suspect, for the group that was present that evening, the tone would not have been radically different. The usual topics would have come up—money, weight gain, politics, what's good on Netflix, and work, all of these topics peppered with jokes—but I know the energy would have been different, a bit guarded with a different flavor of expression. In the past, I witnessed some of my black and brown friends suddenly become extreme introverts in the presence of white people. I have witnessed some of my intelligent white friends suddenly become really stupid in the presence of people of color. Strange, indeed.

In the professional world, it is common and even acceptable for parallel organizations to exist. As a psychologist, I was a member of the American Psychological Association and the Association of Black Psychologists. Black physicians are members of American Medical Association and National Medical Association, which promotes the collective interests of physicians and patients of African descent. Our black medical students are members of Student National Medical Association and our Latino medical students belong to the Hispanic Medical Association. I could name race-specific organizations in every profession and with every racial/ethnic group. Why is this so? These organizations offer racial affinity group forums where racial identity can be fortified, where networks can be established, and where they can collectively forward an agenda of interest to their racial group. The fact that these parallel organizations continue to exist demonstrates that inclusive and representative practices are not fully present in the organizations where there is a large membership by the majority race. These organizations are still perceived to be white organizations.

Similarly, our leisure activity operates in a separate manner. There appear to be leisure activities more associated with whites and those associated with people of color. The data supports this phenomenon. Whites are more prevalent participants of hockey, downhill skiing, fly-fishing, travel, visiting national parks, and in general, physical activities. Blacks are participants in sporting activities like basketball and track, dancing and socializing in clubs, engaging in cooking activities like barbecuing and grilling, and attending church functions. Data shows that Latinos enjoy soccer, picnicking, cooking, and large multigenerational family gatherings. The research on Asian North Americans' leisure activities is limited with the two most studied groups being Chinese and Korean. Traditional Chinese leisure activities find involvement in a range of passive leisure activities including the tile-based strategy game mah-jongg, reading, walking, watching television, gardening, and sewing, to modern Chinese leisure activities that embrace physical activities. Korean North Americans generally identified with more passive activities as compared to other racial groups and prefer doing leisure in groups.[2]

It doesn't take much analysis to know that for most middle- and working-class Americans, leisure time has become a luxury. A weekend is used for errands: grocery shopping, laundry, cleaning the house, visits to barbers and hair stylists. Vacations are increasingly costly and demand time for planning. A trip to the amusement park or a visit to out-of-town relatives suffices. It is a challenge to find large blocks of time for vacations. It is particularly challenging when you want to share your leisure time with other family members or friends and have to try to coordinate your schedules and finances, as the cost of some leisure activities has increased dramatically over the years. The cost of a Disneyland vacation for a family of four is on average over $6,000.[3] The average cost of attending a major league baseball game for a family of four ranges from $95 to $314.[4] Of course, there are many leisure activities that are not associated with high financial costs: walking, jogging, running, playing baseball, football, soccer, playing board games, observing nature, visiting family and friends, listening to music, attending a church, synagogue, or mosque, or just relaxing. Yet, teasing out leisure differences due to class is challenging.

Ironically, although we seem to have less time to devote to leisure activities, we have more choices than ever about how to spend the little leisure time we do have. My colleague Dr. J. Goosby Smith and I worked on a consulting project assisting a museum to increase its patronage by African Americans. We held several African American focus groups on leisure-time activity. Relaxation and having fun topped the list of preferred leisure choices for the focus group participants. When we compared their criteria to what was identified by researchers as "American leisure-choice criteria," relaxation and having fun were nowhere on the list. Maybe "feeling comfortable and at ease in one's surroundings" could be translated as relaxation, but it would be a stretch to translate any of the other five criteria found in our work as fun (social interaction, doing something worthwhile, having the challenge of new experiences, having the opportunity to learn, participating actively).

"Fun" is a relative term. Hanging out at a coffee shop reading aerodynamics magazines and drinking coffee is fun for my husband. It is not fun for me. Thus, the easy answer to the question of why we do not socialize across racial lines may be that we have different ideas about what is fun. Maybe, maybe not. Maybe it is just that we need parallel structures in our social lives as well as in our professional lives.

My sister Felicia knew this from experience, which is why she hypothesizes that we have parallel leisure activities across races. "Yes, we do the same leisure activities, but we do them differently," she tells me. "Like music—we all like to listen to music, but we listen to different music."

These parallel leisure structures go beyond music. For example, many of us read, but are we reading the same books? I have been in several women's book clubs over the years, some predominantly white and others all black. Some of the titles we read did overlap, but the black book clubs sought out and concentrated on black authors or books related to race issues far more often than the white book clubs did. The only exceptions were specifically multicultural book clubs. Because it was a multicultural club, the members intentionally selected books of racially diverse interest. It is interesting that the club has to be designated as multicultural before we move beyond books by white authors and of white interest. It demonstrates that we all tend to read those books whose characters we can identify with and whose plots resonate with our everyday lived experience.

Online book discussions such as Goodreads.com and apps make it easier to express views on books by participants across racial lines. Similarly, mass-media book clubs like Oprah's Book Club, first on *The Oprah Winfrey Show* and now through *O, The Oprah Magazine*, NPR's *Book Club on the Air, Good Morning America's* book club, Despierta Leyendo (Wake Up Reading) on Univision's *¡Despierta América!* (Wake Up America), British TV's *Richard and Judy Book Club*, BBC Radio 4's *Bookclub*, and an Australian TV show, *First Tuesday Book Club*, have provided and continue to provide opportunities for a shared experience, but they do not provide the intimacy associated with leisure time spent with friends.

My sister's hypothesis was confirmed in my interview with researchers Monika Stodolska and Kimberly Shinew, professors in the Department of Recreation, Sports, and Tourism at the University of Illinois Urbana-Champaign, who have studied the racial and ethnic interface with leisure for decades. Stodolska and Shinew offered a deeper, empirical analysis of our leisure choices. Their offices at the university are right next door to each other, and there is an ease in how they discuss and share their thoughts on race and leisure honed from years of studying and writing about the topic. They talk about leisure research with the objectivity and passion that engages others in their work.

Stodolska and Shinew's research focuses on issues of cultural change and quality of life and their relationship to the leisure behavior of ethnic and racial minorities. They explore subjects like racial discrimination in leisure settings, recreation behavior of minority populations in natural environments, physical activity among people of color, and constraints on leisure.

In our interview, they tell me that when there is overlap in the choice of leisure activity that we tend to do them in parallel worlds and the styles of participation are different.[5] For example, whites and people of color enjoy family gathering in parks. However, Hispanics and blacks will tend to stay longer, typically five to six hours, and socialize in much larger groups. This leads to a not-so-uncommon complaint from whites of blacks and browns "taking over the parks" and requests to local officials for them to have "their own parks."

We can do leisure activities for different purposes that are largely driven by the amount of resources, financial and otherwise, available to the participants. In our interview, Dr. Stodolska provides me with an example: "You can buy a fishing rod from Walmart and the activity of fishing can be consumptive. We know that [with] people of lower socioeconomic classes, whatever they catch or hunt, they consume. You take that same activity and you can require a lot of resources. For example, you can go deep sea fishing or safari hunting in Africa, and this recreational activity becomes less consumptive and more expensive."

By definition, leisure activities are optional and not governed by equal opportunity laws as with organizations and school systems. Yet some public places of leisure—beaches, clubs, resorts, parks—have unwritten racial boundaries employed by participants and, as a result, are segregated.[6] It is not the structure but our own choosing that keeps these institutions segregated. Although these institutions have worked hard to be welcoming, we have a long way to go before participants feel a sense of ownership.[7]

The segregation of leisure activities is illustrated in a comedic video for the website Funny or Die. In the video, a black hiker, played by actor Blair Underwood, is stopped by a white couple while in one of America's national parks.

"Are you . . . are you lost?" they gently ask.

Black hiker responds, "No, I'm just taking a breather before I hit the steep part, and checking out these prickly pear cacti. Have you seen these? They're edible."

The white couple is amazed and continues on their way. The hiker then passes two other white hikers; one is wearing an Obama T-shirt with the word HOPE written across it. He gives the black hiker a thumbs-up. A woman walks by and stops to take a photo of him. He views others watching him from a hill. A white woman running toward him turns around and runs the other way. The park ranger then approaches the black hiker to ask if everything is okay.

"You forgot to sign the guestbook that we keep at the base of the trail," he tells the black hiker.

"Oh, well is there a law that says I have to sign it?"

The park ranger laughs. "That's funny. No, we just like all the guests of the park to, umm . . . We just want proof that you're here. This is really amazing for us."

This humorous video, although a bit exaggerated, drives home the point that our leisure activities are typically segregated and another barrier to fostering cross-racial friendships.

Another example is black commentator Rich Benjamin's 2015 TED Talk, in which he chronicles his trip to "Whitopia."[8] He defines Whitopia in three ways: "First, a Whitopia has posted at least six percent population growth since 2000. Second, the majority of that growth comes from white migrants. And third, the Whitopia has an ineffable charm, a pleasant look and feel, a *je ne sais quoi*."[9]

As a cultural critic, anthropologist, and writer, Benjamin travels to St. George, Utah; Coeur d'Alene, Idaho; and Forsyth County, Georgia. His trip is loaded with learning about white culture, particularly that the residents of these towns are not white supremacists or racists; in fact, race is not even a conscious factor.

"They emigrate there for friendliness, comfort, security, safety— reasons that they implicitly associate to whiteness in itself."[10] Along with experiencing the benefits of white privilege he embraces leisure activities associated with whites. He learns to golf. "Golf is the perfect seductive symbol of Whitopia," he states and notes that his best interviews were given on the golf course. He also learns to fish and hunt, attends mega-churches, and hosts a number of dinner parties and gets invited to many of them. After two years and twenty-seven thousand miles journeying in Whitopia, Benjamin details his learning about white culture in his book *Searching for Whitopia*, and he also continues to golf "every chance he gets" while leaving the guns and megachurches behind.[11]

In the last analysis, we self-segregate because of free choice and because people simply enjoy doing things with folks racially and culturally similar to them. Cross-racial friends can be a catalyst for making invisible racial boundaries in leisure activities more apparent and by doing so erase them. The capacity for leisure activities to be experienced in racially mixed settings is there. Professor Shinew tells me that it just needs to be encouraged. She cites a community garden as a collaborative experience and a leisure activity that has demonstrated potential for fostering cross-racial friendships. Sports are enjoyed across racial lines while also fostering relationships among and between diverse groups. Research further indicates that leisure activities with any kind of structure, even if loosely formed, and intentionally created welcoming atmospheres permit racially diverse friends to come together as equal partners in the experience.[12]

Empirically it is hard to determine if racial groups are not engaging in certain leisure activities due to free will or because they do not feel welcomed to participate. There are those who would argue that racial groups continue to self-segregate for leisure activities largely due to free will. They purport that increased efforts have been made to eradicating racism in recreational settings. It begs the question, If leisure is governed by free choice, should it matter if people self-segregate in parks, concerts, book groups, sporting events, clubs, and other social activities?

In many respects, individuals are often judged by the company they keep. From childhood days, parents caution their children about choosing their friends wisely. A primary reason why parents choose to educate their children in private schools is so they will have a wider pool of like-minded, financially resourced children. Similarly, many parents of color also choose same-race social organizations for their children to enhance their chances of success. One such organization is Jack and Jill of America, Inc.

The late Marion Stubbs Thomas founded Jack and Jill of America, on January 24, 1938, in Philadelphia. Twenty mothers came together to discuss creating an organization to provide social, cultural, and educational opportunities for Negro youth between the ages of two and nineteen. In 1946, ten chapters were involved in the national restructuring process. The constitution and bylaws were drawn up, and the organization was incorporated under the laws of the state of Delaware. Today, Jack and Jill boasts more than 230 chapters nationwide, representing more than 40,000 family members dedicated to "nurturing future African American leaders by strengthening children through leadership development, volunteer service, philanthropic giving and civic duty."[13]

Jack and Jill of America is an invitation-only membership organization formed in the time of inflexible segregation. But some believe that in a post–civil rights era it serves primarily as an elitist social organization, planning swimming parties, horseback riding lessons, skiing trips, and debutant socials for upper-middle-class blacks worried that their children will not know their African American roots because they live in predominantly white neighborhoods and attend primarily white schools. Critics state that the organization does not provide access to educational opportunities and professional development for *all* black children from all socioeconomic classes.[14] This controversy dates to the organization's inception and continues today, including via Twitter wars.

There is no doubt that Jack and Jill's philanthropic arm is a force for good, particularly in the African American community, donating millions of dollars for education, reducing poverty, and eliminating healthcare disparities.[15] Yet as an organization that is designed to provide a sense of belonging for its members, it often promotes an elitist stand. It is this nexus of race and class that creates tension within the black community.

Jack and Jill moms tell me they became members and chose to have their children participate in the organization to provide them with a solid sense of racial identity and to offer them a wider social group than the one they experienced in their predominantly white neighborhoods and school systems. They believe the advantages outweigh the disadvantages of being labeled elitist.[16]

Allison was invited into Jack and Jill by a very good friend in 2005 when her daughter, Amaia, was in kindergarten. Now that Amaia is in her junior year of high school, Allison reflects with me on the personal and financial investment she has made in the organization over the past twelve years. Amaia attended an all girls' private school with little to no diversity. "When I say there were a couple of black kids, I mean a couple," Allison states. It became extremely important for Allison and her husband for Amaia to have black friends and to be able to "see black families doing the same things that she saw her white friends' families doing." Amaia also played lacrosse, a predominantly white sport. "She *was* the diversity for that sport and it became even more important that she have a black experience outside of school and lacrosse."

With over forty thousand family members in Jack and Jill, Allison admits that there are women who join the organization "for all the wrong reasons." She believes that these members "buy into the perception of elitism and that being a member makes them think that they are better than others." Allison puts these intentions aside and focuses on the goal of parenting Amaia in a manner that provides a foundation for success.

Amaia's first job came through the support of a Jack and Jill Mom. As the Teen Legislative Chair for her chapter, Amaia enhanced her leadership competencies and honed organization skills that served her so well that she was able to receive a positive letter of recommendation for a coveted slot in the investment club at her school. On balance, the fact that Amaia experiences a fuller expression of her black identity and that she has opportunities to foster positive race esteem along with leadership development far outweighs, in her mother Allison's mind, any labels of elitism that are placed on membership in Jack and Jill.[17]

Similar to Jack and Jill, adult social groups exclusively for specific racial ethnic groups exist across the United States. Sociologists tell us that "similarity breeds connection," and people's personal networks are homogeneous with regard to many sociodemographic, behavioral, and intrapersonal characteristics.[18] Proponents of homophily theory have long argued that individuals are more likely to develop and maintain supportive relationships with others to whom they are similar on important social dimensions such as class, race, age, and education level.

However, social groups that are invitation-only and that are race-based add another barrier to receiving the benefits of socializing across racial lines. As a member of two invitation-only black women's organizations, the Links, Inc., and Northeasterners, Inc., I know the power of these fabulous groups—personally, in satisfying the basic human need of belonging, and professionally, in establishing networks for enrichment and advancement.

These organizations a have long history. The Links was founded in 1946 and Northeasterners in 1930, and another well-respected invitation-only black women's social organization, Girl Friends, Incorporated was founded in 1927. Black men's social organizations also exist and tend to be even more secretive and elite. They were also founded many decades ago—the Boule in 1904, the Guardsmen in 1933, and 100 Black Men of America in 1963. All of these groups were born at a time of rigid segregation, overt racism, and racially encapsulated societies. Although we still have a long way to go for racial equality, perhaps it is time to revisit race-based memberships for these organizations while still maintaining a race-specific thrust in their mission and activities.

By actively working to make an organization's social activities open to and inclusive of other races, the unintentional by-product of exclusiveness could be mitigated. Acknowledging and recognizing other dimensions of diversity that exist even within the membership of the group, such as religious and sexual orientation differences, could also support the organization's embrace of inclusion. These practices would enhance the mission and would not take away from the distinguished and accomplished individuals who make up their memberships. I believe it is possible for same-race social organizations to build both internal bonds that strengthen social belonging and enhance race esteem while simultaneously building external bridges with whites that increase social capital for all.

Whites could benefit by reaching out and supporting the activities of these organizations through active participation. For example, they could attend sponsored galas and planned events, and financially support programs. More whites in attendance at Links and Boule functions and events do not take away from the race-specific mission of these organizations and would demonstrate transracial racial-identity status characterized by fluidity and choice in one's actions thus offering an opportunity to strengthen white racial identity outside of the context of oppressor or a member of the dominant race.

Predominantly white social organizations could benefit from continued diversification of their memberships and ensuring that practices, policies, and procedures that govern these organizations reflect racial inclusivity.

As I write this I am not without my own assessment of these ideas as being a bit utopian. Would racially inclusive social organizations eliminate the need for same-race social groups? I doubt it. I can't imagine that any of the named black social groups or other same-race social groups will be suspended any time in the foreseeable future. In fact, most are still actively growing their memberships.

In a global society with individuals of multiple and intersecting identities do same-race social groups work against social equity and reduce social capital for its members by being ethnocentric? Perhaps. At minimum, it is worth further exploration if we are really serious about fostering racial equality and creating a level playing field for all races.

The formula for achieving social equity is for both same-race and predominantly white social groups to work independently and together to be more inclusive. As a result, same-race social groups and predominantly white social groups will continue to exist but not because of social isolation and intolerant exclusivity. Being more inclusive can only help to enhance their collective missions and strengthen our communities for the good of all. It cannot hurt to move in this direction, and it seems to be the path being set by the younger generations.

Here's an example: Khalida, a black woman, and Micah, a white male, have been friends since elementary school in Cleveland Heights, Ohio. Now that they are in their early thirties, their friendship is stronger than ever. Micah's friends are very diverse and he acknowledges that "Khalida has probably been a factor" in that fact. They recall a time when, in college, Khalida and one of Micah's friends got together and decided they wanted to host a holiday party. "We had everyone's friends come and no one knew each other. And it was amazing. Since then, we made it a point to invite everyone we knew to the party regardless of race and get everyone there and not tell anybody who else was coming. Recognizing and celebrating differences makes it fresh and fun."

Karl Spracklen, a white professor of leisure studies at Leeds Beckett University in the UK, argues that leisure is central to understanding wider debates about identity, postmodernity, and globalization.[19] As a result, leisure activities not only have the power to bring us together across racial lines for enjoyment and renewal but to deepen friendships that build the kind of trust necessary to advance racial equity.

————

Joann, a white woman, speaks fondly of her best friend, Joy, who is black. Relating a time when they were about to go out dancing, she tells me that Joy turned to her and said, "I forgot to tell you, you're going to be the only white person there." "Will I be okay?" Joann asked. "Yes," Joy stated definitively. Joann reports that they had a "great time." On the occasion of Joann's wedding, she recalls that the bridal party members were all going to a spa for facials, hairstyling, and so forth. Joy, a member of the bridal party, asked Joann, "Am I going to be okay?" Joann *guessed* that her friend was not likely to suffer any overt racial discrimination, but she was unsure about unsuspected racial discomfort. Joann is intuitive enough to point out the difference in the dancing episode and the bridal-party spa day. Joann tells me, "I didn't think to bring it up. She [Joy] is more aware of it [racial discomfort]. She brings it up."

Being out of their comfort zones has become so much a part of the daily experience of many people of color that to experience it when crossing racial lines in friendship is somewhat normal. This does not mean that discomfort does not exist—just that it is normal to feel uncomfortable. Similarly, whites who live outside of white settings experience discomfort while in a leisure environment when they are surrounded by people of color. The difference is that white people have less experience being in these uncomfortable situations.

My early research found that race is a source of stress for both white people and people of color, yet whites exhibited fewer coping strategies for racial stress.[20] Racial stress is defined as the psychological discomfort that results from a situation or event that an individual appraises as troubling because of racial discrimination or isolation.[21] I wanted to test my hypothesis that cross-racial friends would help to reduce racial stress so conducted a national survey to study the relationship between quality of life measures and having friends across racial lines. This friendship survey incorporated the Subjective Happiness Scale and the Everyday Discrimination Scale,[22] allowing us to examine the correlation between happiness and perceived discrimination with the number and depth of an individual's cross-racial friendships.[23]

Using a multipronged sampling strategy, we analyzed data from over a thousand respondents across the United States. Approximately 30 percent of these respondents reported having no friends across racial lines. As with our other friendship surveys, we calculated a depth-of-friendship index based on constructs such as socializing together outside of work, vacationing together, calling in times of emotional stress, borrowing money, witnessing a family argument, playing sports together, and working on projects together. For those with cross-racial friends, the average depth of friendship was low (mean score 2.2 on a scale of 0 to 7). Cross-racial friendship depth increased as reported household income increased and was greater for females than males, and the depth of intimacy in the friendship decreased with the age of the respondent.

The Everyday Discrimination Scale measures chronic and routine unfair treatment in everyday life. In our study we found that individuals with a close cross-racial friend of depth had increased levels of perceived racial discrimination. In other words, having cross-racial friends may make you happier, but it also heightens your awareness of racial discrimination in everyday life.

As the number of cross-racial friends increased, reported happiness increased. This finding offers a promise for positive shared leisure activities across races. However, as reported experiences of race-based discrimination increased, the depth of cross-racial friendship increased for persons of color, but not for whites. That is, when race issues were acknowledged and incorporated into the daily experience of the friendship, people of color experienced cross-racial friendships as more important when compared to the experience of whites. This finding is consistent with other research and with what people understand intuitively: people of color are far more facile at navigating race issues than are whites.[24] As the majority racial group, whites enjoy social privilege and do not experience race-based discrimination in an everyday manner as people of color do. Thus, holding socioeconomic class constant, for cross-racial friends, shared leisure activities adds another challenging layer.

So how do we begin to foster cross-racial friendships and have individuals become more proficient in crossing racial lines in friendship? In addition to eradicating discrimination in leisure activities and reducing differential upkeep and management of public parks and spaces, we can learn from programs like Mix It Up Day, which work for school-age children. Mix It Up at Lunch Day, sponsored by Teaching Tolerance, an international program of the Southern Poverty Law Center, encourages students to identify, question, and cross social boundaries.[25] Students are encouraged to sit with someone new in the cafeteria and are given a colored ribbon or piece of candy that tells them where they should sit. They are also provided with conversation starters to support positive interactions. Themes such as wearing their clothes inside out or backwards, celebrity guests, and prizes make the Mix It Up Day fun for students and faculty. These kinds of planned interactions have been shown to reduce prejudice in school-age children and foster a more welcoming school environment.[26]

Meetups are the Mix It Up for adults. The Meetup app helps individuals to find the right people to join them in doing the things they like to do.[27] Since the focus is on individual interest, it provides the common ground necessary for building friends across racial lines. However, if one lives in a geographic area that is not racially diverse, the possibility of making friends of different races is limited. Still, app users have been able to creatively form diverse groups by setting up culturally diverse Meetup groups around the world and then finding individuals in that group who are in their area who share their same interest.

Because neighborhoods remain racially segregated, it takes more effort for adults to "mix it up." Although the Supreme Court ruled against racially restrictive covenants in 1948 and they were outlawed by the federal Fair Housing Act of 1968, it is surprising to find that some of this language still exists in many housing association by-laws without the need or urgency to remove the restrictions.[28] Under these conditions, it is still plausible that our family and our former neighbors, the Maiers and the Fragassis, could be clandestinely prohibited from living in the same neighborhood, making it harder for us to become friends and socialize together.

Moreover, the spirit of the racially restrictive covenant still exists not only in our neighborhoods but in our leisure activities. Whether or not parallel leisure structures represent exclusionary practices resulting from covert racism and unconscious bias or if they simply are reflective of freely chosen self–segregation based on basic human needs of belonging, we can work toward changing the outcome. In order to break down institutional racism and level the playing field, shared leisure activities across racial lines are necessary. Let the party begin!

Chapter 10

THE HEAVENLY VISION
OF RACIAL UNITY

After graduating from a Catholic high school, I did what a lot of girls did at that time and entered a religious community of Catholic nuns. Well, maybe not a lot of girls did that, and maybe only white girls. Well, maybe only a few white girls, and certainly even fewer black girls. Since I wore full religious garb at the time, I was quite an anomaly. "Gee, I've never seen a black nun before" was how I was most often greeted. People never had time to get themselves together and even try to act as if they had some manners when they saw me. All their unedited remarks just came stammering out of their mouths. For the thirteen years that I was part of a religious community, I not only embraced a nontraditional life-style but ran right into the color-blind racism described by Dr. Eduardo Bonilla-Silva, characterized as racial inequality resulting from nonracial dynamics.

When I entered religious life, to my knowledge there were only two black women who preceded my joining that particular community. Being only seventeen years old, my struggles to integrate into community life were acute and not all grounded in racial tension. Over time, like my peers, I weathered bouts of homesickness, adjusted to the controlled schedule that included regimented prayer and meals, and learned to control our boisterous behaviors. Unlike my peers, I couldn't adjust to the lack of racial diversity in my everyday life. I lived with all white people and taught in an all-white school with the exception of one black student, Toni Massey. If Toni happened to be absent from school, I didn't see another black face all day. On weekends I lived in a monoracial white world.

I had been told that the community had not accepted black women for many years and that if I had wanted to enter the community ten years prior to my entrance in 1969, I would have been denied or at least encouraged to enter one of the already desegregated communities or one of the few black religious orders in the South. The rationale I was given was that black women would "feel like a fish out of water." They definitely had that right about how black women would feel. Yet, the burden remained on black women to adjust. For many years I accepted that burden.

I found solace not in advocating for cultural change within religious life but in working to be the human translator about whites for the black community. I focused my energies on social justice issues, particularly in working with black youth, as a way to hold onto my black identity. My apostolate (a nun's term for assigned ministry or assigned job) was teaching English, psychology, and religion at my alma mater, Notre Dame Academy (NDA). In 1980, NDA had not changed in its racial makeup since I had graduated. In fact, Toni Massey was the new Debbie Plummer there, representing the entire black race to that educational environment. It was no mystery to me (and should have been obvious to others) that my work with Black Catholic Input (BCI), a diocesan youth group that I founded for black high school students, was my attempt to put meaning into my world—to make it real.

Starting BCI made my experience as a racial minority a gift for me. Yet the emotional pain also increased as a result of my involvement, and it ultimately served as the catalyst for my leaving the community.

BCI grew from fourteen students to hundreds of students in the course of a few years, and it still exists today as part of the Youth & Young Adult Ministry of the Cleveland Catholic Diocese. We held retreats, did community service activities, and sponsored dances as fund-raisers. Meetings and dances were held at Regina High School, a school that was undergoing a demographic change from white Irish to more racially mixed. As a result, white parents from several elementary schools that served as feeder schools to Regina High School struggled with whether or not they should send their girls to Regina because it was becoming "too black." The presence of Black Catholic Input on the premises was cited as the reason. "We see all of these black kids coming out of the school and it makes us uncomfortable," I was told. The leadership of my religious order presented their rationale that I needed to change the venue for BCI meetings and dances because the principal of the largest feeder school was at a loss as to what to tell the parents who were so upset about Regina's growing "black image."

As the fish out of water in religious life that was still swimming, I was expected to understand and help these black students learn to swim on dry land. However, I was tired of swimming on dry land and had a complete awakening in that moment that not only was I trying to swim on dry land but that whites were doing nothing to make the waters conducive for other kinds of fish. From deep inside me the courage to speak rose and I surprised even myself with my response.

"I am so sorry that Sister can't find something in the Gospels to help her to respond to those parents," I said and left the room. Shortly after that meeting, I began the process for leaving the community.

My leaving religious life was not so much an issue of vocation—I am still drawn to spiritual growth and practice—but it was impossible for me to survive as a black person in an all-white community (disappointingly, even a religious one). For me, being told by community leaders to change the venue for Black Catholic Input activities was what social scientists would define as the "critical incident." Critical incidents are often turning points in decision-making, as the situation often causes significant risk of physical or psychological harm if the condition persists. A critical incident may not be a dramatic event, as the significance lies in the intra-psychic jolt experienced by the individual. The situation serves as a huge wake-up call because it causes one to see the environment and the people in it from a totally different perspective. Until that meeting, I perceived a shared identity as a woman in a religious order living out the charism, a deep experience of God's goodness, with others in community. Race did not matter any more than the different family backgrounds we each brought with us when we entered that religious life. Our collective identity as Notre Dame Sisters trumped individual racial identity and guided our behavior and decisions. After that meeting, I experienced a heightened consciousness of my black identity, and with this, I felt disconnected from my identity as a member of that religious community.

What made my survival in a religious community impossible is at the core of what I believe makes it difficult to cross racial lines in friendship. One has to find a way to maintain one's own racial self while at the same time acknowledging and appreciating another person's racial self. You have to be pretty stable in your own racial identity to be able to take in the experience of the other person's racial identity without losing your own. If religious life were culture-free, I might have been able to survive, but it wasn't. Because of the number of nuns of Irish ethnicity, Saint Patrick's Day was celebrated as if it were a high holy feast. Because of the order's German roots, German customs even influenced how we folded our underwear. Over thirteen years, I ate many meals in the convent and never once was there cornbread and greens (let alone the rice and beans and plantains that I was used to). And although our liturgies were beautiful, never was a Negro spiritual or gospel song even hummed. But it was even more than the feasts we celebrated, the customs we followed, the foods we ate, or the kinds of songs we sang. White European cultures were so embedded in the thinking, values, and ways of knowing in religious life that if I had continued to live in that environment, I would have had no choice but to act like a white person and embrace a white identity. Trying to explain this to some of my religious sisters was like trying to get a fish to understand the concept of wetness. For me, holding on to my black racial identity in religious life would have been like a fish trying to survive outside of water.

"We must face the fact that in America," Dr. Martin Luther King said, "the church is still the most segregated major institution in America. At eleven o'clock on Sunday morning when we stand and sing 'And Christ has no east or west,' we stand at the most segregated hour in this nation. This is tragic."[1]

It was in 1963 when Dr. King made these remarks, and today, Sunday morning remains one of the most segregated hours in American life, with more than eight in ten congregations made up of one predominant racial group. In theory, many would agree with Dr. King that this is a tragic situation. Yet recent polls suggest that most churchgoers are content with the racial makeup of their congregations and are lukewarm about diversity.[2]

There are a number of reasons for this. Religious congregations are a microcosm of an American society suffering from racial fatigue. We are tired of talking about race and tired of race being an issue, so we avoid the topic, particularly outside of work settings. We live in segregated neighborhoods and we're reluctant to travel outside our neighborhoods for worship. Yet, if we are to form authentically Christian and other faith-based communities, dialogues on race are important. Responding to the prayer that we all may be one requires that these dialogues take place.

It is a natural human tendency for people to want to be around others who are like them, and most religious congregations are populated through their members' social networks. Unfortunately, in the United States, most churches, mosques, synagogues, and other places of religious practice have been racially exclusive in terms of their membership, ministry, and mission. Most of us who are churchgoers attend churches that are not diverse, and race is rarely, if ever, mentioned as a topic of interest or pursuit. In 2003, Bishop Fred Caldwell of Shreveport, Louisiana, after unsuccessfully urging his white friends to join, decided to pay whites to attend the five-thousand-member, predominantly black Greenwood Acres Full Gospel Baptist Church in order to reach his dream of "a rainbow in God's church." The offer attracted media attention, and some whites agreed to come for free.[3]

Multiracial congregations are difficult to create and challenging to maintain. It requires advocating for racial justice and practicing racial equity, worshiping together in the same language, integrating diverse music genres and worship styles in the service, sermons that address a diverse membership, and diversifying the leadership of the congregation.[4] Most racially diverse congregations have focused on creating a common social identity rooted in faith that subordinates racial identity. Because churches have historically been the safe haven for people of color, where racial identity becomes stabilized and integrated, fostering a common neutral racial identity disadvantages people of color. For many people of color, faith communities are places where race can be fully owned, accepted, and seamlessly integrated into one's being, so much so that expressions of racial identity are natural and easily apparent to others through manner of speaking, practices, dress, and expressions. The majority of whites have not had experiences of not being in the majority and often interpret racial-identity expression as exclusionary or even inauthentic expressions of a collective identity as faith community members.

There have been many attempts to design programs and strategies that address this dilemma. Racial reconciliation, an effort that grew out of the civil rights movement by African Americans in conservative Protestant churches, is one of them. Racial reconciliation works to promote racial equality and the fostering of cross-racial relationships.[5] Influenced by racial reconciliation, the Promise Keepers' movement, an Evangelical Christian organization for men, made racial inclusion one of its seven promises: "Promise 6: A Promise Keeper is committed to reaching beyond any racial and denominational barriers to demonstrate the power of biblical unity."[6]

As a strategy to enhance racial equality and promote cross-racial relationships in the church, racial reconciliation efforts have been criticized for managing race more as a social issue than a gospel value.[7] Not only does its implementation vary from church to church but there is hardly consensus on whether or not the church should even be involved in the work of racial reconciliation, perceiving it to be a political issue.[8] The concept of racial reconciliation is complex and nuanced. It requires deep understanding of race as a social construct and of peacemaking and peacekeeping as strategy. Most church leadership does not possess this knowledge base or skill set.

Another criticism of racial reconciliation is that it has been equated with having racially diverse congregations. The assumption is that if the congregation is representationally or compositionally diverse in its racial makeup, then reconciliation is automatic. That is not the case. It takes a great deal of work to tie diversity to inclusion.

Lagging behind organizational efforts for understanding diversity and developing strategic initiatives necessary to manage it effectively, faith communities have neglected to tie diversity to inclusion. In doing so, organizations now place emphasis on understanding and eliminating unconscious biases, microaggressions, and microinequities in the workplace.

I have often used the example that inclusion is like being at home in someone else's home rather than just being a guest. As a guest in someone's home, the standard is to be treated respectfully. Being given an invitation to "make yourself at home" gives you a piece of the ownership.

Although people understand this inclusion analogy of "being at home in someone else's home," it is still is a bit too subjective. To quote Benjamin Franklin, houseguests, like fish, seem to smell after three days. Inclusion extends way beyond a three-day invitation. Inclusion is more than visiting one another's churches as welcomed guests. Our gospel choir goes and sings at your suburban white church. Everyone brings a dish to share from his or her culture. Don't get me wrong: this is a good start, but it is simplistic in orientation. It does not usually lead people to deal with the differences in racial expression of cultural values and norms that are generally the source of racial clashes and miscommunication. If I visit your church for a multicultural feast and while there I ask why you moved to a new neighborhood when two black families moved onto your street, you may start to feel as if you need some Pepto-Bismol.

Inclusion is creating *conditions* that leverage differences. In the workplace, we leverage differences in order to drive business outcomes, spur innovation, and achieve the mission of the organization. In our communities, we leverage differences to create peaceful environments and transform our society for the good of all. In faith communities, we leverage differences to achieve our destiny as people of God. This is a very difficult and challenging process and measured not by whether or not someone *feels* that they are included. Feeling included is a by-product of an inclusive culture.

As a psychologist, I know that there are a number of variables that load into someone's feeling state and that it is possible for someone to not feel included despite the existence of inclusive practices and policies. The reverse of that is also true. It is possible for someone to feel included despite discriminatory policies and inequitable practices. We evidence this phenomenon in many faith communities when an unbalanced responsibility is placed on people of color for accepting existing norms and practices, gaining access to information and social support and opportunities for exercising formal and informal power.

Full acceptance of membership in the church depends on an individual's ability to be seen as the prototype of that organization. The prototypical member will personify the norms, behaviors, values, and even external appearance seen as important to maintaining the culture of the church. As a result, diversity or divergence from the prototype introduces tensions around who belongs in the church. Creative tensions appear and are negotiated through social dynamics that influence inclusion as it is experienced by individuals. This tension naturally exists with diversity, and until it is recognized and reckoned with, there is no chance for racial reconciliation.

The Pew Research Center ranks the Catholic Church as one of the highest-ranking racially diverse religious groups in the United States, largely due to its high percentage of Latino members.[9] Immigrants, particularly Hispanics, make up a significant proportion of Catholic America.[10] However, this aggregate high ranking does not take into account the racially segregated parishes that make up the Catholic Church. Thirty-eight percent of Catholic parishes are identified as "multicultural parishes," meaning they meet one of the three following criteria: (1) regularly celebrating Mass in a language other than English or Latin; (2) the percentage of parishioners who are non-Hispanic white is less than 40 percent; and/or (3) the parishioner diversity index, or probability that two randomly selected parishioners identify as different race or ethnicity, is 33 percent or higher.[11] Of note is that the definition of "multicultural church" is the composition of nonwhites or races other than white. In other words, the parish could be predominantly black, as is my parish, St. Agnes–Our Lady of Fatima in Cleveland, Ohio, which is considered a multicultural parish. Ironically, this conceptualization of cultural diversity in the US Catholic Church is born out of a framework of privilege by making white the norm and racial minorities the other. Because of its racially segregated parishes, the Catholic Church does not offer any more opportunities for advancing racial reconciliation than in the Protestant church.

Although the Catholic Church ranks high among faith traditions with racial diversity in aggregate, that speaks little to what emphasis on racial reconciliation might be given at the local parish level. At my predominantly white parish in Massachusetts, race has never been a topic for discussion, although pro-life concerns abound in the sermons, along with much intercession for the New England Patriots to keep winning football games. Indeed, most Catholics (64 percent) had not heard a homily on racism or racial justice over the entire three-year cycle of the Sunday lectionary, according to research by Bryan Massingale, a priest, moral theology professor, and author of *Racial Justice and the Catholic Church*.[12] Perhaps even more telling of the lack of understanding of the impact of racism and the predominance of white privilege is that, when questioned about this discrepancy, white Catholics believed that it was "not a problem," owing to the fact that "it wasn't necessary to address racism in our church" because it simply did not apply. This assertion was supported by stories where they applauded their efforts for being welcoming and responsive to the needs of the one black and the one Hispanic family in the church that they could identify by name, even though they could not recall any personal encounter with these families; but they knew and had proof of outreach efforts.[13]

It is a very different case for my church home, Cleveland's St. Agnes–Our Lady of Fatima, under the vibrant leadership of Reverend Bob Marva. In this predominantly African American parish, the liturgy and its expression is "authentically black and truly Catholic," a term that came out of the 1960s black Catholic movement within the church when activists fought to weave racial-identity expression in liturgies and to see the determination of black parishes and, most importantly, the right to identify as both black and Catholic.[14] The struggle for the Catholic Church to be identified as truly racially diverse in the leadership of church chanceries, diocesan staffs, parish staffs, schools, institutions of higher education, and Catholic organizations remains today.[15]

Despite the inability of some local parishes to address racism in the Catholic Church, the response was swift to the formation of an Ad Hoc Committee Against Racism after the Charlottesville Unite the Right Rally in August 2017. Soon after, the committee was formed upon the unanimous recommendation of the US Bishops Conference Executive Committee and in consultation with members of the United States Conference of Catholic Bishops.[16] The committee will work to support the implementation of the 2018 pastoral letter on racism, which, in turn, built on the ideas on racism presented in the 1979 Pastoral Letter of Racism, Brothers and Sister to Us: "Racism is a sin: a sin that divides the human family, blots out the image of God among specific members of that family, and violates the fundamental human dignity of those called to be children of the same Father."[17]

Racial reconciliation efforts in the church have also been criticized for focusing more on interpersonal relationships and overcoming personal biases while ignoring structural racism inherent in poverty, education, health outcomes, and the criminal justice system. As a result, the church, with its segregated worship spaces, remains an American institution reflective of the residuals of slavery. Dr. Love L. Sechrest, associate professor of New Testament at Fuller Theological Seminary, states:

> Interdependence is critical for healing racial schisms in the church not because there is a Bible verse that demands it, but because the lingering

legacy of our troubled racial past demands the greater sensitivity and sacrifice of a higher righteousness going forward. We will know when we have finally overcome when local congregations reflect the ethnoracial composition of their communities, towns and neighborhoods, when the draw of the Christian family supersedes the pull of cultural comfort. We will have finally overcome the legacy of destructive ethnic and racial stereotypes when skin color or speech patterns do not inhibit the affirmation of leadership gifts in these multifaceted congregations. We will have finally arrived in the territory about which Dr. King dreamt when our best friends in the church really are people from other races and ethnic groups, when the people who know our greatest fears and deepest longings do not look anything like us.[18]

The involvement of Jews in the civil rights movement is a long and noted involvement, often symbolized by the presence of Rabbi Abraham Joshua Heschel in the front row of the Selma march. Rabbi Heschel was able to bring Dr. King's message to a wide Jewish audience, and Dr. King made Rabbi Heschel a central figure in the struggle for civil rights.[19] Over fifty years later, David Stern, senior rabbi of Temple Emanu-El synagogue in Dallas, noted in response to the fatal shooting of five police officers in Dallas,

The racial healing we seek will be painful, and the pain will be evidence that we're healing. The involvement of Jews in the civil rights movement fifty years ago does not grant us a free pass today. As Jews, we will need to expand our circle of prophets—because the voices of Jeremiah and Amos are carried forward in our day by writer/activists like Ta-Nehisi Coates and Bryan Stevenson.

Instead, the God who heard the cry of the oppressed requires us to listen—to narratives of racism, to exposures of white privilege and educational inequities and mythic meritocracies. We do not need to agree with everything we hear, but we need to hear it. And when that hearing produces pain, then we need to feel it. And if that pain motivates us to create a more just and safe society instead of silencing the truths that disturb us, we will know that we have broken through the silence towards hope. The books of the Hebrew prophets are fundamental to our identity as Jews, but they do not make good bedtime reading. This healing will sting before it salves.[20]

How do we move toward this healing? Sociologist Michael Emerson believes that involvement in multiracial congregations over time leads to fundamental differences. Friendship patterns change.[21] In his research he found that people in multiracial congregations have significantly more friendships across race than do other Americans. Over 80 percent of the people in racially mixed congregations reported that most of the racial diversity in their friendships stemmed from their involvement in a racially mixed congregation. The Bahá'í religion is one such example.

The Bahá'í religion is an independent, monotheistic world religion. It is the youngest of the world's religions and one of the fastest growing.[22] Oneness of humanity is a central principle of the faith; thus, where there are Bahá'ís, there is diversity. Melodie and Richard, an interracial couple, have been Bahá'ís most of their married life. "When we had children," Richard tells me, "we felt like we had to have a spiritual group where our kids would feel whole."

I gathered at their home one evening with twelve members of the Bahá'í faith to learn more about their quest for racial unity in the context of spirituality and how friendships nourished this belief. Not surprisingly, it was by socializing in diverse groups that most of these people came to know of the Bahá'í faith, or, if Bahá'í from birth, their faith had made them automatically a part of a diverse environment. Susanne, a forty-seven-year-old white woman, related, "I grew up in Canada in an all-white environment. When my parents became Bahá'í, all of a sudden there were people in our home from all races. I can't imagine going back to anything different. It would be like taking a rainbow and taking all the colors out of it." Barbara, another participant, affirmed that when the Bahá'ís come together, it is like "a big family reunion and just not knowing all the family yet."

The rationale or motivation for cross-racial friendships is rooted in the spiritual. For some, the spiritual is realized in formal religious practices. For others, the spiritual is lived as a philosophical orientation or a basic approach to life. Whether the basis of one's spirituality is an organized religion or a personal belief system, socializing across racial lines can only be practiced in a spiritual context because we have to transcend all of the factors outlined earlier: how our brain forms prejudices, our tribal nature, cultural encapsulation, personal-choice tendencies, geographical distance, and demographic differences with respect to racial groups. Even faith communities are challenged to offer us a way beyond these barriers to develop transracial identities and cross racial lines in friendship.

Yet if we are to form authentically Christian, faith-based, or spiritually oriented communities, dialogues on race are important. As humans, we have a natural tendency toward ethnocentrism—the belief that our culture is the standard by which to judge all other cultures. We also have a natural tendency toward culturally myopic thinking—the belief that our culture is relevant to all others. Moving away from ethnocentrism and cultural myopia helps us to be more authentic and fully functioning. Friends who cross racial lines reflect our transcendent core.

Chapter 11

FRIENDS IN
THE BIG TENT

It was a rare autumn day in Cleveland, Ohio, when two seasons didn't overlap. The temperature gently rose to the low seventies by the time we entered St. Agnes–Our Lady of Fatima for 10:30 a.m. Mass. My husband, Mike, had to make the pitch for increased tithing at both the 8:30 and 10:30 Masses, so Joan joined Mom and me as the driver so that only one car was needed. Over a series of texts to my sister Felicia on the way to Mass, we decided to take Mom to brunch after services. For Mike, this presented a perfect opportunity for a family-free home (my ninety-one-year-old mom lives with us) filled with football and only our pug to distract him.

As she waited for us to arrive, Felicia read the news on her iPad while enjoying coffee and a mimosa. My sister, with her own brand of passion for racial equality, was heavily invested in forwarding the rights of Colin Kaepernick and the NFL players to kneel during the anthem. She had even made an unsuccessful attempt to get her husband to boycott watching football (he was home watching the game). As we got seated, Felicia began making comments about a recent tweet by President Trump about the NFL players. She then paused and directly addressed Joan: "I have to stop and ask all white people because I just don't know any more who believes what and who to trust, and I don't want to assume. If you are a Trump supporter, I can respect your right to support his agenda, but I just can't . . ."

I didn't know if it would be the mimosa reacting to what Joan might say or if the response would come from my generally nonaggressive sister, who values diverse political viewpoints. So I cut her off. Joan had voted for Trump. I sat next to Joan but did not look at her. I swore I felt her muscles tightening. Perhaps a projection on my part. My muscles were tightening.

"Joan would not call herself a Trump supporter," I said directly to my sister, overfunctioning, a "jump in and fix it" habit I have been trying to break since 1985 when I first read about the concept in Harriet Lerner's *The Dance of Anger.*[1] I took a purposeful, long pause, then said, "Although she did vote for Trump." My sister stared at Joan, not in disbelief but in dismay that her mistrust of whites was grounded in reality and before her was living proof. Mom, who over her ninety-one years has mastered the art of quickly changing the topic when a conversation becomes uncomfortable, did just that. Thank God for Mom.

Yes, one of my closet friends had voted for a candidate whom I believed to have espoused racist beliefs and acted on racist practices and therefore was a racist.[2] "Racist" is an ugly label that I have rarely used in all my years as a psychologist working to further the goals of diversity and inclusion. After casting our votes for president, Joan and I had some animated conversations about this, and we had some transformative ones as well. Before casting our votes, it was a conversation we avoided.

This avoidance is not atypical for long-term cross-racial friends. The pair intuitively knows that as adults, race is now a taboo topic. Race changes from a topic that perhaps you were able to be curious about in elementary school, one that you shared advocacy about in high school and joked about in college. But when it comes to accomplishing adult developmental tasks such as getting a good job, making a significant investment in buying a home, choosing a life partner, parenting children, and voting, race can become a divisive factor in decision-making. When cross-racial relationships have a long, positive history, consciously or unconsciously, for many cross-racial friendship dyads, the participants try to preserve the relationship and simply do not talk about race.

For most people, all politics is local. I don't mean in the sense of voting for our councilors, our school board committee members, or on issues on our local ballot. I mean politics with a small p, which is about how we use our personal power and the ways we influence one another and make our positions known. We do this all the time in our everyday lives when we negotiate over resources at work, create compromises among family members, and use our energy to build coalitions to advance our goals, like hosting Thanksgiving dinner at our home or getting another family member to host it.

A black American focus group participant shared a conversation she had with a Nigerian American cab driver while in DC shortly after the 2016 election. "I thought the conversation was going to go a different way. He [the driver] immediately went into, 'Man, I love that Trump guy.' I was shocked. He told me that not only did he vote for Trump but that several in his Nigerian American community in New York, his network, had also voted for him. He was aware that many black Americans had not voted for him. Because he was an immigrant I found this confusing and told him so. He told me that he had only been in the country about ten years and didn't have the whole civil rights movement as baggage. 'The economy . . . that's my thing,' he said. 'I like him because his message is about jobs. He's a successful businessman and he could run the country like how he runs his business.'"

All politics is local and personal. Then there is the politics with the capital letter *P* that is about the governance of our nation and the party ideologies that influence its practices and policies. When we vote, the small-*p* politics gets translated into the large-*P* politics, and that is when it gets messy.

Henry Tsai grew up hearing stories of ordinary people told to him by his mother, the owner of a small restaurant. As a result, twenty-four hours after the 2016 election, Henry created the website Hi From The Other Side, designed to get people to share their stories.[3] By listening to each other's stories, Henry believes we can bridge the deep political divide:

> I think I am not alone in my observation that we, generally as a country, are talking past each other. There's not a lot of direct engagement and there's a lot of demonizing of others' political opinion. Obviously it hasn't always been this way and it doesn't have to be this way. The weekend after the election, I went down to the JFK Presidential Library and spent an entire afternoon there and after watching the debates between JFK and Nixon, was just taken aback and struck by how civil it was . . . that they were disagreeing passionately but cordially. It seems like people who don't know each other, get into fights over someone's

posting. So, my solution to that is, in order to get to the place where there is better engagement of ideas, step one has to be listening. That's how democracy works.[4]

As a former Silicon Valley worker and a Harvard graduate, Henry held an ethos of seeing a need and trying to address it with a technology solution. The website was an attempt to get people to talk to each other, launched with a friend who is a computer scientist at MIT. The website matches voters and political supporters from across the aisle. It works like a dating site except that you are introduced to people of a different political ideology from your own. Through an algorithm based on a short survey about your likes and dislikes outside of politics and childhood aspirations, you are matched with someone "from the other side" with whom you also hold common ground. The website offers a discussion guide that lays out ground rules and ways to begin the dialogue. They suggest that people talk face-to-face as much as possible— by phone, video chat, or in person. He says,

> I am trying to get people to recognize that there are a lot of parts of our identity. If we could listen a little better, we could do some good for public discourse. In our discussion guide, we ask people to think back to certain points in their lives and talk about what they were hoping for. There's a lot that you can learn about a person from the way they talk about their hopes and dreams.

Henry has "a little hope and a big hope" for what the website will achieve. "The little hope is that people are having quality conversations. There is nothing that makes me happier than receiving emails for someone who said, 'I just had a three-hour conversation with someone who I would completely disagree with,' or 'I could not believe how much we have in common,' or that 'our conversation was productive.' Some have agreed to follow up or they have invited the other person over to their home after the conversation. That's the thing I care about the most."

Henry's big hope is for wider-spread conversations that matter. He gets requests from other countries to create customized versions of the website, including, for example, one from the UK for a website that can bridge the Brexit divide. He and partners Yasif and David, who manage the technical aspects, know that "the technology is agnostic to the issues." The goal is to pair people up who are different yet have common ground. "We are hyperfocused to make this experience good."

He goes on, "I didn't create this website so that one side could convince the other side that they are right. My observation is that we are not even close to being able to have persuasion if we are not listening. I think that the mission is not to convince; let's just understand. Just because you disagree vehemently on politics doesn't mean that you can't become friends or that you don't have a lot of other things in common."

American democracy has a remarkable resiliency, for it has withstood demagogy for decades, in fact, since before the founding of the nation. But today, the aggravating of strains, the cultural lag (i.e., the failure of social skills to keep pace with the technological) have made the appeal greater than ever before. It is not a movement that is born overnight. Its seeds are always present, and in its growth may be gradual and imperceptible up to a point, and then sudden and alarming. It waxes and wanes with the rise and fall of particular demagogues. But sometimes its roots gain a firm hold in congressional committees, in local and state political groups, in certain newspapers, and among certain radio commentators.[5]

Harvard social psychologist Gordon Allport published those words in 1954 in his seminal work on the roots and nature of prejudice. What is not surprising about the findings reported in *The Nature of Prejudice* is that its simple truths, born out of massive empirical research on prejudice across many dimensions (race, ethnicity, religion, age, class), are so profoundly embedded in how we operate. We all have "a propensity to prejudice. This propensity lies in the normal and natural tendency to form generalizations, concepts, categories, whose content represents overrepresentation of his world of experience."[6] In other words, we all, on some level, believe ourselves to be the center of the universe and use ourselves as the standard by which we judge everyone else. Those who are like us are good and wonderful. Those who are not like us, not that good and certainly not as wonderful.

What is surprising is that how we hold prejudice toward others still permeates modern society, even though Allport and many researchers since his time have offered recommendations for reducing or even eliminating many of the negative effects of prejudice. We praise the work but do not change our behaviors.

Allport suggested that legislative solutions were only one of several possible channels for improving race relations and changing prejudiced attitudes. We can have all the equal employment opportunity regulations and race discrimination laws in the world (and we do), but it is not enough to eliminate prejudice. Included in Allport's list of recommendations to eliminate the negative effects of prejudice are "equal status relationships and for more intimate acquaintance which are likely to make for increased tolerance."[7] In sum, we need cross-racial friendships.

In my humble opinion, two of the most enlightening chapters in this book are the ones on the correlations between visibility and strangeness with prejudice and how victims of oppression operate in society. The research findings explain the inherent challenges in cross-racial interactions, such as the one described at the beginning of this chapter about the brunch conversation on contemporary race issues that Felicia, Joan, and I had.

The visibility and its associated strangeness of blacks in their minority status from the white dominant group always place blacks in the "other" position. We are "readily fitted into a category of prejudgment because some visible mark is present to activate the category in question." Allport used as examples of the "strikingly visible character of some (not many) group differences" as "a Negro, an Oriental, a woman, a policeman in uniform." Today we would have to change the word "Negro" to "black" and "Oriental" to "Asian." And we would need to include whites in that group and identify the race of the policeman.

When my younger sister Felicia stopped to consider her words about the current racially charged events of the day, she suddenly saw Joan as white and not the person that she had known since she was nine years old. Allport demonstrated that all people use stereotypes as mental shortcuts that then become the foundation for prejudice. Joan was white and therefore in that social loading, knowingly or unknowingly, held racist views and was not to be trusted.

Similarly, Joan found it baffling that her vote in the past election could be translated by my sister as an endorsement of any kind of racist beliefs, which she so abhorred. She now began to see my sister not only as black but as a social activist. Allport noted that when minority groups embrace political action, they are viewed as militant, as troublemakers or agitators. Joan now became susceptible to Felicia in her social loadings as radical, perhaps even irrational and angry.

Of course, most of us don't talk about race and share our thoughts and perceptions in this manner. In fact, Joan, Felicia, and I, like most people, avoid talking about race in casual conversations because these conversations can be extremely discomforting. Recall how my mom quickly changed the conversation and all of us were relieved. These kinds of situations happen repeatedly and routinely across racial lines. Among cross-racial friends lacking the competencies to manage all of the negative social loadings in an efficient and productive manner, we unwittingly reinforce that race is a taboo topic for discussion, particularly if we value the relationship. Yet, where there is discomfort there is learning, if we stay with the discomfort long enough. That is the value of talking about race across racial lines with trusted friends.

This dynamic is further explained by the formation of in-group loyalties (in this case, blacks vs. whites) explored by Allport. In addition, the work of many social psychologists building on Allport's research helps us to understand how the intersection of "capital P" and "small p" politics plays out in cross-racial friendships.

Here is how it works: Because of the visibility of race in our skin color, our hair texture, the size of lips and nose, and other racial identifying features, people of color evoke different reactions from the world. When I walk in the room, people see a black woman and are automatically loaded with social information that may or may not fit for me. What race evokes from the world influences our thinking, behavior, and decisions, particularly about politics, how power and governance affect us. It is as if a different data set gets uploaded in us depending on our race and, as a result, we download different reactions. I uploaded data from my parents, a file that is now permanently on my hard drive and which includes a deep understanding of America's diversity rooted in their immigrant status and an appreciation for the role of government in creating programs that stabilize our society with jobs and education regardless of cultural background. I personally uploaded a deep desire to have a chorus of all voices contributing to the creation of a new reality that works for all and a belief that equal access to healthcare and educational opportunities would result in a stable society. I am an independent voter who espouses progressive ideologies and who leans almost always with the Democratic Party.

Joan got data uploaded from her parents as business owners, now placed on her hard drive, on the need for a limited role for government and a concern for fiscal responsibility and sensible budgeting that spurs businesses and innovation. Joan personally uploaded an emphasis on religious liberty and deep concern for life from womb to the tomb. She leans toward the Libertarian Party but has always been positioned as Republican.

You would think that there would be plenty of common ground between Joan's and my political ideologies as we are both somewhat conservative in our personal behaviors and far more liberal in our thinking. Yet, race tips that balance every time. As a black woman, I am firmly positioned with Black Lives Matter. As a white woman with family who are police officers, Joan positions herself in almost every case of a shooting of an unarmed black man with the police officer. Our conversations help us to understand both sides better, but our understanding does not change our voting patterns. We could worship together, enjoy brunch on a beautiful fall day, and share a history spanning decades, but our vote would be filtered through a racial lens.

Joan, like all white Americans, enjoys racial social privilege and the freedom of choice that comes with it. They can vote for issues and candidates in support of their personal beliefs that can further their position of social advantage in the world. I, like most people of color, who do not have racial social privilege, feel compelled to vote for issues and candidates who will not further disadvantage our social position in the United States.

For example, the economy continues to be one of the top voting issues for all Americans, and treatment of racial minorities ranks toward the bottom of voting priorities.[8] White American voters can afford to vote for a candidate who they believe will strengthen the economy, even if that candidate holds racist beliefs, as they will experience little or no personal consequences as a result of that vote. Whites can disassociate themselves from that aspect of the candidate's ideology while maintaining their personal egalitarian beliefs and positive intentions to work toward eradicating racism. Whites can put aside the candidate's racist beliefs or even dismiss them as a mischaracterization by the media. Whites can even affirm the candidate's racist beliefs as justified. Whites have lots of options on how they can vote for a candidate who will advance their top voting priority and still maintain psychological integrity.

Voters of color, on the other hand, presented with a candidate who promises an improved economy yet espouses racist beliefs, are faced with risking the everyday and long-term physical and psychological effects of being targeted by racist ideologies.[9] We may benefit financially from the improved economy but at great personal cost to the quality of our lives. We may suffer an increase in microaggressions, the everyday public verbal and non-verbal slights based on minority group membership. We can be subjected to questions and assumptions about one's American identity. Hiring and promoting practices of underrepresented racial groups in organizations can be criticized as unnecessary affirmative action. Utilizing minority-owned businesses can be denied due to the perception of substandard work. Our children can be subject to disproportionate discipline in schools and biased curriculum choices. For people of color, there is a lot of risk for not considering a candidate's racist ideology in voting. All politics is local, and stem from small-p politics.

The job of the interviewer as a qualitative researcher, is to not only be comfortable with the questions and make sure they are clear, concise, and relatable, but to make the interviewee comfortable with the process in order to solicit candid responses rather than socially approved answers. Great interviewers like Oprah Winfrey balance their own vulnerability with objectivity, which leads to deeper conversation and new insights. That is what I tried to achieve when I interviewed Derek Black.

I had never spoken with someone associated with white nationalism before, and I wanted to make sure I balanced my feelings while remaining objective. I also wanted to make sure that he was comfortable enough talking to a black woman to be honest and open. I heard about Derek's talk at the Nantucket Project from my good friend Jill. She and I share the big, audacious goal of eliminating racism, anti-Semitism, and bigotry in the world. We have animated conversations, share books and articles on how to do this, and challenge ourselves to be inclusive in our behavior and thinking. Jill eagerly shared what she had learned from Derek's talk at the Nantucket Project. The Nantucket Project "brings fresh ideas to curious audiences in live talks, short original films and unforgettable experiences," such as Black speaking about his journey from being a staunch white nationalist to rejecting its tenets.[10]

I had read Derek's op-ed piece in the *New York Times*, "What White Nationalism Gets Right About American History," and the article on his exit from white nationalism in the *Washington Post*.[11] And now I had the opportunity to interview him to discuss how his friendships had helped to change his beliefs about race.

Derek Black is the son of Don Black, the creator of Stormfront, an online news site and "voice of the new, embattled white minority."[12] The website is "a community of racial realists and idealists" and the largest white nationalist website, which claimed more than three hundred thousand users in 2015.[13] His mother, Chloe Black, was married to the white supremacist David Duke, who is Derek's godfather. Derek's roots in white nationalism are deep and he actively professed and advocated for these principles along with his family all of his life. As a young adult he was considered the "future of white nationalism."[14] That is what makes it so remarkable that his thinking changed through his friendships with diverse friends that he met as an undergraduate student in a liberal arts college.

To be clear, it wasn't friends of color who changed Derek's thinking. He explains to me that he "put more weight" on the opinions of those who disagreed with him who were not affected by his ideology. "My ideology doesn't have anything to say about white people. So when you challenge what I have to say, I have to take it on a more neutral playing field."[15]

Ostracized on campus after he was "outed" while away at a conference, Derek credits his friend Matthew, who invited him to Shabbat dinner, for reaching out and including him. Matthew had regularly invited a diverse group of his friends to Shabbat dinner, some of whom at first refused to come when they found out that Derek would be there. "It took like eight people in general to be like no, we are not affected by what you are saying and we think it's totally wrong."

The extended-contact effect is at play here. This theory, born out of contact theory research, hypothesizes that knowing that a member of your social identity group has a positive relationship with a member of an out-group can lead to more positive attitudes toward that out-group.[16] In other words, whites who have cross-racial friends can influence other white friends to have less negative attitudes toward people of color. This was the case with Derek Black. If he had only heard arguments against white nationalism from Matthew, who is Jewish, or from people of color, it would not have influenced him as much. Derek tells me, "It's significant that white nationalists don't think that Jews are white, and Matthew knew that, so him inviting me to Shabbat was a significant act." Yet, what was even more significant was that Matthew had white friends along with his friends of color who disagreed with his thinking. This was the catalyst and the bridge to thinking more about the effect on Jews and people of color.

"My friend Juan and several people of color who I hung out with, I think were conscious that, like Matthew, they were demonstrating by their presence that ideas of racial separation weren't abstract. White nationalism meant removing them, real people, from these spaces. I know that that can't have been easy for them to do, but it was a very significant context to me, engaging with arguments against white nationalism with more sincerity then I had done before," says Derek.

In 2008, Derek Black made an impassioned speech to a white nationalist group in Memphis about the future of their ideology. "The Republican Party has to be either demolished or taken over," he said. "I'm kind of banking on the Republicans staking their claim as the white party."[17]

At that time, Derek honestly did not perceive anything wrong in an ideology of racial separation. He was particularly confused about why people of color would fear him for what was, after all, an ideology. He didn't wish harm to any person of color; he just wanted the races to live separately.

"I found out that one of the Jewish student life groups had a meeting on campus when they found out I was there," he says. "They didn't want to be in the same room together and I was horrified by it. And I wrote a short piece to the campus community on my opinions and why they shouldn't be afraid of me. So, I wanted to convey that my ideas were not a threat to the well-being of their community."

Five years later, through his contact with friends who challenged his thinking, he had radically changed that position. "I think I wrote in my original letter in 2013 denouncing white nationalism that I couldn't get my head around chatting with an African American friend about their summer plans, but simultaneously advocating for an ideology that thought it would be better if they weren't in the country."

Although white nationalism is considered a fringe movement, Derek explains to me that monoracial environments are the way our society functions. As Americans, we interact in pretty much a version of racial separatism most of the time. White nationalism is born out of that culture, and on even the most subtle level many whites buy into it.

"White nationalists' thinking is that they want everybody to be separated so therefore everywhere should be monoracial. Lots of people buy into it on some level. Black neighborhoods are dangerous and blacks are more likely to commit crimes. These are ideas a lot of people buy into on some level, even if they think it's so unfortunate that this is happening to blacks. They want to be a sympathetic liberal, but those are the exact same arguments they use to make the case for white nationalism. On some level, they believe that white people are the most normal group in America and the most stable and the most liked and who [are] more homogenous."

What is scary is that Derek tells me these ideas are so prevalent among whites that it makes it very easy for whites to make the leap to white nationalism, even if they do not do it consciously or formally join a white nationalist group. In fact, he discussed with me how easy it is to travel and interact in all white environments, making it challenging to have friends across racial lines. The enrollment in his undergraduate college was 90 percent white, as is the institution where he is a history doctoral student.

"The fundamental thing that white nationalists want is for everybody in the room to be white. And there are so many settings that qualify for that, whether it is my graduate program or the [Universalist] church. I know a lot of affluent white nationalist leaders who would find a way to speak to these groups just because of who is in the room."

After our interview, I sat for a long time just taking in what Derek had shared, especially the last part, where he responded to my question about how we might change the direction our society was headed in terms of race relations.

"The only way you can undermine white nationalism is by changing the thing that drives American society," he said. "You cannot have these rooms where everybody in them is white."

I sit in a lot of rooms where everybody, with the exception of me, is white. As a chief diversity officer, I am there to remind my colleagues that people of color do exist and that it is all of our jobs to increase diversity. I am there to integrate diversity into our mission and business practice, to make it "go plaid," as I like to say.[18] Organizations pay a lot of attention to this and work hard to achieve diverse workforces, but after work hours, we go into our separate societal rooms, which in the long run makes it even harder to achieve business goals.

I am struck by Derek's account of his genuine surprise that people would be afraid of him because of an ideology. It provides me with insight as I compare his surprise to the feeling of amazement that I have when white friends fear blacks and browns and believe them to be militant when they are in advocacy mode for racial justice. It makes little sense, for in Derek's case, fearing white nationalism is rational as that ideology has led to violence and death as recently as the Charleston church massacre and the Charlottesville protests.

Advocacy by blacks and browns for racial justice has led to inflamed cultural wars used by politicians to incite more fear in white Americans. Claims that assert the moral equivalence of whites' fear of people of color to people of color's fear of whites further establishes a racial and political divide. These fears drive how we translate small p into capital P with our vote.

Here's the scariest part of it all. Before we sit in shock of white nationalism or to those who listen to black and brown advocacy and label them as militant, recall how the brain works when managing differences and how we go into fight or flight response. Recall Gordon Allport's research, over sixty years ago, naming our propensity for prejudice and demonstrating how victims of oppression operate and how they are labeled as troublemakers or agitators. Recall Allport's recommendation that equal-status relationships are likely to make for increased tolerance. Recall the research that states that most Americans do not have friends who cross racial lines. Recall Derek Black's experience and firsthand knowledge that the capacity for whites to be white nationalists is rooted in our society and reinforced by our all-white environments. Recall the power of extending oneself in friendship evidenced by Derek's friend Matthew and, by extension, all of his diverse friends. Then examine your own patterns of friendships.

Catherine Epstein is the 2017 recipient of the Facing History and Ourselves Margot Stern Strom Innovation Grant for educators who "think out of the box, solve problems and inspire students."[19] Catherine is a white woman who teaches eleven- to thirteen-year-olds in a private school in Massachusetts and noted that her students made "sweeping and negative generalizations about people who are politically different than themselves." In her case, that meant Republicans or conservatives or Southerners. Catherine knew that people in other parts of the country were making "sweeping, negative, and dangerous assumptions about people like my students, some of whom are Muslim, some of whom have gay or lesbian parents, some of whom are first-generation Americans and some of whom are transgender." She wondered how she could help her students get beyond rejection and fundamental disinterest or lack of curiosity about each other.

Inspired by the radio program *On Being*'s "Pro-Life, Pro-Choice, Pro-Dialogue," which featured a conversation about abortion between pro-life Christian ethicist David Gushee and reproductive rights activist Frances Kissling, Catherine conceived of the Correspondence Project with the same aim for coming together not to change opinions on controversial topics, but from changing our perspectives about each other. Gushee and Kissling were asked why they kept talking to each other when they never actually reached common ground. Gushee's response was that it "reminded him that she [Kissling] was a human being."[20]

Catherine's Correspondence Project creates tangible engagement between students on different ends of the political spectrum who exchange letters over the course of one school year. Through a Facebook invitation reaching out to teachers in conservative regions, she became connected with a junior high teacher in a "very rural, ultra conservative public school in Arkansas." On Catherine's visit to the town, on her drive from Little Rock Airport heading west, she stopped in Plumerville for a drink. Catherine recalls that "hanging from the ceiling were two T-shirts for sale: one said 'I was deplorable before deplorables were cool' and the other featured a map of the US with the states shaded blue or red based on how they voted in 2016. At the top, large text read 'Deplorable Lives Matter.'"[21] In that moment Catherine faced the fundamental challenge of the project. "As much as I love and believe in the idea of generating dialogue across difference, as I looked up at the T-shirts hung from the ceiling, I felt alienation, because their presence seemed to assume that everyone who passed through would agree."

Her partnership with her fellow teacher from Arkansas has been "a real gift," allowing her to talk with someone who "shared a desire to make our communities more curious about each other." Together, they carefully planned the project, setting norms and using best practices for creating dialogue across differences. They decided to ground each month's letter that the students would exchange in a particular topic, providing trigger questions for them to write about. On patriotism: "What do you think it means to be an American?" On politics: "What cause would get you into the streets for a protest?"

They began with letters as an intentional way to slow students down and to create a material connection between the sender and the receiver. The two teachers also participated in the letter writing, which began with answering, What assumptions do you think others might make about you? Before the students opened their first letters from Arkansas, Catherine read her first letter from the Arkansas teacher. In it, she wrote:

> Being from the South and Arkansas, people make lots of assumptions about me. Because I have a Southern accent, people think that I am dumb. Since our school wears Hillbilly mascot t-shirts, people think we are backward and slow. I do not think that I am any of these things, and it hurts my feelings that people have these prejudices.

Catherine notes that "in many of my students' first letters to Arkansas, they wrote, 'I know this might sound stupid, but what's a hillbilly?'"

Their letters have served to humanize the students to one another through an ongoing correspondence about both their daily lives and their perspectives on the world. They have cultivated a long-term dialogue between two teachers and students who might not otherwise thoughtfully engage with one another. It is also helping them come to a more nuanced understanding about political difference and to make a few friends along the way.

––––––––

When faced with diversity, we may start off with the involuntary process of fight or flight but we can choose to stay, learn, and grow. It is a tough process, because to have the smaller letter p influence the capital letter P requires us to have diversity in our lives through friendships and then move into the bigger political tent together.

Cheryl, an administrator who is black, shares in a focus group the experience of working closely with a group of white women in a school system. Although they never had a political conversation, she assumed they were Democrats. "They were so friendly, interested in getting to know me and my family, and we prayed together, did Bible study together. They gave me lists of people to pray for on our prayer calls. But amazingly, when it came to the 2016 election, I found out that they were Republicans and their whole family lines were Republicans. It's all they knew. I know this sounds crazy, and it falls true for many of us too. Our parents were Democrats and that is all we know. It is astounding to me and truly a rude awakening, and very backwards thinking to make those kinds of assumptions, I admit."

David, an executive director of an arts institute who is black, says he has a very diverse group of friends. "I grew up having Asian friends, and Jewish friends, and Mormon friends. And all my life I've had these friends from Tennessee, and in December came together with some of these buddies of mine and I know they voted for Trump, and so we are sitting at the bar, and one of the guys who said he was more liberal than the other guys asked, 'Oh, David, how was it growing up in Tennessee?' One of my most conservative friends said, 'Oh, I'm sure it was fine.' I said, 'You have no frickin' idea.' Here was a moment to talk about this. We were just happy that we were together. But I said, 'Let's talk about this.' We have to have the courage and the bravery and the vulnerability to actually invite this kind of conversation. It is incumbent on all of us."

In 2016, the word of the year, as designated by the Oxford Dictionaries, was "post-truth"—an adjective defined as "relating to or denoting circumstances in which objective facts are less influential in shaping public opinion than appeals to emotion and personal belief."[22] When we live in racially segregated environments and socialize in segregated settings, get information filtered through news media aligned with our interpretation and then add racial distrust, that becomes a perfect formula for a separatist society. *Fox & Friends* cable news program consistently ranks as number one in viewers, though reportedly only 1 percent of those viewers are black and the percentage of other viewers of color is most likely as low.[23] With the lack of diversity in its viewership and in its staff representation, the news program sets up the kind of all-white environment that Derek Black observes easily lead to white nationalist beliefs. Getting information from trusted, fact-checked media sources, interacting with diverse friends, and exercising multicultural competences is a formula for democracy.

However, America's democracy is characterized by a duality around race that has existed since its founding. As Thomas Jefferson penned his signature to the Declaration of Independence proclaiming that "all men are created equal," he owned and sold hundreds of slaves, some of whom were his own children.[24] In addition, America is a nation of immigrants with racial diversity as a core part of our identity. Our borders hold the Statue of Liberty, a gift of friendship from the people of France and a symbol of "liberty enlightening the world." The statue stands as a welcome sight for immigrants amidst increasing xenophobia and echoes of "build the wall" chants from the 2016 presidential election cycle. It is also symbolic of freedom and America's diversity. Cross-racial friendships as equal-status relationships entered into freely by the individuals give witness to our attempt to resolve the duality of America as both racist in its practice and postracial in its aspirations.

Democracy is predicated upon diversity under the big tent. It comes with relationships across different social identity groups that allow for gentle bumping and learning from each other in an effort to resolve that duality. That struggle firmly grounds us in reality that can be challenging to navigate but that leads to assurance that we can create the kind of society that we all want and can live in. Without this diversity, we maintain a separatist society and one where we live in fear of each other.

Jane, who is white, and Dolores, who is black, have been friends for over twenty years. Despite their twenty-year age difference, they have a lot in common. They share a love of the arts and sing together in choirs and just for the pure joy of hearing their voices together. They have influenced each other's thinking and behavior about race. "I don't watch the news without seeing it through her eyes as well," Jane said. "I used to fear walking in the room where I was the only black person there," Dolores said. Being close friends has not made it all easier. In fact, they speak to the complexity of the relationship. "It's always layered; there's no simple answer to race and its impact on politics," said Jane. "Yet understanding it is easier to do, because with friends across racial lines you become more fearless."

Chapter 12

SOME OF MY FRIENDS ARE...

In my previous book, *Racing Across the Lines: Changing Race Relations Through Friendships*, I began each chapter by describing a conversation with my close friend Yvonne Sims.[1] These conversations became the catalyst for my now decades-long research into adult cross-racial friendship patterns. Much to my surprise, for many readers, these chapter introductions were their favorite parts of the book. It was because the conversations testified to the nature of true friendship. In my research, I was so immersed in the challenges and benefits of cross-racial friendships that I had given little thought to the inherent challenges of and general lack of knowledge about maintaining and nurturing friendships in general.

Friendship expert Shasta Nelson coined the term "frientimacy," defining it as "the experience of a meaningful friendship; a heartfelt, supportive closeness among friends. In her book *Frientimacy: How to Deepen Friendships for Lifelong Health and Happiness*, she outlines steps for addressing the intimacy gap found in most friendships. Nelson adds her work to a body of research that demonstrates a strong correlation between well-being, quality of life, and strong social relationships."[2] Her work posits three requirements for a healthy mutual friendship: positivity, consistency, and vulnerability. Achieving these three requirements is challenging enough. When racial differences are thrown into the equation, it creates a dynamic that imbalances the relationship.

Research demonstrates that cross-racial friendships reduce prejudice, particularly for whites.[3] However, the potential for cross-racial friendships to reduce the impact of white privilege and unconscious bias toward people of color depends on the nature of the relationship. Not every cross-racial friendship addresses the challenges fostered by institutional racism and white privilege in a beneficial manner. My research over many years has led me to define five kinds of cross-racial friendships: bubble friends, fantasy friends, calendar friends, fellowship friends, and heart friends.

Bubble cross-racial friends set up an experience of racial utopia that they live in and then defend to others. The denial of racial inequities allows persons of color and whites with similar sensibilities to enter cross-racial friendships with ease. As "postracialists," they agree that racial disparity exists but attribute its cause to individual attributes such as ignorance, laziness, and/or immoral behavior. They are color-blind and assimilationist in their thinking, focusing more on the promise of a benevolent and just America than on its speckled history of racism and discrimination against people of color. As a result, bubble friends dismiss racial inequalities in everything from wealth to health.

During a presentation in August 2017 at the National Association of Black Journalists Conference in New Orleans, Omarosa Manigault, then an assistant to President Trump, responded to a question about Trump's policies, defending her position: "I sit at a table where I am not only the only African American woman, but the only African American at all," she said, dismissing the previous questions about her community service. "If you're not at the table, you're on the menu."[4]

Omarosa's former role in the White House in a nebulous communications position was largely perceived to be a reward for her deep loyalty to and friendship with Trump, stemming from her antagonist role over a decade before in his reality television show *The Apprentice*. Although she now claims opposing views from Trump's, she continues to be ridiculed on social media for reinforcing Trump's postracialist views and thus furthering racist ideas. As Ibram X. Kendi writes in the National Book Award winner *Stamped from the Beginning*, "If the purpose of racist ideas had always been to silence the antiracist resisters to racial discrimination, then the postracial line of attack may have been the most sophisticated silencer to date."[5]

This is what makes bubble friends so dangerous for positive race relations. Unlike fantasy and calendar friends, who at least give witness to the goals of racial equality, bubble friends promote propaganda of a racial utopia and attribute racist attitudes and behaviors to individuals rather than institutional policies, practices, and structures.

Bubble cross-racial friends are tokens for each other, allowing each friend to deflect any accusations or claims of racial discrimination. As tokens, persons of color get the benefit of believing there is no difference between members of the dominant race and themselves. Whites give themselves a get-out-of-jail-free card by having a person of color they can claim as a close friend.

Fantasy cross-racial friendships exist for both people of color and whites. Many adults endorse having friends of different races and then when pressed for specifics on those friendships conjure up the person who sat next to them in a high school English class, or a coworker who is on the same United Way team, or the family who sits a couple of pews in front of them in their church whose names they don't know, or the neighbor who lives on their street whom they know only as the "Pomeranian dog's mom."

We claim fantasy friendships because we intuitively understand that having a diverse group of friends is a socially warranted and morally enlightened response in a global society. We perceive ourselves as holding egalitarian attitudes that do not prevent us from crossing racial lines in friendships, and when questioned about our own friendships will quickly catalog our history, searching for confirmation. Respondents to our friendship surveys from across the nation have acknowledged that the survey questions caused them to examine their friendship patterns and the assumptions they had made about the racial composition of their own friendship lists.

Because fantasy friendships involve very little contact and particularly no depth or intimacy, they perpetuate the myth of a color-blind society where positivity exists and serves as a necessary and sufficient requirement for advancing race relations. The election of Barack Obama reinforced this fantasy and the belief in a postracial society.

Living the fantasy has some benefits. It promotes tolerance and supports the premise that not only is it okay to have friends across racial lines but that almost everybody does, or would if they could. It assumes that if you live in a segregated area and never socialize in mixed-race groups, this is simply the by-product of making choices for safe neighborhoods, better schools, and community services that enhance one's quality of life.

It makes the assumption that there is a level playing field and that everyone wants these by-products but that there are outside forces that prevent these conditions for everyone.

Barb, a white woman, noted that as she listened to others in the focus group talk about their interracial friendships that she had "nothing from which to pull," citing her Catholic school experience and white neighborhoods as leaving her without any history of cross-racial socializing. She could talk with great excitement about a friend of a different race on social media. "I wished she lived [in Cleveland] so we could take the friendship to the next level," she says, "because she is everything I would look for in a friend. She is intelligent. We have the same interests. She has answered all of my blogging questions even though I am sure many of them are very stupid, and she patiently answers them."

One problem with having fantasy cross-racial friends is that fantasies live in our imagination and are often impossible or improbable realities. When we honestly examine our friendship patterns and come to understand that our friends of a different race may be just fantasy friends, it offers an opportunity for growth and renewing our commitment to diversity.

Shortly after the launch of one of our friendship surveys, I received an email from a respondent. She thanked me for doing "this important work" but went on to tell me that taking the survey made her "very sad" because she realized any cross-racial friends that she thought she had, she rarely saw. And a close friendship that she did have with a black woman was one where she had not seen that person in over ten years. As a university professor she "felt good about having mentored a few black women with whom I maintain warm relations, but these are not peer relations—the kind that seems to be what you are asking about, and what I don't have."

The beauty of this kind of insight about any fantasy cross-racial friends is that it can lead us to change that pattern if we choose to reach out, renew former acquaintances, or establish new friendships across racial lines. Even if we choose not to bring fantasy friends to reality or no longer have the opportunity to do so, fantasy friends do allow us to put a positive tag on having cross-racial friendships and provide a glimmer of hope for a different future if we so choose to move in that direction.

Calendar cross-racial friends are those who are generally part of a group of friends connected by shared experiences that are typically recreational. I call them calendar friends because they aren't the friends you would call at 3:00 a.m. in a crisis, but movie buddies, foodie groups who restaurant hop, church members who participate in social justice and charitable activities, or coworkers who regularly eat lunch together. Calendar friends operate with the expressed philosophy that racial differences do not matter. They function with an emphasis on race sameness. Instead of being blind to race, they deny that race even exists: "We are all human beings." "We are all Americans." "We all put our pants on the same way." "We all have red blood inside." The denial of racial heritage and the historical impact and variance in the experience of American dreams and ideals are forever strong in these cross-racial friendships. While interacting these friends avoid race talk or assume it is not necessary. The friendship of Charlotte and Patricia is an example.

Charlotte, a white woman, and Patricia, a black woman, get together once a month for dinner, choosing a different restaurant every time, as they both love to dine out even though they both struggle with their weight.[6] Over the years, their families had shared a number of social events and even visited in each other's homes. Their fathers had been coworkers in the same company for over thirty years, and in their final years before retirement found themselves fast friends. When Patricia's dad passed weeks after he retired, it was Charlotte's dad, having been a human resources executive at the company, who organized an outpouring of support from the company and helped Patricia's mom navigate a messy retirement-benefit situation to assure her financial security. Years later, Patricia's mom remained forever grateful to Charlotte's family and thought of them as dear friends.

When Charlotte and Patricia found themselves in the same city due to work relocation and with no established friends, they committed to finding an evening on their busy calendars to get together once a month for dinner. It was an enjoyable experience for them both for many months, until race entered the conversation.

Patricia described the experience to me as "the Last Supper." During a meal in the city's only authentic Vietnamese restaurant, they chatted about family, work stress, and their most recent weight losses. Then

Charlotte brought up a conversation she'd had with an elderly black woman whom she helped at church, who "got really mad at me when I said this." She paused and looked at Patricia as if suddenly realizing her friend's racial identity. "You probably will too," she said, "but I am going to say it anyway."

She went on to give her views on the controversy surrounding Colin Kaepernick and other NFL players who took a knee during the singing of the national anthem in protest of police brutality and discrimination against blacks, which sparked a national outcry as well as national support. Charlotte believed the football players had a right to kneel, but that it was wrong for them to do so, and not the way for them to get their message across. It was an opinion that Patricia understood, and she mentioned an article she had just read that morning by *New York Times* opinion writer David Leonhardt, "The Choice Between Kneeling and Winning."[7] In citing the article and another op-ed piece by Charles Blow, "Divert, Divide, Destroy,"Patricia thought she would finally be having a meaningful conversation about race, a topic that had been forefront in her mind since the election of Donald Trump.[8] She knew Charlotte was not a Trump supporter and assumed that she, being an intelligent, caring, generous person, would understand the complexity of the situation.

"What I got was a heavy dose of white fragility in action," Patricia tells me. "We both saw taking a knee through our racial lens. She kept saying it was wrong and unpatriotic. Patriotism to her was supporting your country all the time despite how it treats you. She didn't want to acknowledge that we have laws that disadvantage black people and a criminal justice system that profiles you if you are black."

It was a conversation that Patricia described as "uncomfortable for both of us." From Patricia's perspective, the conversation was witnessing white privilege in action. Charlotte had wanted to switch the topic and not discuss race ever again at their dinners. "Let's just have fun" was how she phrased it to Patricia. "We don't need to talk about race." This statement infuriated Patricia, as she did not feel that she had the luxury of putting race aside. "When we left dinner we were not sure if there would ever be another dinner together. She knew that I was very upset and I could tell that she was upset. Race was just a topic for her when for me it was my lived experience. I can't run away from race."

Over time, Patricia decided that Charlotte's role in her family's history was worth preserving, at least for her mother's sake. She privately decided not to talk about racially charged topics with Charlotte. In doing so, she felt that she was compromising a bit of herself by cutting off a significant part of her identity expression whenever she met with Charlotte. She knew that relationship would never be the same and that Charlotte would be "a friend on my calendar to share dinner with on a monthly basis."

When both individuals involved in the relationship share the same status in their racial-identity resolution, calendar cross-racial friendships generally do not disrupt the trajectory toward positive race relations in society. Like fantasy friends, they promote a healthy level of tolerance and genuine acceptance. Like fantasy friends, they allow the friends to put positive tags on others who do not share their race. However, unlike fantasy friends, calendar friends are real. If one party in the dyad moves out of racial encapsulation to venture into an exploration of how race impacts the respective worldviews in the relationship, tension is the inevitable result. In the case of Patricia and Charlotte, there's a high probability that their friendship will fade over time for many reasons. The friendship was rooted in family history rather than shared interests and complementary personalities. With this weak foundation and lacking the capacity to have meaningful conversations about race, the relationship becomes static and, as a result, fertile ground for unconscious biases and microaggressions to take root.

Patricia, with heightened awareness of Charlotte's whiteness and its associated privilege, begins to create an emotional relationship triangle by including a third party (typically another same-race friend) used to debrief and process challenging racial encounters, now that her friendship with Charlotte has that boundary and they are not able to talk about race directly. These debriefing conversations begin something like this:

"Girl, you won't believe what she said . . . I had to bite my tongue."

"I had to resist taking her to school on what she said . . ."

"She's such a nice person, but like most white people, she just doesn't get it."

Charlotte, with heightened awareness of Patricia's race as black, goes into "fight or flight" mode. She experiences a physiological reaction whenever she interacts with Patricia within the context of black culture. The reaction makes her psychologically uncomfortable and Patricia's behaviors then get translated as a threat. It can be as simple as Patricia using a slang term that Charlotte is not familiar with or talking about a movie, book, or song that is popular among blacks that causes Charlotte's muscles to tense. It might be the way that Patricia freely laughs and embraces a black friend that they run into when Patricia and Charlotte are out together that causes Charlotte to feel uneasy. Now attuned to the subtle racial differences between her and her friend, Charlotte feels like a racial outsider—something she is not accustomed to feeling. She works to keep both the social loadings of stereotypes about blacks and stereotypic thinking at bay and not "mess up" when speaking to Patricia. This thinking causes Charlotte anxiety and reinforces her implicit belief that blacks are overly sensitive and keep "the race thing" going simply by wanting to talk about it all the time. Charlotte remains confused about Patricia's feelings of racial discrimination. Patricia holds a much better job with a much higher salary than Charlotte's. Patricia travels freely and socializes with a much wealthier crowd than Charlotte could ever imagine socializing with. Charlotte wonders how all of this access and inclusion translates into racial discrimination.

Understandably, this is a hard concept to grasp. Unfortunately, Charlotte and Patricia's relationship, as is typical with calendar friends, does not support transformational conversations during which they can explore this question within the parameters of a trusted friendship.

For middle- and upper-class people of color, the experience of racial discrimination often stems not from being treated badly but from the unequal distribution of the benefits resulting from white privilege. This can be a hard concept to grasp. It is what author and longtime *Newsweek* contributor and editor Ellis Cose calls the "rage of a privileged class."[9]

Over time, Patricia and Charlotte's friendship becomes exhausting for both of them. In general, calendar friends pose the risk of reinforcing stereotypes and widening the racial divide. Since the commitment level of these kinds of friendships is only a deleted calendar event away, they offer little promise of a brighter future for race relations. Yet many people maintain them. They offer the positivity and consistency of friendship without the risk of vulnerability. As one focus group participant stated, cross-racial friends allow you to "grab a quick nugget of happiness and then keep moving before it disappears."

Fellowship cross-racial friends have the capacity to sustain those "nuggets of happiness" even while navigating society's racial divide. Fellowship friendships are forged across racial lines by people working on mutual goals for social justice, achieving a mission, or meeting business objectives. The relationship is formed on the basis of shared goals and frequent contact in working together toward those goals. The level of vulnerability varies depending on the extent to which the relationship enters into the personal or private domain. Shasta Nelson states that "vulnerability, in its healthiest form, is incremental, thoughtful, and predicated on commitment. It is a two-way street paved by both positivity and the trust we feel from the track record of consistency."[10]

Many survey respondents and focus group participants described these kinds of cross-racial friendships in their lives. They regularly see these friends at work, church, or civic meetings. They spend many hours on work teams, planning church fund-raisers, and campaigning for candidates, volunteering for benefit dinners, or at committee meetings to advance a variety of causes.

One interviewee tells me, "I talk to these two women from my church a lot and even share personal things . . . but not necessarily private things that I would with my close friend. Yet they are important to me."

Fellowship cross-racial friends are important not only to the individuals involved but to closing the racial divide. Fellowship friends differ from friends of the heart only in that the commitment is external to the parties rather than between them, the depth and continuity of the relationship depends on the level of engagement in the shared goal, and vulnerability is optional. Once the shared experience disappears, the friendship is changed or diminished. However, "emotional contagion" often results from these relationships, which extends long after the friendship ends.

Group emotional contagion, or the transfer of moods among people in a group, has been researched by psychologists for decades under a number of social and professional settings.[11] What we know about how emotional contagion works is that there is a significant influence and exchange of emotions within group behavior. These emotional packages are given to one another either consciously or unconsciously.

Stacey, a fifty-three-year-old black focus group participant in New York City, provides a good example: "So, I have a good friend from college and she's Asian. An incident happened where some advertising was done by a big corporation that depicted Asians in a poor light. And I didn't see it and other people noticed. And she got upset about it. So, I didn't realize until I saw her upset. It didn't even dawn on me that, yes, I knew she was Asian, but I didn't realize that she would have that reaction, and it made me a little more sensitive to people of other races. I was more sensitive and more aware, and even though I'm black and I know things happen, but I just lumped everyone together until things happened to close friends of mine. It's like okay, they have problems now and now I'm more tuned in and I'm offended by it."

The positivity derived from fellowship cross-racial friendships leads to improved cooperation, increased understanding between races, and, by extension, reduced racial conflict. Often, the bonds of these friendships continue beyond the work commitment, beyond the fund-raiser, beyond the election cycle.

Ernest "Rip" Patton participated in the first sit-ins in Nashville, Tennessee, and in 1961 was one of the twenty-seven Freedom Riders whose bus made it to Jackson, Mississippi, where they were arrested for entering a "whites only" Greyhound bus station waiting room. A twenty-one-year-old music major at Tennessee State University, he was an active member of the Student Nonviolent Coordinating Committee (SNCC). The first twenty-seven Freedom Riders, who included Congressman John Lewis, were arrested and ultimately sent to Parchman Penitentiary in Raymond, Mississippi, after weeks in the city and county jail. Now, at seventy-seven years old, Rip Patton's memories are still strong and kept alive through his work as a civil rights activist.

Dr. Patton describes how during his incarceration, the prison guards did everything they could to break the activists' spirits—putting the heat on during blisteringly hot days, freezing them out with air conditioning at night, putting stool softeners in their food, taking away their thin mattresses. Still, through it all they sang parodies of familiar gospel songs to communicate with one another and maintain solidarity.

At Parchman Penitentiary they were segregated. "They had all black males in one section, all white males in one section, all white females in one, and all black females in another," Dr. Patton explains to me during our interview. "And we would put our heads against the wall and start singing a song which would mean, 'We are okay over here.' And then we would listen and the black women would get their mouths against the wall and they would sing so that everyone knew they were okay . . . and then the white men and white women. I don't remember all the words but it was to a song that went, 'I know we'll meet again. I know, I know we'll meet again.'" He sings the line in his rich baritone voice.[12]

The struggle for racial equity continues, and as cross-racial friends we continue to meet again and again in that fight. Relationships between people of color and whites struggling together for racial equality and social harmony are the foundation for the "beloved community" Dr. Martin Luther King fostered and promoted. Dr. King described the beloved community as the end product of reconciliation and redemption. We create a beloved community through cross-racial fellowship, friendships allowing us to expand our vision and our dreams. We create a beloved community when we imagine and create. The work of imagining and creating is best done in community with cross-racial fellowship. In that beloved community we are joined with other imaginers, creators, and dreamers. The more widely spread imagination, creativity, and dreaming are, the better the society we create. These friendships hold great promise for galvanizing racial unity. Yet we can go deeper.

———

Heart cross-racial friendships support lessening the divide by removing the deep structures of bias through trust. Characterized by depth or intimacy, these friends are able to acknowledge each other in their full racial identity while appreciating and respecting differences. With this foundation they are able to have meaningful, challenging conversations about race. The three frientimacy requirements: positivity, consistency, and vulnerability are embedded in the relationship breaking the boundaries caused by ethnocentrism and racial myopia.

Being vulnerable makes them different from cross-racial calendar friends, who may be tolerant and caring but carefully keep race at bay. Being committed to each other absent an external cause is what makes them different than cross-racial fellowship friends. Cross-racial friends of the heart are open and vulnerable, allowing the traces of institutional racism and the impact of everyday racism to enter into their relationship as part of their lived reality. They manage and risk the anxiety that comes when they step into stereotypes, unintentional microaggressions, and attitudes and behaviors stemming from unconscious bias. They are emotionally resilient and able to adapt to change because their security in the relationship is in knowing that the relationship fosters a natural discomfort given the external realities they inevitably face in a racially charged society. They turn that discomfort into a creative tension, which fuels their activism. Sometimes it is a silent personal activism witnessed and experienced only among each other and others in their friendship circle. The relationship influences their voting patterns, work habits such as mentoring practices and management styles, and how they treat and think about others of a different race. Sometimes the activism is more expressive and they publicly give witness, like Dr. Martin Luther King and Rabbi Joshua Abraham Heschel, to the broader societal racial inequalities.

The frequency with which they spend time together helps to balance the intensity that often comes with different worldviews rooted in race. Ultimately, this relationship reduces bias and changes cultural beliefs. It happens one cross-racial friendship at a time.

Jay Kaufman and Charlie Shorts have been friends for over fifty years, having met and maintained a friendship since their undergraduate years at Princeton. Jay recalls being aware of Charlie practically from his arrival on campus, as Charlie was the only black student in the class of over six hundred. In their freshman year, Jay was impressed by the number of friends Charlie had and described him as "somebody who was very socially adept, had a lot of friends and was generally an admirable individual."

They had friends in common and roommates in common, but both agree they were really just acquaintances that first year. The friendship developed and cemented during senior year when they were carrel mates, sharing one of many small office spaces in the library. They call themselves academic roommates, each studying side by side and preparing their thesis. "We literally spent many hours a day next door to each other in tight quarters," says Jay.

Jay was an English major and French minor who then went on to medical school (go figure). His thesis was "Three Went to Spain: The Influence of the Spanish Civil War on George Orwell, Arthur Koestler and Andre Malraux." Charlie states that he was "this African American student deep, deep, deep, into the study of the creation of modern Germany and writing his thesis on the Nazi period, sitting next to this very nice Jewish boy."

Charlie does not recall himself being as well known or socially adept as Jay claims, especially during his first year at Princeton. In fact, he stated that the university assigned him a single room in a building a distance from the freshman dormitory. Charlie played football, had a job, and says wearily that he worked "virtually every minute that I was at Princeton." He admits that he wasn't a good student at that time and was struggling academically. As we continue the interview, Jay finds this hard to believe as the obvious respect that he has for his friend is almost tangible. As a result of his academic struggles, Charlie began to emulate Jay's study patterns and in his junior year "attached himself" to Jay. "I'd go into the library when he was in the library. Getting up, I used to joke, when he'd go to the restroom, I'd go to the restroom." As Jay tries to convince Charlie that he is "overstating my influence on you scholastically," Charlie, now a trustee for the City University of New York, among many career accomplishments, counters that in his junior year his grades did improve.

After graduation, they remained close friends, with Jay recalling staying at Charlie's aunt's house when traveling to secure a medical residency. "It was the first time I stayed overnight in the home of an African American. What was amazing to me was that it was exactly like being in my own home. We both used the same brand of toothpaste. It struck me as, what a strange occurrence: I'm in the home of an African American and it is exactly the same things we do."

Charlie recalls meeting Jay's parents as "an amazing experience. . . . His mother and father were so gracious and so responsive to me. And that was a new experience for me in terms of any white family being suddenly open to me, and then we corresponded especially when Jay went to Vietnam. I asked Jay to be a godparent at my first son's baptism. So here was Jay standing in a Catholic church being a godfather to my son."

Jay confirms that, saying, "I have been a very participatory godfather, thank goodness." He then recalls that his parents "loved Charlie" and even had a photograph of Charlie and Jay in their home.

To this day, despite the fact that they live in different cities, the two make plans to get together for dinner and regularly communicate by phone and email. Their humor serves as energy for the positivity that is deeply characteristic of their friendship. They are exceptionally witty and clever in their communications, for example, in emails arranging to have dinner together read like this:

From Charlie:

Dear Dr. Kaufman:

Mr. Shorter has made reservations on the 28th of April for 4 persons at 7:00 at a restaurant just off Broadway. This will, he says, provide you with an easy walk to and from your hosts' home. He also asks that you send him your credit card number for holding the reservation. Be certain to include the expiration date and card code. Thank you. He looks forward to a pleasant evening on the 28th.

Sincerely,

Bob Schwartz

Personal Assistant

Jay's Response:

Dear Mr. Schwartz:

If that is indeed your name, I am appreciative of the dinner reservation but must decline your request for my credit card information. The last time that I provided this to Mr. Shorter, I found that I had been billed for 18 cases of Colt 45 Malt Liquor. In any event, Mr. Shorter has assured me that this meal is his treat as a result of the windfall from his recent consulting gig.

Sincerely,

JHK

"It's also enjoyable getting voicemail messages from Jay," Charlie tells me, "in which he's imitating someone from Princeton Alumni Office, letting me know that I am not giving enough money. I've gotten some that I've archived."

They both admit that their humor and their keen sense of irony have been part of their bonding as a way to release tension, a tension often stemming from societal race relations. In my interview with them, they discuss, review, and analyze the 1958 "sympathy sit-ins" happening in the

North in support of black youths sitting at segregated drug-store food counters attempting to be served. The "sympathy sit-ins" were happening at Harvard, Princeton, and Yale. The Princeton students and faculty were met with resistance and roughing up by the protestors.

Jay recalls, "As I witnessed it, I went down to watch. I watched this and did absolutely nothing. I watched it and I knew something was wrong, but my first comparative was to be able to get along at Princeton and be accepted there myself. So I did nothing. My life since that moment has been a very slow and gradual progression toward activism to make up for that moment. Charlie, along the way, humanizes this. I mean, here is a person that I can think about whom I love who is actually a part of this issue that goes on. And so Charlie is never far from my mind when I talk about the global issue of racism. It is very personal to me now."

Charlie reflects and shares with Jay, "I was there too and I did absolutely nothing. To tell you the truth, I didn't understand what was going on. I was just so isolated and I wondered why . . ."

Both friends continue to process the 1958 sit-ins and their responses through their present-day lens. They talk about the eight years under the Obama administration and the contrast to the Trump administration. They discuss who they believe are the potential new leaders who can support the kind of optimism and diversity they witness with their children and grandchildren. Charlie tells me why they are strong supporters of cross-racial friendships:

"Jay is part of a small cadre of people who have influenced my attitudes and made me less bitter and more optimistic about America, both from a religious and racial standpoint. Jay is one person, but because of him, I certainly understand far better, due to the actual experiences we have had, my beliefs in the core values of America."

They do not shy away from talking about race. Charlie states, "When I talk to Jay it's always with a high degree of respect, which it should be with any friendship. Therefore, we can talk about racial problems, we can talk about religious problems, political problems, and I feel very comfortable with that. I listen to his position. He doesn't always agree with mine. The thinking is that Jay and I have a good, close relationship. I cannot and I do not expect Jay to understand what it means to be called a 'nigger' or to be treated like one. It's a core experience as an African

American. The same is true in terms of anti-Semitism. I cannot understand in my core what that is really like."

As trust is a major barrier to establishing deep cross-racial friendships,
I asked Jay and Charlie if they found it to be true that they trusted their
same-race friends more than they trusted their cross-racial friends. In
general, although they acknowledged a deep level of trust between them,
they found that the research was true in their own lives. Charlie cites examples of being in African American settings and the sense of belonging it
creates. Jay cites experiences being only with Jews and the natural affinity
that happens with shared experiences. They are facile at "identity pulling"
or selecting from their multiple and intersecting identities the one most
important at the time. The fact that they acknowledge that it is easier to
build trust with their same-race friends does not diminish the trust they
experience. It just took longer to develop, but it is nonetheless as strong.

Like Jay and Charles, Perpetua and Clara first met in an introductory
freshman class. Only they were introduced fifty years later, at Florida
Southern College, in Lakeland, in 2009. They shared two classes together and were assigned a semester-long group project that provided
them with the opportunity to meet and not only work together but share
their views on a number of topics, particularly their faith. They both
agree that it was their in-depth conversations about faith that drew them
closer as friends. Although Perpetua is black Haitian American and Clara
is white from a small Southern town, they can quickly list all of the traits
they share: both are introverts; they have the same sense of humor; they
love the same books; they are both fashionistas; they have the same celebrity crushes; and while in college they were not into the Greek scene.

Their shared faith and interests led them to believe that they saw the
world through the same lens. They had many conversations about race
and the conservative county where Clara grew up and experienced racial
stereotypes. Clara gives credit to their friendship as helping her understand the racial tensions and views their friendship in nothing but positive terms. They had a rough spot, five years into their friendship, when
the news was announced that Darren Wilson, the white police office in
Ferguson, had been indicted in the shooting of eighteen-year-old Michael Brown, who was unarmed. Making meaning out of the unrest that

erupted in Ferguson and across the nation took a toll on their friendship. For the first time in their relationship, they disagreed vehemently. They decided to take a break, each processing whether or not the friendship was worth continuing.

Perpetua experienced herself as being "a little militant," and that it was necessary to fight every battle and "insert myself into every conversation." She became very much aware of Clara's privilege and her "power to refuse" to even talk about race. She acknowledged that she was impatient with Clara and "kept bombarding her with information" so much so that she understood Clara's resistance. Still, she wasn't sure if Clara "had the willingness to listen and learn alongside me."

Clara admitted that she was "looking at it from a white person's perspective." She noted that Perpetua seemed to understand white culture because she had lived in predominantly white settings all of her life. She didn't feel she had much to "bring to the table" on race. She had to ask herself, "Am I really willing to let my blinders stay up and sacrifice this wonderful human that God has blessed me to find? No, it wasn't worth it to me. I just had to remind myself of all the ways that this person lifts me and encourages me and is really a true friend. I was willing to work through that to set aside my judgments and opinions. I wanted to hear her and her whole side of the situation."

Similarly, during this time Perpetua began to ask herself "the real questions," like "Who is this person?" She looked to the past to understand the present. "It's an exercise in patience for me in recognizing that we are not all starting from the same point and I couldn't just telepathically throw that information into her head. When there is genuine good intentions and you can see an effort being made to meet somewhere in the middle, then it is good to reach an understanding and move forward."

Their advice on getting through racially charged situations in cross-racial friendships is to first expect that racial tension will occur. Perpetua calls this "letting it all happen." During this time it is important to concentrate on the foundations of relationship and stay committed. This must be the ground from which you work to move forward. Both parties have to be willing to put aside biases and prejudices, to reflect and ask real questions of themselves and each other. They also tell me that it is important to consider the tension a time of opportunity to grow and learn from each other. They acknowledge that it requires a lot of patience and caution to "take the time and don't be in a hurry to fix everything." Pushing through it is tough work.

As a result of this rough patch in their friendship, Perpetua and Clara believe that their relationship is now so "full of depth" and is "so fulfilling." They continue to communicate daily through texting, sending Snapchats, or voice calls. They make the time to be together using vacation days to visit each other. "We depend on each other like our hearts are connected," says Perpetua.

Ramona, Etaine, Sharon, Alyce, and Ronnie Mae have been friends for over twenty years. Like most friends of long standing, there is ebb and flow to their group interview conversation as they describe how they quickly transitioned from colleagues to friends. Sharon and Ronnie Mae are white. Ramona and Alyce are black Americans, and Etaine hails from Jamaica. They meet once a month for what they call a club meeting, not to be mistaken with a book club or a women's group or a professional affinity network, even though they are all HR executives working at MIT or Harvard University. The "club meeting" has its roots in their personal history.

Alyce's aunt had been a budget analyst in the 1950s and 1960s, a time when there were very few blacks in their work settings. "She told me that when somebody new came into the organization, the first question was 'Are they a club member'?" Ramona explains that it was code language to indicate if the individuals were black. This code language was used in a social context as well. "My mom was a stay-at-home mom and if her parents were going to social gatherings she would ask if other club members would be there."

Now, for Ramona, Etaine, Sharon, Alyce, and Ronnie Mae, race is integral to the sense of belonging and connectedness that is the requirement to be in "the club." Club membership is based on being able to bring their full and authentic self to the experiences they share. They vacation together on the Cape every summer. They get together on weekends and go to plays and concerts, and they call each other in good times and bad. They also talk a lot about race, but from the framework of their shared values.

Sharon puts it this way: "I think part of the reason we are friends is because we have been pretty simpatico. We went to the Women's March together. We've gone to a march supporting immigrants' rights. We are pretty like-minded on things like that. When I think back to the death of Trayvon Martin, I know Alyce in particular was affected by that especially because she is the mother of a young black male, and I'm thinking gun control. We've talked about that."

As we discuss their friendship in the context of our current political climate, the impact of social media, and their experience of generational differences seen through the eyes of the children, we come to the conclusion that their club is a microcosm of the world, or at least the world as they would want it to be. Any signs of white fragility are addressed head-on. "They never protect me," Sharon laughingly says.

"There's no way white fragility has affected Sharon or Ronnie Mae," Etaine says. "I think the way we formed our friendship, we first found our commonalities based on that we never look at a white face or a black face."

"I don't look at Sharon as a white women," Ramona says. "If somebody calls my attention to it, it's like, 'Oh, right, she is,' but in general, if some white person pissed me off, she knows I'm going to call her and tell her about it, and I'm comfortable saying it, and she offers her opinion on it."

Because of this level of comfort and intimacy, there is a stark realization that this club protects them and nurtures them from a racially divisive world. Even when they disagree, they note that "what survives is the friendship." When events like Charlottesville happen, they contact each other and say, "We need a club meeting."

THE WAY FORWARD

When Joan and I decided to meet for lunch at Brio in Legacy Village, we didn't realize that the restaurant that was once so familiar to us that we knew what we wanted to order before we got there now had a new menu. Not only was the menu new but the interior had been remodeled to reflect a coastal bar restaurant. The Italian rustic decor was replaced with an aquatic theme in its colors, and the menu featured more seafood and seasonal dishes. Everything had a fresh and open feel to it, and the conversation Joan and I had seemed to pick up that vibe.

Our decades of friendship, fortified by shared values, had weathered dissenting perspectives on politics and cultural issues of the day. I could hold her reality as sacred just as she held mine, but we couldn't really talk about race.

Somehow on this day, we went deep, talking about religion, politics, and racism in the way that I went deep with my friends who share my race. Although we have always stood on the same precipice looking out at the world, sometimes we saw the same things in the horizon and sometimes we did not. My view came through a racial lens as if I were wearing tinted sunglasses. Although Joan's view was filtered through many of the same conditions we jointly experienced, she admitted that race was not a filter. Ethnicity was a filter for her, though, as she recalled at one time trying to claim only the Irish and German aspects of her heritage, leaving out her dominant Italian roots. She sensed that being Italian was not considered as respectable and that Italians often fell into the stereotype of being thuggish, coarse individuals who used vulgar language and were too familiar with the underground world of crime. Still, Joanie was aware that her skin color gave her the option to slip into another aspect of her racial identity that was acceptable and that whiteness came with social privilege. More importantly, she understood my passion for race equity. As a close friend, she remained committed to helping me in that quest, even if it was simply by witnessing and acknowledging the impact of racism in my life or by living herself with heightened awareness to racial innuendos. For example, just that past week she had confronted a teacher who evaluated a community program the class had attended as being a bit too "urban" for the students. "You mean black?" Joan asked and began a discussion on the benefits of diversity.

The learning has not been one-sided. I learn from Joan how to truly hold multiple perspectives. Through our friendship, I actually experience a white person as cautious, uncomfortable, and even fragile when it comes to talking about race not simply because white privilege dictates that she doesn't have to talk about it, but because she *loves* me and does not want to hurt or offend. Like anyone who loves someone and finds themselves in a position where they are desperately trying to understand them, she feels pain. It is not a pain born out of sympathy, because she knows of my strength that is rooted in race esteem. Sometimes, she explains that passion for my race unsettles her. It is also not a discomfort born out of empathy, because she acknowledges that her "world is small" compared to mine, limiting her capacity to identify with my experiences.

She is honest enough about these feelings because she *loves* me and the trust is deep. It opens me up to love her even more.

Yet she feels pain when we talk about race issues and she knows it is not my pain. It is like we are in the same theater watching the world on the same screen, sitting in seats distant from one another yet in eyesight. It presents a conundrum for both of us that can't be easily explained or articulated. But we want to get closer. So, I respect where she is in her racial-identity resolution process and coming to terms with whiteness. After all, as a member of the dominant race, she has had the luxury of not having to think about race. She respects that racial identity is an aspect of me that cannot be ignored or experienced through the lens of her color blindness. She honors the fact that every day I wake up a black woman and that has implications for how I experience my world and what gets evoked from that world. We enter race talk with this knowledge and re-spect and begin and end conversations in a rhythmic manner sensing when the other can manage its weight without feeling strangled. We hold sacred conversations about race that will not leave either of us feeling like we overshared with little or no return on that emotional investment. Over time, and with deepening trust and love, we have more and more honest conversations about race and learn more and more from each other. Sometimes these conversations leave us feeling like we have closed the racial divide. It's a feeling that we can only live out. We can't put it in a how-to manual. We can't market it. We can just be friends.

Almost two decades ago, I began this journey of exploration into the nature of cross-racial friendships after a conversation on a walk with my sister-friend Yvonne. I began with the belief that cross-racial friends are essential to our personal development and an effective and necessary means to improve race relations. I am still on the path of discovery, often disheartened to discover more road bumps to navigate, and gleeful when the way is straight and fast to Dr. King's beloved community.

What I know to be true of cross-racial friendships is that those of the heart, which offer the most potential for racial equity, require three con-ditions: (1) consistent, lifelong examination of oneself as a racial being and its influence on one's behavior and thinking; (2) intentional lifestyle choices that lead to multicultural living; and (3) heightened awareness of the impact of racism in our society and a commitment to work with friends toward eradicating it. It seems like a lot to ask of a friendship but it is really a lot simpler than one might think.

RACIAL-IDENTITY SELF-ASSESSMENT

Start with understanding your racial identity or the psychological connection you have with your race. Have a clear sense of yourself as a racial being in order to understand how race has affected your life and influenced your thinking and behavior. This isn't just an exercise for whites but for people of color as well, although people of color tend to do this naturally in their daily life. Think about yourself as a racial being for a day (or even just an hour), pulling race from your multiple and intersecting identities as just that one aspect of your identity. Examine your thoughts, behaviors, and decisions through that racial lens. If there is no difference in how you experience yourself, that tells you something about the degree of social privilege you hold. Share your experience of "racial identity pulling" with your friends—same race friends and those across racial lines. Other reflection exercises on racial identity and racial identity assessment tools can be found by visiting my website, www.dlplummer.com.

LIFESTYLE CHOICES LEADING TO MULTIRACIAL LIVING

Examine your racial lifestyle choices: Where you choose to live, worship, shop. What you choose to read; the shows you watch; the music you listen to; the organizations you work for, belong to, and support; where you vacation; who you buy goods and services from; who you friend and unfriend on social media; who you have conversations with on issues that matter. Mix it up racially. Through making intentional choices to live, work, and play in multiracial settings, you are bound to meet potential friends of a different race. Socialize with your friends of different races and strive for living, working, worshipping, and playing in diverse environments. Create those kinds of environments for yourself.

ACKNOWLEDGING RACISM AND UNCONSCIOUS BIAS

Know and believe that racism exists, not just in the overt intentional form that the majority of us detest and work against, but in the subtle, everyday form that is often unintentional and unconscious. This form of modern racism seeps into our organizations, places of worship, leisure activities, and politics. It is time for us to talk about how that is so and to use the collective wisdom of diverse racial groups to manage unconscious biases effectively, reduce prejudices, and dismantle racism. It is a long, arduous process best achieved with diverse friends.

If you do not know where to start, discover your own hidden biases by taking the race dimension of the Implicit Association Test (IAT).[13] Review your results and, if you are comfortable doing so, share them with others, particularly cross-racial friends. If you are not comfortable sharing your results with others, use journal writing to unearth what informs any negative racial attitudes. After taking the IAT, move on to understanding how biases show up in your everyday life and work to understand how biases seep into institutions, businesses, churches, mosques, synagogues, school systems, sports, recreational activities, politics, and other aspects of daily living.

With your cross-racial friends, work to turn societal racial mistrust (which I outlined in the first two chapters of the book) into interpersonal racial trust (demonstrated in cross-racial friendships, especially those of the heart I described in the final chapter). You can do that by having those honest and difficult conversations about racially biased institutional policies, racially charged events, and political views with negative racial undertones. If your friends of a different race fit into the Fantasy or Calendar Cross-Racial Friends category, you may have to ease into these conversations slowly and with preparation. For example, you could start with "Hey, I just read in this book about cross-racial friendships and wondered what you thought about . . ." Or start with discussing a racially themed movie, television show, or book. If, like my friendship with Joan and Rita, your cross-racial friends are long-term friends and you have rarely talked about race, remember that bumping needs to be gentle. With all of your friends, start and continue to talk about racial equality as an important and necessary topic in your daily life, just as you would other topics important to your health and well-being. Don't be afraid to ask what might seem like naive or stupid questions about race. Give each other permission to make mistakes by taking a pledge that you will give each other the benefit of the doubt, that you will not quickly label the impact of an honest question as a microaggression without giving the person an opportunity to provide his or her intention. Marrying intention with impact will get you to a shared understanding. Don't be afraid to give or hear the honest responses. Turn fear into a challenge by creatively managing racial tension through writing a "Dear [fill in the race] Friend letter," stating (1) this is what I said; (2) this is what I really wanted to say; (3) this is what I learned, or was inspired by, or will do differently, or simply stating, "I still don't get what was so upsetting but here's an invitation to discuss more." As the saying goes, even the flattest of pancakes has two sides; be willing to explore each side.

Although cross-racial friendships are hard to form, require deep nurturing, and are challenging to maintain in a racially divided society, you don't need to have many cross-race friends to contribute to positive race relations on a societal level. It's the quality of the friendship and not the quantity of friends that matters.

MOVING FORWARD TOGETHER

Cross-racial friendships that foster intergroup contact remain one of the most effective methods of improving race relations. They are successive approximations toward the goal of the beloved community, bringing us closer to a shared American experience, moving us from separate and unequal to together and equal. Cross-racial friends, especially those of the heart, reduce bias and change cultural beliefs not just for the individual dyad; they hold the potential for positive change for their families and their circle of friends. Over time, these friendships have profound effects on healing divisions among different racial groups and fostering racial equity. Racial equity takes place one cross-racial friend at a time.

ACKNOWLEDGMENTS

My hope in writing this book was that it would spark a different conversation about race relations, and for that reason it could not have found a better home than with Beacon Press. I am proud to be published by Beacon, whose books create a more informed, inclusive, and engaged society. I am especially grateful for the enthusiastic support and seasoned guidance of my editor, Helene Atwan, and the fresh wisdom of Maya Fernandez. I know that many writers claim their agent as the best but their claims are weak compared to mine, as Esmond Harmsworth and Jane von Mehren are indeed the best. Along with your confidence in me as a writer, you recognized the potential for this topic to be more than a simplistic response to the urgent need to improve race relations. Thank you for being allies in this work.

The Friendship Study would not have been possible without the ever-present support from my research partner at UMass Medical School and my dear friend, Jeroan Allison. You are brilliant and challenge me to always dig deeper and keep questioning. My research assistant, Renee Lucas, deserves an extended round of applause for her attention to detail and timely execution of tasks. My research is grounded and built on the work of a number of esteemed social scientists who have my deepest respect, especially Linda Tropp, Eduardo Bonilla-Silva, Monika Stodolska, Kimberly Shinew, and Raúl Pérez. Thank you for your insights and your support. To the thousands who have completed surveys, participated in focus groups, or provided key informant interviews, please know that your contributions are greatly valued. Your voices are represented in this book.

It takes a village to get from idea to published work, and I am most grateful to my GrubStreet village. To Eve Bridburg goes deep gratitude for your expert guidance and free therapy sessions. You are simply one wonderful human being. To Christopher Castellani goes awe and admiration of your brilliance as a writer and teacher. Thank you for your kindness and encouragement. To my respected Grub instructors and consultants, Chip Cheek, Michelle Hoover, Ethan Gilsdorf, Matthew Frederick, and Sorche Fairbank, a very big thank-you. I have greatly benefited from your talents. Special thanks to fellow Grub board member and book lover Jeffrey Mayershon, for being a valued cheerleader for my writing projects.

Through writing this book I sought to sharpen my thinking, challenge assumptions, expand worldviews, and enlighten and inspire others on an issue that matters greatly to me. Readers of early drafts of the manuscript helped me to do that. Special thanks to Karen Tucker, Jerry Avorn, Rachel Mitchum Elahee, Eve Bridburg, Evan Rosen, and Jacqueline McLemore for your insights. Your feedback was invaluable and helped to strengthen this important message.

I would be remiss if I did not mention the leadership, staff, and fellow advisory board members of Facing History and Ourselves, especially Roger Brooks, Marc Skvirsky, Farrell Boucher, Patricia Keenan, Fran Colletti, Jill Karp, and Karen Tucker. This fabulous organization has been the source of deep, rich learning for me over the years and, most importantly, many wonderful and lasting friendships across racial and religious lines. I am so glad and proud that this organization exists for the good of our society.

I continue to learn from those whom I am privileged to call friends. Loving thanks to my cherished friends Joan Agresta and Rita Klement for allowing me to share our friendship story. Enduring thanks to my long-term, fierce white women friends, Donna Skurzak, Jo Salvatore, Lori Stevic-Rust, and Patty Marshall-Razzante, who were all once my students and now, as true upstanders, are my teachers. Heartfelt thanks to my sister-friend, Yvonne Sims, who walks beside me physically and spiritually. You make my world a better place.

I close with a shout-out to my family, especially best-friend sisters Felicia, Simone, and Nancy for your belief in me as a writer and your sincere interest in the topic. I am so blessed to have you as friends, confidantes, and coaches. My parents, Phyllis and Leroy, were my first "diversity management educators." They shared with me many of the lessons in this book. Please know that even from your heavenly seats, the lessons continue. To my loving sisters Brenda and Chris, and brother Paul, I give a big thank-you hug. And most of all to my ever-supportive husband, Michael Bussey, I extend deep gratitude and much love. You have provided warm encouragement every step of the way for this book, along with a few opinions on the topic.

NOTES

INTRODUCTION: CAN WE BE FRIENDS?
1. The names in this case are pseudonyms.

CHAPTER 1: LIVING "SEPARATE AS FINGERS"
1. Booker T. Washington, "Atlanta Exposition Address," presented at the Cotton States and International Exposition, Atlanta, GA, September 1895, available via SharpSchool, http://wwphs.sharpschool.com/UserFiles/Servers/Server_10640642/File/bugge/Chapter%2017/washingtonvsdubois.PDF.
2. "Booker T. Washington," TheBiography.com, https://www.biography.com/people/booker-t-washington-9524663, last modified April 27, 2017.
3. Adekemi Adesokan et al., "Diversity Beliefs as Moderator of the Contact-Prejudice Relationship," *Social Psychology* 42 (2011): 273, doi:10.1027/1864-9335/a000058.
4. Malcolm X and Alex Haley, *The Autobiography of Malcolm X* (New York: Grove Press, 1965), 434.
5. William H. Smith and Richard W. Thomas, *Race Amity: A Primer on America's Other Tradition* (Sudbury, MA: WHS Media Productions, 2016), 43.
6. "Eleanor Roosevelt," Blackhistoryreview.com, last modified 2013, http://www.blackhistoryreview.com/biography/ERoosevelt.php.
7. "My Day," June 6, 1940, Eleanor Roosevelt Papers Digital Edition, http://www2.gwu.edu/~erpapers/myday/displaydoc.cfm?_y=1940&_f=md055599, accessed June 13, 2017.
8. "My Day," April 22, 1942, https://www2.gwu.edu/~erpapers/myday/displaydoc.cfm?_y=1942&_f=md056166.
9. "My Day," May 3, 1952, https://www2.gwu.edu/~erpapers/myday/displaydoc.cfm?_y=1952&_f=md002212.
10. James M. Burns and Susan Dunn, *The Three Roosevelts: Patrician Leaders Who Transformed America* (New York: Grove Press, 2002), 394.
11. Mary McLeod Bethune, interview by Eleanor Roosevelt, WSAI Cincinnati, February 11, 1949, available via New York Public Radio, https://www.wnyc.org/story/209566-mary-mcleod-bethune.
12. "My Day," May 20, 1955, Eleanor Roosevelt Papers Digital Edition, https://www2.gwu.edu/~erpapers/myday/displaydoc.cfm?_y=1955&_f=md003174, accessed June 13, 2017.
13. Dovid Efune, "Fresh Controversy Hits 'Selma': Daughter of Rabbi Abraham Joshua Heschel 'Shocked' by Exclusion of Her Father from Film," *Algemeiner*, January 18, 2015, https://www.algemeiner.com/2015/01/18/fresh-controversy-hits-selma-daughter-of-rabbi-abraham-joshua-heschel-shocked-by-exclusion-of-her-father-from-film.
14. Ibid.
15. Sian Gibby, "King and Heschel and Moses," *Tabletmag*, January 15, 2016, http://www.tabletmag.com/jewish-life-and-religion/196332/king-and-heschel-and-moses.
16. Susannah Heschel, "A Friendship in the Prophetic Tradition: Abraham Joshua Heschel and Martin Luther King, Jr.," *Telos* 182 (Spring 2018): 67–84.
17. Susannah Heschel, interview by Deborah Plummer, September 28, 2017.

18. Heschel, "A Friendship in the Prophetic Tradition," 2.

19. Deborah L. Plummer et al., "Patterns of Adult Cross-Racial Friendships: A Context for Understanding Contemporary Race Relations," *Cultural Diversity & Ethnic Minority Psychology* 22, no. 4 (2016), doi:10.1037/cdp0000079.

20. David Card, Alexandre Mas, and Jesse Rothstein, "Tipping and the Dynamics of Segregation," *Quarterly Journal of Economics* 123 (2007): 1, doi:10.1162/qjec.2008.123.1.177.

21. Maria Krysan et al., "Does Race Matter in Neighborhood Preferences?" *American Journal of Sociology* 115 (2009): 2, doi:10.1086/599248.

22. Paula McAvoy, Rebecca Fine, and Ann H. Ward, "State Standards Scratch the Surface of Learning About Political Parties and Ideology," *Center for Information and Research on Civic Learning and Engagement*, November 1, 2016, http://civicyouth.org/wp-content/uploads/2016/09/State-Standards-and-Political-Ideology.pdf.

23. Kris Olds, "Global Citizenship: What Are We Talking About and Why Does It Matter?," *InsideHigherEd*, March 11, 2012, https://www.insidehighered.com/blogs/global highered/global-citizenship-%E2%80%93-what-are-we-talking-about-and-why-does -it-matter.

24. Robin J. Ely and David A. Thomas, "Cultural Diversity at Work: The Effects of Diversity Perspectives on Work Group Processes and Outcomes," *Administrative Science Quarterly* 46, no. 2 (2001): 229–73, doi:10.2307/2667087; Frank Dobbin and Alexandra Kalev, "Why Diversity Programs Fail," *Harvard Business Review*, July-August 2016, https://hbr.org/2016/07/why-diversity-programs-fail.

25. Todd L. Pittinsky, *Us Plus Them: Tapping the Positive Power of Difference*, Leadership for the Common Good (Boston: Harvard Business Review Press, 2012).

26. Todd L. Pittinsky, Seth Rosenthal, and Matthew Montoya, "Measuring Positive Attitudes Toward Outgroups," *Cultural Diversity and Ethnic Minority Psychology* 17 (2011): 2, doi:10.1037/a0023806.

27. "Race and Social Connections: Friends, Family, and Neighborhoods," Pew Research Center, June 11, 2015, http://www.pewsocialtrends.org/2015/06/11/chapter-5-race-and -social-connections-friends-family-and-neighborhoods.

28. K. Davies et al., "Cross-Group Friendships and Intergroup Attitudes: A Meta-Analytic Review," *Personality and Social Psychology Review* 15 (2011): 4, doi:10.1177/1088868311411103.

29. D. L. Plummer and J. Allison, "Friendship Survey II," March 2, 2017.

30. L. Dunsmuir, "Many Americans Have No Friends of Another Race: Poll," Reuters, August 8, 2013, http://www.reuters.com/article/2013/08/08/us-usa-poll-race-idUSBRE 97704320130808.

31. Bill Clinton et al., *One America in the 21st Century: Forging a New Future*, September 1998, https://clintonwhitehouse2.archives.gov/Initiatives/OneAmerica/PIR.pdf.

32. Barack Obama, "Barack Obama's Speech on Race," presented at the Constitution Center, Philadelphia, PA, March 18, 2008.

CHAPTER 2: LIVING "ONE AS THE HAND"

1. The names in this case are pseudonyms.

2. Dunsmuir, "Many Americans Have No Friends of Another Race."

3. Robert P. Jones, Daniel Cox, and Juhem Navarro-Rivera, "American Values Survey," Public Religion Research Institute, 2013, https://www.prri.org/wp-content/uploads/2013 /10/2013.AVS_WEB-1.pdf.

4. "Race and Social Connections: Friends, Family, and Neighborhoods," Pew Research Center.

5. Plummer et al., "Patterns of Adult Cross-Racial Friendships."

6. Jennifer A. Richeson et al., "An fMRI Investigation of the Impact of Interracial Contact on Executive Function," *Nature Neuroscience* 6 (2003): 1323–28, doi:10.1038/nn1156.

7. Ibid., 1326.

8. Jennifer A. Richeson and Sophie Trawalter, "Why Do Interracial Interactions Impair Executive Function? A Resource Depletion Account," *Journal of Personality and Social Psychology* 88 (2005): 6, doi:10.1037/0022-3514.88.6.934.

9. Daniel Goleman, *Emotional Intelligence: Why It Can Matter More Than IQ* (New York: Bantam, 2005).

10. Jason Marsh, Rodolfo Mendoza-Denton, and Jeremy Adam Smith, *Are We Born Racist? New Insights from Neuroscience and Positive Psychology* (Boston: Beacon Press, 2010), 41–44.

11. Mark Shanahan, "Just How Hard Is It to Make It onto 'Jeopardy'?," *Boston Globe*, July 21, 2015, https://www.bostonglobe.com/lifestyle/2015/07/20/take-out-league-for-alex/Liia88Ueq2MawhZx6FYLhJ/story.html.

12. Andrew Campbell, Jo Whitehead, and Sydney Finkelstein, "Why Good Leaders Make Bad Decisions," *Harvard Business Review*, February 2009, https://hbr.org/2009/02/why-good-leaders-make-bad-decisions.

13. Ibid.

14. Cheryl Staats et al., *State of the Science: Implicit Bias Review* 2015 (Columbus: Kirwan Institute for the Study of Race and Ethnicity, Ohio State University, 2015), http://kirwaninstitute.osu.edu/wp-content/uploads/2016/07/implicit-bias-2016.pdf.

15. Jacob L. Vigdor and Edward L. Glaeser, "The End of the Segregated Century: Racial Separation in America's Neighborhood, 1890–2010," Manhattan Institute, January 22, 2012, https://www.manhattan-institute.org/html/end-segregated-century-racial-separation-americas-neighborhoods-1890-2010-5848.html.

16. Francis Cardinal George, "Dwell in My Love," *Catholic Online*, April 4, 2001, http://www.catholic.org/featured/headline.php?ID=390.

17. Linda R. Tropp and Elizabeth Page-Gould, "Contact Between Groups," in *APA Handbook of Personality and Social Psychology* 2 (2015), doi:10.1037/14342-020.

18. John Dovidio, Samuel L. Gaertner, and Tamar Saguy, "Another View of 'We': Majority and Minority Group Perspectives on a Common Ingroup Identity," *European Review of Social Psychology* 18, no. 1 (2007): 296–330, doi:10.1080/10463280701726132.

CHAPTER 3: TWO-BUTTON CHOICE: ACQUAINTANCE OR LOVER

1. Plummer et al., "Patterns of Adult Cross-Racial Friendships."

2. Melanie Killen and Adam Rutland, *Children and Social Exclusion: Morality, Prejudice, and Group Identity* (Malden, MA: Wiley-Blackwell, 2011), http://onlinelibrary.wiley.com/book/10.1002/9781444396317.

3. Online report for, CNN *Anderson Cooper 360°* special report *Kids on Race: The Hidden Picture*, March 5, 2012, http://i2.cdn.turner.com/cnn/2012/images/03/29/ac360.race.study.pdf.

4. Ibid.

5. Tana Gilmore and Kelli Fisher, "Top 7 Reasons Why Single Black Men Don't Approach Black Women," *Essence*, February 17, 2015, https://www.essence.com/galleries/top-7-reasons-why-single-black-men-dont-approach-black-women#624166.

6. Danielle Kwateng-Clark, "Social Media Checks Man Who Says Black Women Are Not 'Coachable,'" *Essence*, March 16, 2017, https://www.essence.com/culture/social-media-man-calls-black-women-not-coachable.

7. "Who We Are," Jack and Jill Foundation, last modified 2017, https://jackandjillfoundation.org/who-we-are.

8. Beverly D. Tatum, *Why Are All the Black Kids Sitting Together in the Cafeteria? And Other Conversations About Race* (New York: Basic Books, 2003).

9. Kristen Bialik, "Key Facts About Race and Marriage, 50 Years After *Loving v. Virginia*," Pew Research Center, June 12, 2017, http://www.pewresearch.org/fact-tank/2017/06/12/key-facts-about-race-and-marriage-50-years-after-loving-v-virginia.

10. Sheryll Cashin, *Loving: Interracial Intimacy in America and the Threat to White Supremacy* (Boston: Beacon Press, 2017).

11. Jennifer L. Bratter and Rosalind B. King, "But Will It Last? Marital Instability Among Interracial and Same-Couples," *Family Relations* 57, no. 2 (2008): 160–71, doi:10.1111/j.1741-3729.2008.00491.

12. The names in this case are pseudonyms.

13. The names in this case are pseudonyms.

14. *Kids on Race.*

15. Jason Johnson, interview by Deborah Plummer, part 1, September 11, 2017.

16. *A Review of EEOC Enforcement and Litigation Strategy During the Obama Administration—A Misuse of Authority*, US Chamber of Commerce, June 2014, https://www.uschamber.com/sites/default/files/documents/files/021449_LABR%20EEOC%20Enforcement%20Paper_FIN_rev.pdf.

17. Devon W. Carbado and Mitu Gulati, "Working Identity," *Cornell Law Review* 85 (2000): 1259, http://scholarship.law.cornell.edu/cgi/viewcontent.cgi?article=2814 &context=clr.

18. Adia Harvey Wingfield, "Being Black—but Not Too Black—in the Workplace," *Atlantic*, October 14, 2015, https://www.theatlantic.com/business/archive/2015/10/being -black-work/409990/; William E. Cross Jr, et al., "Identity Work: Enactment of Racial-Ethnic Identity in Everyday Life," *International Journal of Theory and Research* 17 (2017): 1, doi:10.1080/15283488.2016.1268535.

19. See Jennifer Lee and Min Zhou, *The Asian American Achievement Paradox* (New York: Russell Sage Foundation, 2015).

20. Stefanie K. Johnson and Thomas Sy, "Why Aren't There More Asian Americans in Leadership Positions?," *Harvard Business Review*, December 19, 2016, https://hbr.org /2016/12/why-arent-there-more-asian-americans-in-leadership-positions; "The Model Minority Is Losing Patience," *Economist*, October 3, 2015, https://www.economist.com /news/briefing/21669595-asian-americans-are-united-states-most-successful-minority -they-are-complaining-ever.

21. "Often Employees, Rarely CEOs: Challenges Asian-Americans Face in Tech," NPR, last modified May 17, 2015, https://www.npr.org/2015/05/17/407478606/often-employees -rarely-ceos-challenges-asian-americans-face-in-tech.

22. "The Model Minority Is Losing Patience."

23. Ellis Cose, *Envy of the World: On Being a Black Man in America* (New York: Washington Square Press, 2003).

CHAPTER 4: SAME TREATMENT DOES NOT MEAN EQUAL TREATMENT

1. David Rock and Heidi Grant, "Why Diverse Teams Are Smarter," *Harvard Business Review*, November 4, 2016, https://hbr.org/2016/11/why-diverse-teams-are-smarter.

2. Robert D. Putnam, *Bowling Alone: The Collapse and Revival of American Community* (New York: Simon & Schuster, 2001), and Robert D. Putnam, *Our Kids: The American Dream in Crisis* (New York: Simon & Schuster, 2016).

3. Jonathan Easley, "Trump Casts Inner Cities as 'War Zones' in Pitch to Minority Voters," *Hill*, August 22, 2016, http://thehill.com/blogs/ballot-box/presidential-races /292283-trump-casts-inner-cities-as-war-zones-in-pitch-to; Adam K. Causey, "To Some, Trump's 'Bad Hombres' Is Much More Than a Botched Spanish Word," PBS, October 20, 2016, https://www.pbs.org/newshour/politics/trumps-bad-hombres-draws-jeers -spanish-lessons.

4. Rodolfo Mendoza-Denton, *Stigma and Prejudice: Achieving Positive Intergroup Relations* (San Diego, CA: Cognella, 2011), 291–301.

5. Hillary B. Bergsieker, J. Nicole Shelton, and Jennifer A. Richeson, "To Be Liked Versus Respected: Divergent Goals in Interracial Interactions," *Journal of Personality and Social Psychology* 99, no. 2 (2010): 248–64, doi:10.1037/a0018474.

6. Ibid., Wendy B. Mendes and Katrina Koslov, "Brittle Smiles: Positive Biases Toward Stigmatized and Outgroup Targets," *Journal of Experimental Psychology: General* 142, no. 3 (2013): 923–33.

7. Claude M. Steele, *Whistling Vivaldi: How Stereotypes Affect Us and What We Can Do* (New York: W. W. Norton, 2011).

8. Ibid., 147.

9. K. Migacheva and L. R. Tropp, "Learning Orientation as a Predictor of Positive Intergroup Contact," *Group Processes and Intergroup Relations* 16 (2013): 426–44.

10. K. Migacheva, L. R. Tropp, and J. Crocker, "Focusing Beyond the Self: Goal Orientations in Intergroup Relations," in *Moving Beyond Prejudice Reduction: Pathways to Positive Intergroup Relations*, ed. Linda R. Tropp and Robyn K. Mallet (Washington, DC: American Psychological Association, 2011), 99–115.

11. "Project Implicit," Harvard University, last modified 2011, https://implicit.harvard .edu/implicit/takeatest.html, accessed June 12, 2018. See Mahzarin Banaji and Anthony Greenwald, *Blindspot: Hidden Biases of Good People* (New York: Delacorte Press, 2013).

12. Christopher L. Aberson, Carl Shoemaker, and Christina Tomolillo, "Implicit Bias and Contact: The Role of Interethnic Friendships," *Journal of Social Psychology* 144, no. 3 (2004): 335–47, doi:10.3200/SOCP.144.3.335-347.

13. Cheryl Staats et al., *State of the Science: Implicit Bias Review* (Columbus, OH: Kirwan Institute for the Study of Race and Ethnicity, 2017), http://kirwaninstitute.osu.edu/wp -content/uploads/2017/11/2017-SOTS-final-draft-02.pdf.

14. Elizabeth Page-Gould, Rodolfo Mendoza-Denton, and Linda R. Tropp, "With a Little Help from My Cross-Group Friend: Reducing Anxiety in Intergroup Contexts Through Cross-Group Friendship," *Journal of Personality and Social Psychology* 95, no. 5 (2008): 1080–94, doi:10.1037/0022–3514.95.5.1080.

15. Todd M. Michney, "Race, Violence, and Urban Territory: Cleveland's Little Italy and the 1966 Hough Uprising," *Journal of Urban History* 32, no. 3 (2006): 404–28, doi:10.1177/0096144205282573.

16. Natalie Proulx, "Should the United States Celebrate Columbus Day?," *New York Times*, October 5, 2017, https://www.nytimes.com/2017/10/05/learning/should-the-united -states-celebrate-columbus-day.html.

17. Daria Roithmayr, *Reproducing Racism: How Everyday Choices Lock in White Advantage* (New York: New York University Press, 2014).

18. W. Brian Arthur, "Competing Technologies, Increasing Returns, and Lock-in by Historical Events," *Economic Journal* 99 (1989): 116–31, http://www.haas.berkeley.edu /Courses/Spring2000/BA269D/Arthur89.pdf.

CHAPTER 5: WHAT'S IN A RACE?

1. W. E. Cross Jr., "The Psychology of Nigrescence: Revising the Cross Model," in *Handbook of Multicultural Counseling*, ed. Joseph G. Ponterotto et al. (Thousand Oaks, CA: Sage, 1995), 93–122; Haresh Sabnani, Joseph G. Ponterotto, and Lisa Borodovsky, "White Racial Identity Development and Cross-Cultural Counselor Training," *Counseling Psychologist* 19, no. 1 (1991): 76–102, doi:10.1177/0011000091191007.

2. Rita Hardiman, "White Identity Development: A Process Oriented Model for Describing the Racial Consciousness of White Americans," *Dissertation Abstracts International* 43, 1-A (1982), 104; Janet E. Helms, *Black and White Racial Identity* (Westport, CT: Greenwood Press, 1990).

3. Janet E. Helms, "An Update of Helms's White and People of Color Racial Identity Models," paper presented at the Psychology and Societal Transformation Conference, University of Western Cape, South Africa, January 1994.

4. W. E. B. Du Bois, *The Souls of Black Folk* (Chicago: A. C. McClurg, 1903), Bartleby .com, 1999, www.bartleby.com/114.

5. Deborah L. Plummer and Sabin Fernbacher, "Racial Identity Resolution Process: A Gestalt Perspective," *Gestalt Review* 20, no. 2 (2016): 129–46, http://www.jstor.org/stable /10.5325/gestaltreview.20.2.0129.

6. "An Expat in Panama: Is There Racism in Panama?," video, 12:56, July 21, 2016, https://www.youtube.com/watch?v=Jtat-vvCWts.

7. Plummer and Fernbacher, "Racial Identity Resolution Process," 129–46.

8. "Our Work," Facing History and Ourselves, last modified 2017, https://www.facing history.org/our-work.

9. *Salute*, dir. Matt Norman (Burbank, CA: Warner Brothers and Paramount Pictures, 2008), DVD.

10. Harry Edwards, "The Olympic Project for Human Rights: An Assessment Ten Years Later," *Journal of Black Studies and Research* 10, no. 6/7 (1979): 2–8, doi:10.1080/00064246 .1979.11414041.

11. Damian Johnstone, *A Race to Remember: The Peter Norman Story* (Melbourne, Australia: JoJo, 2009).

12. "Carlos, Smith Pallbearers at Norman's Funeral," ESPN, October 9, 2006, http:// www.espn.com/olympics/trackandfield/news/story?id=2618107.

13. Tommie Smith, Delois Smith, and David Steele, *Silent Gesture: The Autobiography of Tommie Smith* (Philadelphia: Temple University Press, 2007).

14. Charmaine L. Wijeyesinghe and Bailey W. Jackson, *New Perspectives on Racial Identity Development: Integrating Emerging Frameworks*, 2nd ed. (New York: New York University Press, 2012), 161–91; Evangelina Holvino, "Intersections: The Simultaneity of Race, Gender and Class in Organization Studies," *Gender, Work & Organization* 17, no. 3 (2010): 248–77, doi:10.1111/j.1468–0432.2008.00400.x.

15. Marta Calás and Linda Smircich, "1.8 From the 'Woman's Point of View' Ten Years Later: Towards a Feminist Organization Studies," *Sage Handbook of Organization Studies* (2006): 284, doi:10.4135/9781848608030.n9; Aurelia Mok and Michael W. Morris, "Managing Two Cultural Identities: The Malleability of Bicultural Identity Integration as a Function of Induced Global or Local Processing," *Personality and Social Psychology Bulletin* 38, no. 2 (2011): 233–46, doi:10.1177/0146167211426438.

16. Deborah L. Plummer, "Identity Aspect Most Important to You?," questionnaire, March 11, 2017.

17. A. J. Umaña-Taylor et al., "Ethnic and Racial Identity During Adolescence and into Young Adulthood: An Integrated Conceptualization," *Child Development* 85 (2014): 21–39, doi:10.1111/cdev.12196.

18. F. E. Aboud and S. R. Levy, "Interventions to Reduce Prejudice and Discrimination in Children and Adolescents," in *Reducing Prejudice and Discrimination*, ed. Stuart Oskamp, Claremont Symposium on Applied Social Psychology Series (Mahwah, NJ: Lawrence Erlbaum Associates, 2000), 269–93; Frances E. Aboud, Morton J. Mendelson, and Kelly T. Purdy, "Cross-Race Peer Relations and Friendship Quality," *International Journal of Behavioral Development* 27, no. 2 (2003): 165–73, doi:10.1080/01650250244000164; Lisa Hunter and Maurice J. Elias, "Interracial Friendships, Multicultural Sensitivity, and Social Competence," *Journal of Applied Developmental Psychology* 20, no. 4 (1999): 551–73, doi:10.1016/S0193-3973(99)00028-3; Matthew Taylor, "Cross-Race Friendships," in *Encyclopedia of Child Behavior and Development*, ed. Sam Goldstein (New York: Springer, 2011), 441–44.

19. Maureen T. Hallinan and Richard A. Williams, "Students' Characteristics and the Peer-Influence Process," *Sociology of Education* 63, no. 2 (1990): 122–32, doi:10.2307/2112858.

20. Thomas F. Pettigrew and Linda R. Tropp, "How Does Intergroup Contact Reduce Prejudice?" *European Journal of Social Psychology* 38, no. 6 (2008): 922–34, doi:10.1002/ejsp.504; Thomas F. Pettigrew and Linda R. Tropp, "Does Intergroup Contact Reduce Prejudice?: Recent Meta-Analytic Findings," in Oskamp, *Reducing Prejudice and Discrimination*, 93–114.

CHAPTER 6: GENTLE (AND NOT SO GENTLE) BUMPING

1. Deborah J. Schildkraut, "White Attitudes About Descriptive Representation in the US: The Roles of Identity, Discrimination, and Linked Fate," *Politics, Groups, and Identities* 5 (2017): 1, doi:10.1080/21565503.2015.1089296.

2. "Parable of Ups and Downs" in Robert W. Terry, *Authentic Leadership: Courage in Action* (San Francisco: Jossey-Bass, 1993), 194–204.

3. Rohini Anand and Mary-Frances Winters, "A Retrospective View of Corporate Diversity Training from 1964 to the Present," *Academy of Management Learning & Education* 7, no. 3 (2008): 356–72, doi:10.5465/AMLE.2008.34251673.

4. Hilary Miller, "Nick Cannon Wears Whiteface, Sparks Internet Debate," *Huffington Post*, March 24, 2014, https://www.huffingtonpost.com/2014/03/24/nick-cannon-whiteface_n_5022676.html.

5. J. D. Vance, *Hillbilly Elegy: A Memoir of a Family and Culture in Crisis* (New York: HarperCollins, 2016).

6. Ibid., 194.

7. Rita Hardiman, "White Identity Development: A Process Oriented Model for Describing the Racial Consciousness of White Americans," PhD diss., University of Massachusetts, Amherst, 1982; Mark M. Leach, John T. Behrens, and N. Kenneth LaFleur, "White Racial Identity and White Racial Consciousness: Similarities, Differences, and Recommendations," *Journal of Multicultural Counseling & Development* 30, no. 2 (2002): 66–80, doi:10.1002/j.2161-1912.2002.tb00480.x; Janet E. Helms, *A Race Is a Nice Thing to Have: A Guide to Being a White Person or Understanding the White Persons in Your Life* (Topeka, KS: Content Communications, 1992); Janet E. Helms, "An Update of Helms's White and People of Color Racial Identity Models," in *Handbook of Multicultural Counseling*, ed. Joseph G. Ponterotto et al. (Thousand Oaks, CA: Sage Publications, 1995), 181–98.

8. Helms, *Black and White Racial Identity*.

9. Debby Irving, *Waking Up White, and Finding Myself in the Story of Race* (Cambridge, MA: Elephant Room Press, 2014).

10. "Confederate Statues Were Built to Further a 'White Supremacist Future,'" NPR, August 20, 2017, https://www.npr.org/2017/08/20/544266880/confederate-statues-were-built-to-further-a-white-supremacist-future.

11. "Do Confederate Statues Make You Uncomfortable?," *America Inside Out with Katie Couric*, April 6, 2018, National Geographic Channel, http://channel.nationalgeographic.com.

12. Robert McClendon, "Mitch Landrieu on Confederate Landmarks: 'That's What Museums Are For,'" *Times-Picayune*, June 24, 2015, http://www.nola.com/politics/index.ssf/2015/06/lee_circle_statue_new_orleans.html.

13. "Nathan Bedford Forrest Monument—Selma, Alabama," Explore Southern History, accessed December 3, 2017, http://www.exploresouthernhistory.com/selmaforrest.html; Erin Edgemon, "Nathan Bedford Forrest Bust Back in Alabama Cemetery," *Al*, May 26, 2015, http://www.al.com/news/index.ssf/2015/05/nathan_bedford_forrest_bust_ba.html.

14. Jess Bidgood et al., "Confederate Monuments Are Coming Down Across the United States. Here's a List," *New York Times*, August 28, 2017, https://www.nytimes.com/interactive/2017/08/16/us/confederate-monuments-removed.html; Carolyn E. Holmes, "Should Confederate Monuments Come Down? Here's What South Africa Did After Apartheid," *Washington Post*, August 29, 2017, https://www.washingtonpost.com/news/monkey-cage/wp/2017/08/29/should-confederate-monuments-come-down-heres-what-south-africa-did-after-apartheid/?utm_term=.a9be702e17b9; Frank Camp, "Four Perspectives on Removing Confederate Monuments," *Daily Wire*, August 15, 2017, https://www.dailywire.com/news/19768/four-perspectives-removing-confederate-monuments-frank-camp#.

15. Peggy McIntosh, *White Privilege and Male Privilege: A Personal Account of Coming to See Correspondences Through Work in Women's Studies* (Wellesley, MA: Wellesley College Center for Research on Women, 1988); Helen A. Neville, Roger L. Worthington, and Lisa B. Spanierman, "Race, Power, and Multicultural Counseling Psychology: Understanding White Privilege and Color-Blind Racial Attitudes," in *Handbook of Multicultural Counseling*, 2nd ed., ed. Joseph G. Ponterotto et al. (Thousand Oaks, CA: SAGE, 2001), 257–88.

16. Maria Perez, "Diversity Is Not America's Strength, Republican Congressman Steve King Says," *Newsweek*, December 9, 2017, http://www.newsweek.com/diversity-not-americas-strength-republican-congressman-steve-king-says-743463; Jonah Goldberg, "What If Diversity Isn't America's Strength?" *Los Angeles Times*, January 15, 2018, http://www.latimes.com/opinion/op-ed/la-oe-goldberg-diversity-strength-20180115-story.html; "Tucker: Diversity Isn't Our Strength. Unity Is," Fox News, last modified January 18, 2018, http://video.foxnews.com/v/5714755098001/?#sp=show-clips.

17. Schildkraut, "White Attitudes About Descriptive Representation."

18. James Baldwin, "Letter from a Region in My Mind," *New Yorker*, November 17, 1962, https://www.newyorker.com/magazine/1962/11/17/letter-from-a-region-in-my-mind.

19. Ta-Nehisi Coates, "What We Mean When We Say 'Race Is a Social Construct,'" *Atlantic*, May 15, 2013, https://www.theatlantic.com/national/archive/2013/05/what-we-mean-when-we-say-race-is-a-social-construct/275872/; Megan Gannon, "Race Is a Social Construct, Scientists Argue," *Scientific American*, February 5, 2016, accessed August 30, 2017, https://www.scientificamerican.com/article/race-is-a-social-construct-scientists-argue.

20. Linda A. Tropp and Rebecca A. Bianchi, "Interpreting References to Group Membership in Context: Feelings About Intergroup Contact Depending on Who Says What to Whom," *European Journal of Social Psychology* 37 (2007): 153–70, doi:10.1002/ejsp.340.

21. Linda R. Tropp, "How White Teachers Navigate Racial Diversity in Their Classrooms: The Roles of Contact and Racial Anxiety," paper presented at the Resilience of Racism Conference, Oakland, CA, June 2017.

CHAPTER 7: A NEW GENERATION . . . A NEW FORM OF RACISM

1. Thomas C. Reeves and Eunjung Oh, "Generational Differences and the Integration of Technology in Learning, Instruction, and Performance," in *Handbook of Research on Educational Communications and Technology*, ed. J. Michael Spector et al. (New York: Springer Publishing, 2014), 295–303.

2. Scott Clement, "Millennials Are Just About as Racist as Their Parents," *Washington Post*, April 7, 2015, https://www.washingtonpost.com/news/wonk/wp/2015/04/07/white-millennials-are-just-about-as-racist-as-their-parents/?utm_term=.4602793119ec; Scott Clement, "White Millennials Show Slightly Less Implicit Bias Against Blacks, 2008 Survey Found,"

Washington Post, April 7, 2015, https://www.washingtonpost.com/news/wonk/wp/2015/04/07 /white-millennials-are-just-about-as-racist-as-their-parents/?utm_term=.05f3da9ccc82.

3. "As US Copes with Charlottesville Violence, Protestors Take to the Streets," NPR, August 13, 2017, https://www.npr.org/sections/thetwo-way/2017/08/13/543259431/as-u-s -copes-with-charlottesville-violence-protesters-take-to-the-streets; Katharine Q. Seelye, Alan Blinder, and Jess Bidgood, "Protestors Flood Streets, and Trump Offers a Measure of Praise," *New York Times*, August 18, 2017, https://www.nytimes.com/2017/08/18/us /demonstration-race-free-speech-boston-charlottesville.html.

4. "Nature of the Sample: NPR/PBS NewsHour/Marist Poll of 1,125 National Adults," August 17, 2017, http://maristpoll.marist.edu/wp-content/misc/usapolls/us170814_PBS /NPR_PBS%20NewsHour_Marist%20Poll_National%20Nature%20of%20the%20 Sample%20and%20Tables_August%2017,%202017.pdf.

5. Eduardo Bonilla-Silva, *Racism Without Racists: Color-Blind Racism and the Persistence of Racial Inequality in America* (Lanham, MD: Rowman & Littlefield, 2017).

6. Plummer et al., "Patterns of Adult Cross-Racial Friendships," 4.

7. Peter Levine, "Generational Differences in Attitudes Toward Racism," *Peter Levine*, July 11, 2016, http://peterlevine.ws/?p=17122.

8. Van Jones, *Beyond the Messy Truth: How We Came Apart, How We Come Together* (New York: Ballantine Books, 2017).

9. "Parable of the Polygons: A Playable Post on the Shape of Society," Ncase, http:// ncase.me/polygons, accessed December 3, 2017.

10. Ibid.

11. Eduardo Bonilla-Silva, interview by Deborah Plummer, September 21, 2017.

12. Ibid.

13. Steven Becton, interview by Deborah Plummer, November 17, 2017.

14. "CNN Panel Debate Goes Haywire: Paris Dennard vs. Keith Boykin," video, 7:37, August 14, 2017, https://www.youtube.com/watch?v=u8a3DoKYUfo.

15. Pippa Norris, "The Bridging and Bonding Role of Online Communities," *Harvard International Journal of Press-Politics* 7, no. 3 (2002): 3–8, doi:10.1177/1081180021291 72601.

16. C. Foxx, August 19, 2017 (9:48 a.m.), Facebook comment.

17. Robin DiAngelo, "White Fragility," *International Journal of Critical Pedagogy* 3, no. 3 (2011): 54–70, p. 58, file:///C:/Users/student/Downloads/249-665-1-PB%20(1).pdf.

18. Ibid.

19. Robin DiAngelo, "Why It's So Hard to Talk to White People About Racism," *Huffington Post*, April 30, 2015, https://www.huffingtonpost.com/good-men-project/why-its -so-hard-to-talk-to-white-people-about-racism_b_7183710.html.

20. Angie Thomas, *The Hate U Give* (New York: HarperCollins, 2017), Kindle ed., chapter 14.

21. "Nation of Cowards," video, 4:05, February 18, 2009, https://www.youtube.com /watch?v=2Fy2DnMFwZw.

22. Alexander Zubatov, "The Flipside of White Privilege: Black Entitlement," *Medium*, June 9, 2016, https://medium.com/@Zoobahtov/the-flipside-of-white-privilege-black -entitlement-6208f27a93cc.

23. Peggy McIntosh, "White Privilege: Unpacking the Invisible Knapsack," *Peace and Freedom Magazine*, July/August (1989), https://nationalseedproject.org/images/documents /Knapsack_plus_Notes-Peggy_McIntosh.pdf.

24. John Blake, "It's Time to Talk About 'Black Privilege,'" CNN, March 31, 2016, http://www.cnn.com/2016/03/30/us/black-privilege/index.html.

25. McIntosh, "White Privilege."

26. Nicholas Epley, *Mindwise: Why We Misunderstand What Others Think, Believe, Feel, and Want* (New York: Vintage, 2015).

27. Ibid.

28. Marsh, Mendoza-Denton, and Smith, *Are We Born Racist?*

29. "Jane Elliott's Blue Eyes/Brown Eyes Exercise," Jane Elliott, http://www.janeelliott .com, accessed December 3, 2017.

30. Tracie L. Stewart et al., "Do the 'Eyes' Have It? A Program Evaluation of Jane Elliott's 'Blue-Eyes/Brown-Eyes' Diversity Training Exercise," *Journal of Applied Social Psychology* 33, no. 9 (2003): 1898–1921, doi:10.1111/j.1559-1816.2003.tb02086.x.

31. Cathy J. Cohen et al., "The 'Woke' Generation: Millennial Attitudes on Race in the US," October 2017, https://genforwardsurvey.com/assets/uploads/2017/10/GenForward -Oct-2017-Final-Report.pdf; Jeff Fromm, "GenZ Is on the Rise, Here Is What You Need to Know," *Forbes*, January 4, 2017, https://www.forbes.com/sites/jefffromm/2017/01/04/gen-z -is-on-the-rise-here-is-what-you-need-to-know/2/#28fa4fca1d62.

32. Ta-Nehisi Coates, "The First White President: The Foundation of Donald Trump's Presidency Is the Negation of Barack Obama's Legacy," *Atlantic*, October 2017, https:// www.theatlantic.com/magazine/archive/2017/10/the-first-white-president-ta-nehisi-coates /537909.

CHAPTER 8: DIFFICULT LAUGHS MADE EASIER

1. "How to Navigate Race-Based Humor," *The Daily Show*, video, 2:42, April 13, 2016, https://www.youtube.com/watch?v=FdErPLSD_94.

2. Anthony J. Chapman, "Humor and Laughter in Social Interaction and Some Implications for Humor Research," in *Handbook of Humor Research*, ed. Paul E. McGhee and Jeffrey H. Goldstein (New York: Springer, 1983), 135–57; Rod Martin and Nicholas A. Kuiper, "Three Decades Investigating Humor and Laughter: An Interview with Professor Rod Martin," *Europe's Journal of Psychology* 12 (2016): 3, doi:10.5964/ejop.v12i3.1119; "Laughter Is the Best Medicine: The Health Benefits of Humor and Laughter," last modified October 2017, https://www.helpguide.org/articles/mental-health/laughter-is-the-best-medicine.htm.

3. "Stress Relief from Laughter? It's No Joke," Mayo Clinic, https://www.mayoclinic .org/healthy-lifestyle/stress-management/in-depth/stress-relief/art-20044456, accessed December 3, 2017; Rod A. Martin, *The Psychology of Humor: An Integrative Approach* (Cambridge, MA: Academic Press, 2010).

4. "The Niggar Family," *The Chappelle Show*, http://www.cc.com/video-clips/mlg0y7 /chappelle-s-show-the-niggar-family—uncensored, last modified January 28, 2004.

5. *Chris Rock: Bigger and Blacker*, dir. Keith Truesdell (1999; DreamWorks, 2000), DVD.

6. Soraya Nadia McDonald, "Amy Schumer Responds to Criticism by Insisting She's Not Racist, Just Funny," *Washington Post*, June 29, 2015, https://www.washingtonpost.com /news/arts-and-entertainment/wp/2015/06/29/amy-schumer-responds-to-criticism-by -insisting-shes-not-racist-just-funny/?utm_term=.82956041f425.

7. Chris Hayes, *A Colony in a Nation* (New York: W. W. Norton, 2017).

8. Greg Willard, Isaac Kyonne-Joy, and Dana R. Carney, "Some Evidence for the Nonverbal Contagion of Racial Bias," *Organizational Behavior and Human Decision Processes* 128 (2015): 96–107, doi:10.1016/j.obhdp.2015.04.002; Joanna Robinson, "How *Black-ish's* Searing Political Commentary Transcended 'Very Special Episode' Territory," *Vanity Fair*, February 26, 2016, https://www.vanityfair.com/hollywood/2016/02/blackish-black-lives-matter.

9. Robinson, "How *Black-ish's* Searing Political Commentary Transcended 'Very Special Episode' Territory."

10. Aliya Saperstein and Andrew M. Penner, "Racial Fluidity and Inequality in the United States," *American Journal of Sociology* 118, no. 3 (2012): 676–727, https://www.socsci .uci.edu/~penner/media/2012_ajs.pdf.

11. US Department of Labor Office of Policy Planning and Research, *The Negro Family: The Case for National Action* (Ann Arbor: University of Michigan Library, 1965); James T. Patterson, *Freedom Is Not Enough: The Moynihan Report and America's Struggle over Black Family Life—From LBJ to Obama* (New York: Basic Books, 2012).

12. Saperstein and Penner, "Racial Fluidity and Inequality in the Unites States," 676–727.

13. "ABC's 'Black-ish,' 'Cristela,' 'Fresh Off the Boat' a Win for Racial Diversity in Television Comedy," *LaughSpin*, http://www.laughspin.com/abcs-black-ish-cristela-and -fresh-off-the-boat-a-win-for-racial-diversity-in-television-comedy-videos, last modified May 14, 2014.

14. Renee Graham, "A Sad Day for Late Night," *Boston Globe*, August 17, 2017, https:// www.bostonglobe.com/opinion/2016/08/17/sad-night-for-late-night/SiFcR9ih56zMYJ 6004BS1I/story.html.

15. Raúl Pérez, "Ethnic Humor in Multiethnic America," *Ethnic and Racial Studies* 38, no. 3 (2015): 514–15, doi:101080/01419870.2014.943781.

16. Raúl Pérez, interview by Deborah Plummer, January 5, 2017.

CHAPTER 9: WHAT WE DO WITH OUR LEISURE TIME

1. Marian Morton, "Deferring Dreams: Racial and Religious Covenants in Shaker Heights, Cleveland Heights and East Cleveland, 1925 to 1970," Teaching Cleveland, February 27, 2010, http://teachingcleveland.org/deferring-dreams-racial-and-religious -covenants-in-shaker-heights-and-cleveland-heights-1925-to-1970-by-marian-morton.

2. Monika Stodolska et al., eds., *Race, Ethnicity, and Leisure: Perspectives on Research, Theory, and Practice* (Champaign, IL: Human Kinetics, 2013).

3. Brad Tuttle, "What It Really Costs to Go to Walt Disney World," *Time*, May 15, 2017, http://time.com/money/4749180/walt-disney-world-tickets-prices-cost.

4. "How Much Will It Cost Your Family to Attend an MLB Game," *TimesUnion*, April 9, 2014, http://www.timesunion.com/blogs/article/How-much-will-it-cost-your-family -to-attend-an-5388916.php.

5. Dr. Stodolska and Dr. Shinew, interview by Deborah Plummer, October 16, 2017.

6. Kimberly J. Shinew, Myron F. Floyd, and Diana Parry, "Understanding the Relationship Between Race and Leisure Activities and Constraints: Exploring an Alternative Framework," *Leisure Sciences* 26, no. 2 (2004): 181–99, doi:10.1080/01490400490432109.

7. "Black Hiker with Blair Underwood," Funny or Die video, 3:23, November 23, 2009, http://www.funnyordie.com/videos/24b56caf3e/black-hiker-with-blair-underwood.

8. Rich Benjamin, "My Road Trip Through the Whitest Towns in America," filmed 2015, TED video, 13:01, https://www.ted.com/talks/rich_benjamin_my_road_trip_through _the_whitest_towns_in_america/up-next.

9. Ibid.

10. Ibid.

11. Ibid.

12. Stodolska et al., *Race, Ethnicity, and Leisure*.

13. "Jack and Jill of America Incorporated," Jack and Jill, Inc., http://jackandjillinc.org, accessed December 3, 2017.

14. "The Problem with Jack and Jill," *Clutch Magazine*, http://clutchmagonline.com /2016/07/the-problem-with-jack-and-jill, accessed November 12, 2017.

15. "Who We Are," Jack and Jill Foundation, 2017, https://jackandjillfoundation.org /who-we-are.

16. Jack and Jill Mothers, interview by Deborah Plummer, November 11, 2017.

17. Allison Cunningham, interview by Deborah Plummer, November 13, 2017.

18. Miller McPherson, Lynn Smith-Lovin, and James Cook, "Birds of a Feather: Homophily in Social Networks," *Annual Review of Sociology* 27 (2001): 415–44, doi:10.1146 /annurev.soc.27.1.415.

19. Karl Spracklen, *Whiteness and Leisure*, Leisure Studies in a Global Era (Basingstoke UK: Palgrave Macmillan, 2013).

20. Deborah L. Plummer and Steve Slane, "Patterns of Coping in Racially Stressful Situations," *Journal of Black Psychology* 22, no. 3 (1996): 302–15, doi:10.1177/00957984960223002.

21. Plummer and Slane, "Patterns of Coping in Racially Stressful Situations," 302–315.

22. S. Lyubomirsky and J. Lepper, "A Measure of Subjective Happiness: Preliminary Reliability and Construct Validation," *Social Indicators Research* 46 (1999): 137–55; D. R. Williams et al., "Racial Differences in Physical and Mental Health: Socioeconomic Status, Stress, and Discrimination," *Journal of Health Psychology* 2, no. 3 (1997): 335–51.

23. Deborah L. Plummer and J. Allison, Friendship Survey IV, August-November 2017; Y. Culfee, J. Allison, and D. L. Plummer, "Some of My Friends Are . . . Correlations of Happiness and Well-Being with Cross-Racial Friendships," forthcoming.

24. Linda R. Tropp and Rebecca A. Bianchi, "Interpreting References to Group Membership in Context: Feelings About Group Contact Depending on Who Says What to Whom," *European Journal of Social Psychology* 37 (2007): 153–70, doi:10.1002/ejsp.340.

25. "Mix It Up," Teaching Tolerance, https://www.tolerance.org/mix-it-up, last modified 2017.

26. Ibid.

27. "What Do You Love?" Meetup, https://www.meetup.com/?_cookie-check=y8an -8kM2bXGg9-e.

28. Motoko Rich, "Restrictive Covenants Stubbornly Stay on the Books," *New York Times*, April 21, 2005, http://www.nytimes.com/2005/04/21/garden/restrictive-covenants

-stubbornly-stay-on-the-books.html?mtrref=www.google.com&gwh=DED8180BF4F545
D4BD175C18303A824A&gwt=pay.

CHAPTER 10: THE HEAVENLY VISION OF RACIAL UNITY

1. Martin Luther King Jr., speech at Western Michigan University, Kalamazoo, December 18, 1963, Q&A session, Western Michigan University Archives and Regional History Collections and University Archives, http://wmich.edu/sites/default/files/attachments /MLK.pdf.

2. Bob Smietana, "Sunday Morning Segregation: Most Worshippers Feel Their Church Has Enough Diversity," *Christianity Today*, January 15, 2015, http://www .christianitytoday.com/news/2015/january/sunday-morning-segregation-most-worshipers -church-diversity.html.

3. "Bishop: I'll Pay White People to Attend My Church," CNN Access, August 1, 2003, http://www.cnn.com/2003/US/08/01/cnna.caldwell.

4. Korie L. Edwards, Brad Christerson, and Michael O. Emerson, "Race, Religious Organizations, and Integration," *Annual Review of Sociology* 39 (2011): 211–28, doi:10.1146 /annurev-soc-071312-145636.

5. Ibid.

6. "7 Promises," https://promisekeepers.org/about/7-promises, last modified 2017.

7. Michael O. Emerson and Christian Smith, *Divided by Faith: Evangelical Religion and the Problem of Race in America* (New York: Oxford University Press, 2001).

8. Jarvis J. Williams, "Racial Reconciliation, the Gospel, and the Church," 9 Marks: Evangelism & Gospel, September 25, 2015, https://www.9marks.org/article/racial -reconciliation-the-gospel-and-the-church.

9. Michael Lipka, "The Most and Least Racially Diverse US Religious Groups," Pew Research Center, July 27, 2015, http://www.pewresearch.org/fact-tank/2015/07/27/the -most-and-least-racially-diverse-u-s-religious-groups.

10. Michael Lipka, "A Closer Look at Catholic America," Pew Research Center, September 14, 2015, http://www.pewresearch.org/fact-tank/2015/09/14/a-closer-look-at -catholic-america.

11. Mark Gray, Mary Gautier, and Thomas Gaunt, "Cultural Diversity in the Catholic Church in the United States," Center for Applied Research in the Apostolate, October 2016, http://www.usccb.org/issues-and-action/cultural-diversity/upload/Cultural-Diversity -Summary-Report-October-2016.pdf.

12. Bryan N. Massingale, *Racial Justice and the Catholic Church* (Ossining, NY: Orbis Books, 2010).

13. Ibid.

14. Matthew J. Cressler, *Authentically Black and Truly Catholic: The Rise of Black Catholicism in the Great Migration* (New York: New York University Press, 2017).

15. M. Shawn Copeland, *Uncommon Faithfulness: The Black Catholic Experience* (Ossining, NY: Orbis Books, 2009).

16. "US Bishops Establish New Ad Hoc Committee Against Racism," United States Conference of Catholic Bishops, accessed September 25, 2017, http://www.usccb.org/news /2017/17-149.cfm.

17. "Brothers and Sisters to Us: US Catholic Bishops Pastoral Letter on Racism 1979," United States Conference of Catholic Bishops, accessed December 4, 2017, http://www.usccb .org/issues-and-action/cultural-diversity/african-american/brothers-and-sisters-to-us.cfm.

18. Love L. Sechrest, "Race Relations in the Church in the Age of Obama," Fuller Studio, https://fullerstudio.fuller.edu/race-relations-in-the-church-in-the-age-of-obama, last modified 2017.

19. Heschel, "A Friendship in the Prophetic Tradition."

20. Quoted in Jerry Silverman, "A Conversation About Race, Identity, and Equality," Jewish Federation of Greater Hartford, https://www.jewishhartford.org/news/a-conversation -about-race-identity-and-equality, last modified July 15, 2016.

21. Michael O. Emerson, *People of the Dream: Multiracial Congregations in the United States* (Princeton, NJ: Princeton University Press, 2006).

22. Todd M. Johnson and Brian J. Grim, *The World's Religions in Figures: An Introduction to International Religious Demography* (Hoboken, NJ: Wiley-Blackwell, 2013).

CHAPTER 11: FRIENDS IN THE BIG TENT

1. Harriet Lerner, *Dance of Anger: A Woman's Guide to Changing the Patterns of Intimate Relationships* (New York: William Morrow, 2014).

2. Coates, "The First White President," Charles M. Blow, "Trump Is a Racist. Period," *New York Times*, January 14, 2018, https://www.nytimes.com/2018/01/14/opinion/trump-racist-shithole.html; Michael D'Antonio, "Is Donald Trump Racist? Here's What the Record Shows," *Fortune*, June 7, 2016, http://fortune.com/2016/06/07/donald-trump-racism-quotes/; Nicholas Kristof and Ian Prasad Philbrick, "Donald Trump's Racism: The Definitive List?," *New York Times*, January 15, 2018, https://www.nytimes.com/interactive/2018/01/15/opinion/leonhardt-trump-racist.html?_r=0.

3. Hi From The Other Side, https://www.hifromtheotherside.com, last modified 2017.

4. Henry Tsai, interview by Deborah Plummer, February 23, 2017.

5. Gordon W. Allport, *The Nature of Prejudice: 25th Anniversary Edition* (New York: Basic Books, 1979), 417.

6. Ibid., 27.

7. Ibid., 489.

8. "Top Voting Issues in 2016 Election," Pew Research Center, July 7, 2016, http://www.people-press.org/2016/07/07/4-top-voting-issues-in-2016-election.

9. Alvin N. Alvarez, Christopher T. H. Liang, and Helen A. Neville, *The Cost of Racism for People of Color* (Washington, DC: American Psychological Association, 2016).

10. "The Nantucket Project Is About What Matters Most," Nantucket Project, https://www.nantucketproject.com, accessed December 4, 2017.

11. R. Derek Black, "What White Nationalism Gets Right About American History," *New York Times*, August 19, 2017, https://www.nytimes.com/2017/08/19/opinion/sunday/white-nationalism-american-history-statues.html?mtrref=www.google.com&gwh=7CB45BF33CF6C2299B45732862183D7F&gwt=pay&assetType=opinion; Eli Saslow, "The White Flight of Derek Black," *Washington Post*, October 15, 2016, https://www.washingtonpost.com/national/the-white-flight-of-derek-black/2016/10/15/ed5f906a-8f3b-11e6-a6a3-d50061aa9fae_story.html?utm_term=.a236bc2bffab.

12. "Welcome to Stormfront Radio," Stormfront, https://www.stormfront.org/forum, accessed December 4, 2017.

13. "Stormfront," https://www.splcenter.org/fighting-hate/extremist-files/group/stormfront, last modified 2017.

14. *All Things Considered*, NPR, December 12, 2016.

15. Derek Black, interview by Deborah Plummer, October 5, 2017.

16. Stephen C. Wright et al., "The Extended Contact Effect: Knowledge of Cross-Group Friendships and Prejudice," *Journal of Personality and Social Psychology* 73, no. 1 (1997): 73–90, doi:10.1037/0022-3514.73.1.73.

17. Saslow, "The White Flight of Derek Black."

18. Deborah Plummer and C. Greer Jordan, "Going Plaid: Integrating Diversity into Business Strategy, Structure and Systems," *OD Practitioner* 39, no. 2 (2007): 3–40, https://www.aamc.org/download/454430/data/goingplaid.pdf.

19. "Margot Stern Strom Innovation Grants," Facing History and Ourselves, https://www.facinghistory.org/educator-resources/innovation-grants, accessed December 4, 2017.

20. "Pro-Life, Pro-Choice, Pro-Dialogue," https://onbeing.org/programs/david-gushee-frances-kissling-pro-life-pro-choice-pro-dialogue, last modified October 4, 2012.

21. Catherine Epstein, "The Correspondence Project," presented to Facing History and Ourselves New England Advisory Board, May 15, 2018.

22. "Word of the Year 2016 Is ...," English Oxford Living Dictionaries, https://en.oxforddictionaries.com/word-of-the-year/word-of-the-year-2016, accessed July 12, 2018.

23. Jesse Holcomb, "5 Facts About Fox News," Pew Research Center, January 14, 2014, http://www.pewresearch.org/fact-tank/2014/01/14/five-facts-about-fox-news/; Matt Wilstein, "Only 1% of Fox News Viewers Are Black," *Mediaite*, December 15, 2014, https://www.mediaite.com/tv/only-1-of-fox-news-viewers-are-black.

24. Henry Wiencek, "The Dark Side of Thomas Jefferson," *Smithsonian*, October 2012, https://www.smithsonianmag.com/history/the-dark-side-of-thomas-jefferson-35976004.

CHAPTER 12: SOME OF MY FRIENDS ARE...
1. Deborah L. Plummer, *Racing Across the Lines: Changing Race Relations Through Friendships* (Cleveland, OH: Pilgrim Press, 2004).

2. Shasta Nelson, *Frientimacy: How to Deepen Friendships for Lifelong Health and Happiness* (Berkeley, CA: Seal Press, 2016).

3. Elizabeth Page-Gould, Rodolfo Mendoza-Denton, and Linda R. Tropp, "With a Little Help from My Cross-Group Friend: Reducing Anxiety in Intergroup Contexts Through Cross-Group Friendship," *Journal of Personality and Social Psychology* 95, no. 5 (2008): 1080–94, doi:10.1037/0022–3514.95.5.1080.

4. "Omarosa National Association of Black Journalists 8/11/17," video, 16:16, August 11, 2017, https://www.youtube.com/watch?v=Fm8ovZ75n6s.

5. Ibram X. Kendi, *Stamped from the Beginning: The Definitive History of Racist Ideas in America* (New York: Nation Books, 2016), 499.

6. The names in this case are pseudonyms.

7. David Leonhardt, "The Choice Between Kneeling and Winning," *New York Times*, October 2, 2017, https://www.nytimes.com/2017/10/02/opinion/football-kneeling-winning-trump.html?mtrref=www.google.com&gwh=7389142840BFDDF1A479C8DA1374A36E&gwt=pay&assetType=opinion.

8. Charles M. Blow, "Divert, Divide, Destroy," *New York Times*, October 2, 2017, https://www.nytimes.com/2017/10/02/opinion/columnists/divert-divide-destroy.html?mtrref=www.google.com&gwh=A6C7A074B78C23A0736450A2E4634058&gwt=pay&assetType=opinion.

9. Ellis Cose, *The Rage of a Privileged Class: Why Are Middle-Class Blacks Angry? Why Should America Care?* (New York: Harper Perennial, 1994).

10. Nelson, *Frientimacy*, 42.

11. Sigal G. Barsade, "The Ripple Effect: Emotional Contagion and Its Influence on Group Behavior," *Administrative Science Quarterly* 47, no. 4 (2002): 644–75, doi:10.2307/3094912.

12. Ernest "Rip" Patton, interview by Deborah Plummer, November 16, 2017.

13. "Project Implicit," Harvard, last modified 2011, https://implicit.harvard.edu/implicit/takeatest.html.

INDEX

ABOUT THE AUTHOR

Deborah L. Plummer, PhD, is a nationally recognized psychologist and diversity and inclusion thought leader. She currently serves as vice chancellor/chief diversity officer at UMass Medical School and UMass Memorial Health Care. In 2016 she was named by *Becker's Hospital Review* as one of the Top 15 Chief Diversity Officers to Know.

Dr. Plummer previously held positions as a hospital system chief diversity officer, university psychology professor, founding director of a graduate degree program in diversity management, and staff psychologist. As a licensed psychologist, she maintained a private practice for over twenty years treating individuals, couples, and families while serving a term, by appointment of the governor, on the State of Ohio Board of Psychology.

As consultant and founder of D. L. Plummer & Associates, a firm specializing in diversity management and organizational development, Dr. Plummer worked successfully with over seventy international and national corporations, including Fortune 500 companies, hospital systems, community mental health agencies, public and private school systems, and faith-based institutions developing diversity strategic plans, facilitating diversity training, and conducting organizational development consultations.

Dr. Plummer is the editor of the *Handbook of Diversity Management* and author of *Racing Across the Lines: Changing Race Relations Through Friendships*. She has also authored several book chapters and published numerous journal articles to the professional community on racial identity development and managing diverse work environments. She has written for *Diversity Executive* and the *Boston Globe Magazine*. Her essay

"The Girl from the Ghetto" is featured in the anthology *All the Women in My Family Sing: Writing from Women of Color*, edited by ZZ Packer.

Dr. Plummer is a board member of GrubStreet, one of the nation's leading writing centers, and she works with the New England Advisory Board of Facing History and Ourselves, an organization that empowers people to think critically about history and to understand the impact of their choices.